THE CHRISTIAN ECONOMY OF THE EARLY MEDIEVAL WEST

Fig. 1. Hieronymus Bosch, *Ship of Fools* (1490–1500)

First published in 2022 by Gracchi Books, Binghamton, NY,
an imprint of punctum books, Earth, Milky Way.
https://punctumbooks.com

ISBN-13: 978-1-68571-026-2 (print)
ISBN-13: 978-1-68571-027-9 (ePDF)

DOI: 10.53288/0371.1.00

LCCN: 2022930897
Library of Congress Cataloging Data is available from the Library of Congress

Book design: Vincent W.J. van Gerven Oei
Cover image: mmarftrejo, Toledo, 2012

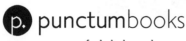

punctumbooks

spontaneous acts of scholarly combustion

GRACCHI

"Too many echoes, not enough voices."
— Cornel West

Ian Wood

The Christian Economy
in the Early Medieval West

Towards a Temple Society

Contents

Preface

This is not a book I had expected to write. I regard myself as a historian of religious culture rather than of the economics of religion. It does, nevertheless, follow logically from some of my recent work. Essentially, it expands on and develops the basic contention of the *Early Medieval Europe* lecture ("Creating a Temple Society in the Early Medieval West") that I was invited to deliver at the Leeds International Medieval Congress in 2019 (and which appeared in *Early Medieval Europe* in 2021). The IMC lecture was itself a spin-off from the plenary lecture that I gave at the International Medieval Congress at Kalamazoo in 2017, on "The Transformation of the Roman West," which I subsequently turned into a short book, published in 2018. A forerunner to that work was the lecture I gave at the Royal Historical Society in 2012, on "Entrusting Western Europe to the Church." Other relevant lectures include "The Early Medieval West as a Temple Society," delivered initially in Beijing in 2018, and subsequently in Vienna and at the University of Bologna in the spring of 2019. At Bologna, I had the good fortune to meet Valerio Neri, as well as Marcello Lusvarghi, to whom I am indebted for some excellent bibliographical advice and help. The text of the Bologna lecture was published in the *Rivista di Storia Antica* at the request of Tommaso Gnolli. Initial versions of parts of the book's argument were also presented in Tübingen, at a seminar organized by Steffen Patzold, in Pisa, at the Scuola normale, at the invitation of Fabrizio Oppedisano, at the University of Lincoln, at the invitation of Jamie Wood, and at Royal Holloway College, London, at the invitation of Kate Cooper. On each occasion I benefitted greatly from the feedback, not least from the organizers. At Royal Holloway College, I also gained much from the comments of Francis Robinson.

In many ways the whole sequence of work is a response to the extraordinary set of publications on Late Antiquity and the Early Middle Ages that appeared between 2005 and 2015, which, however, left me puzzled as to how one could bring together works as disparate as Chris Wickham's *Framing the Early Middle Ages* and Peter Brown's *Through the Eye of a Needle*. Exchanging ideas, usually by email, with a number of friends, and above all with John Haldon, led me to think that the idea of the "Temple Society" was a model that might usefully be applied to interpret the period between 300 and 700 AD. A further set of conversations, with Conrad Leyser, provided the opportunity to put my ideas into their current form.

Both Conrad and I were fortunate enough to be members of Steffen Patzold's *Kollegforschergruppe* in Tübingen in the late winter of 2019, when I was already thinking about the Leeds *Early Medieval Europe* lecture. In the course of numerous conversations, Conrad suggested that what I was trying to say needed more than one lecture, and he offered to arrange for me to deliver a mini-series in Oxford in January/February 2020, which forms the basis of the present text. In making the arrangements Conrad had the support of Neil McLynn, who was able to book the wonderful new auditorium in Corpus Christi College. To both of them I am extremely grateful, all the more so because Corpus was my old college — and for the early medievalist it has a particular attraction, because it has numbered among its alumni more than its fair share of specialists in Late Antiquity and the Early Middle Ages, among them Charles Plummer, Paul Vinogradoff, Michael Rostovtzeff, E.A. Lowe, R.A.B. Mynors, Michael Wallace-Hadrill, John Matthews, Thomas Charles-Edwards, James Howard-Johnston, Mark Whittow, and, currently, Neil McLynn, Jas Elsner, and Marek Jankowiak. I was taught by several of them, including Thomas Charles-Edwards, who was very much present at the lectures. So too was Henry Mayr-Harting, who introduced me to the Early Middle Ages in my first term as an undergraduate.

Among other friends and colleagues who were present, who raised questions, and to whom I am greatly indebted, were Wendy Davies, Peregrine Horden, and Dave Addison. I am also grateful to Worcester College, Oxford, for its support for the lectures. I subsequently circulated a draft of the lectures among several friends, and I am particularly grateful for the comments and criticism I received from Dave Addison, Wendy Davies, Merle Eisenberg, John Haldon, Peregrine Horden, Tom Noble, Helmut Reimitz, and Robert Wiśniewski. I am also indebted for help in securing additional material to Mark Humphries, Paolo Liverani, Fabian Völzing, and Wolfram Brandes. As a result, four lectures have turned into six chapters.

My inclination to draw on social anthropology certainly antedated my conversations with John Haldon. As a student of Peter Brown in 1970, and of Michael Wallace-Hadrill from 1972–1980, I could not but be inspired by the work of Evans-Pritchard, Mary Douglas, and Max Gluckmann. Social anthropology has been in the background, and sometimes the foreground, of much of my thought, most especially the Brixworth Lecture that I gave in 2008, at the invitation of Jo Story, on *The Priest, the Temple and the Moon,* which I guess is where I first started to think about "Temple Societies," without realizing as much — American anthropological writing on the Maya is very much at the root of that lecture. I might add that social anthropology (and Mary Douglas in particular) was at the heart of conversations with Conrad Leyser and Kate Cooper, and with Paolo Tedesco, who provided guidance on the literature relating both to "Temple Societies" and to the economic history of early medieval Italy while I was in Tübingen — for which I am extremely grateful. I was also sensitized to the need for thinking comparatively about churches and temples when working on a bid (unsuccessful as it turned out) to have Monkwearmouth and Jarrow listed as a World Heritage Site in 2011/2012. In the course of helping to prepare the application I had numerous discussions with Richard Morris over the comparability of religious monuments across the globe in the early medieval period.

Placing land and landholding at the heart of my interpretation derives directly from my involvement in what has been called the Bucknell or Woolstone group — hosted by Wendy Davies since its inception in 1979 — which led me to write about Merovingian precaria (1995) and then about the property of Wearmouth and Jarrow (2010). Without the discussions of the group (Wendy Davies, Leslie Brubaker, Ann Christys, Roger Collins, Marios Costambeys, Paul Fouracre, David Ganz, Rosemary Morris, Jinty Nelson, Tim Reuter, Richard Sharpe, Jo Story, Chris Wickham, Jenny Wormald, Patrick Wormald, four of them sadly deceased), I doubt that I would have come to place as much emphasis on the ownership of land as I have done.

To all the people mentioned above — and many more, not least the doctoral students I have supervised over the years — I am deeply indebted. In the course of the preparation of this book I have been particularly indebted to my student Michael J. Kelly, and also to Catalin Taranu (who attended many of my seminars). Finally, I extend my thanks to copyeditor Kristen McCants Forbes and the publishers at punctum books, Eileen A. Fradenburg Joy and Vincent W.J. van Gerven Oei. As an inadequate thanks for over forty years of inspiration, I dedicate the book to fellow members of the Bucknell/Woolstone group, past and present.

1

Towards a Temple Society?

The shift from the years 300 to 600 has been the subject of numerous recent studies, and it has been presented in radically different terms, which have variously encompassed continuity,[1] total discontinuity,[2] and transformation.[3] These differing interpretations of course involve some downright disagreement, but to an extent the differences are also a reflection of the general line of investigation taken by individual studies, whether political, social, economic, cultural, or religious, with the political and economic readings being more likely to stress breakdown or radical change, and the religious to emphasize transformation.

Most of the major readings have privileged one aspect or other of the story, although social and economic issues have often

---

1 Elisabeth Magnou-Nortier, *Aux origines de la fiscalité modern: le système fiscal et sa gestion dans le royaume des Francs à l'épreuve des sources (V^e–XIe siècles)* (Geneve: Droz, 2012); Jean Durliat, *De l'Antiquité au Moyen-Âge: L'Occident de 313 à 800* (Lyon: Ellipses, 2002).

2 Bryan Ward-Perkins, *The Fall of Rome and the End of Civilization* (Oxford: Oxford University Press, 2006).

3 Peter Brown, *The Rise of Western Christendom: Triumph and Diversity, A.D. 200–1000*, 10th Anniversary Revised Edition (Oxford: Oxford University Press, 2013); Ian Wood, *The Transformation of the Roman West* (Leeds: ARC Humanities Press, 2018).

been considered together,[4] as have cultural and religious. Peter Brown has consistently combined social and religious history, most recently in his surveys of the spiritual economy in *The Ransom of the Soul, Treasure in Heaven*, and *Through the Eye of a Needle*.[5] Related in approach is Daniel Caner's elaboration of Vincent Déroche's concept of a "miraculous economy."[6] Raising similar questions there is Valentina Toneatto's *Les banquiers du Seigneur*.[7] In all of these, the spiritual economy tends to be interpreted symbolically, rather than in hard economic terms. Paul Fouracre, however, has located what he calls "the moral economy" (making use of the French concept of *l'économie morale*) very firmly in the realities of financial renders in his study of the history of Church lighting.[8]

There is also a longstanding tradition in Italian scholarship which has looked at the Church and the economy in tandem. Most obviously there is Lellia Cracco Ruggini's study of *Italia Annonaria*,[9] followed by Rita Lizzi Testa's examination of *Vescovi e strutture ecclesiastiche nella città tardoantica* in the

---

4   Chris Wickham, *Framing the Early Middle Ages: Europe and the Mediterranean 400–800* (Oxford: Oxford University Press, 2005).

5   Peter Brown, *The Ransom of the Soul: Afterlife and Wealth in Early Western Christianity* (Cambridge: Harvard University Press, 2015); Peter Brown, *Treasure in Heaven: The Holy Poor in Early Christianity* (Charlottesville: University of Virginia, 2016); and Peter Brown, *Through the Eye of a Needle: Wealth, the Fall of Rome, and the Making of Christianity in the West, 350–550 AD* (Princeton: Princeton University Press, 2012).

6   Daniel Caner, "Towards a Miraculous Economy: Christian Gifts and Material 'Blessings' in Late Antiquity," *Journal of Early Christian Studies* 14, no. 3 (2006): 329–77.

7   Valentina Toneatto, *Les banquiers du Seigneur: Évêques et moines face à la richesse (IVe–début IXe siècle)* (Rennes: Presses universitaires de Rennes, 2012).

8   Paul Fouracre, "Lights, Power and the Moral Economy of Early Medieval Europe," *Early Medieval Europe* 28, no. 3 (2020): 367–87, esp. 368. See now Paul Fouracre, *Eternal Light and Earthly Concerns: Belief and the Shaping of Medieval Society* (Manchester: Manchester University Press, 2021).

9   Lellia Cracco Ruggini, *Economia e società nell' "Italia annonaria": Rapporti fra agricoltura e commercio dal IV al VI secolo d.C.* (Milan: A. Giuffre, 1961).

same region.[10] The tradition is, of course, not limited to Italian scholarship. Bishops and patronage feature strongly in a volume of *Antiquité Tardive* devoted to *Économie et religion*.[11] There is a short but vital article by A.H.M. Jones.[12] The economy of the Egyptian Church, for which there is incomparable material, has been examined by Ewa Wipszycka.[13] The Church's approach to poverty is central to Valerio Neri's discussion of the poor and the marginal (in the West),[14] and to Évelyne Patlagean's ground-breaking analysis (in the East).[15]

But whereas some historians of religion have investigated what has been termed the spiritual economy (a concept which tends to privilege the spiritual rather than the economic), most economic historians have paid scant attention to religion. Jairus Banaji, for instance, presents the Church as if it were no more than a representative section of the elite.[16] Yet, I would argue that the early medieval economy cannot be understood without paying proper attention to the Church as an institution in its own right, nor indeed can the Church be understood without recognition of its economic infrastructure. As Jean-Michel Carrié has noted, "superimposing a transcendent, eschatological discourse on top of economics [...] had practical implications by calling to behave in given ways in everyday economic life."[17]

10 Rita Lizzi Testa, *Vescovi e strutture ecclesiastiche nella città tardoantica: l'Italia Annonaria nel IV–V secolo d.C.* (Como: Edizioni New Press, 1989).

11 *Antiquité Tardive* 14, *Économie et religion dans l'Antiquité tardive* (2006).

12 A.H.M. Jones, "Church Finance in the Fifth and Sixth Centuries," *Journal of Theological Studies* 11, no. 1 (1960): 84–94.

13 Ewa Wipszycka, *Les ressources et les activités économiques des églises en Égypte du IVe au VIIIe siècle* (Brussels: Fondation Égyptologique Reine Élisabeth, 1972).

14 Valerio Neri, *I marginali nell'Occidente tardoantico: poveri, "infames" e criminali nella nascente società cristiana* (Bari: Edipuglia, 1996).

15 Évelyne Patlagean, *Pauvreté économique et pauvreté sociale à Byzance, IVe–VIIe siècles* (Paris: Mouton, 1977).

16 E.g., Jairus Banaji, *Exploring the Economy of Late Antiquity: Selected Essays* (Cambridge: Cambridge University Press, 2016), 152, 156.

17 Jean-Michel Carrié, "Pratique et idéologie chrétiennes de l'économie (IVe–VIe siècles)," *Antiquité Tardive* 14 (2006): 17–26, at 17.

It is the relationship between religion and the economy that I wish to explore in what follows. Although I am clearly indebted to Peter Brown's recent work, I wish to examine what he and others have seen as the spiritual economy in terms of hard numbers, and I wish to do so along lines indicated by John Haldon, who has directed attention to models of temple societies in his exploration of the "tributary mode of production,"[18] although he himself has not applied these models directly to the early medieval West, using them rather as points of comparison.

The term "tributary mode of production" is sometimes used as a synonym for the "feudal mode" in Marxist analysis of economic development.[19] But it has also been presented as a more appropriate term than "Asiatic mode of production,"[20] although for Haldon this latter expression "tends to be used negatively of all those social formations which cannot be fitted into one of the other established modes."[21] Both terms, "tributary" and "Asiatic," have been brought into play by Gerald West in his analysis of the Temple State of the Old and New Testaments, which takes as its point of departure the First Book of Samuel, Chapter 8, together with the Gospel of Mark, Chapter 12.[22] For West, the account of the political reorganization of the tribes of Israel described in the Book of Samuel is a classic statement of the creation of a temple state, in which the funding of the

---

18 John Haldon, "Mode of Production, Social Action, and Historical Change: Some Questions and Issues," in *Studies on Pre-Capitalist Modes of Production,* ed. Laura da Graca and Andrea Zingarelli (Boston and Leiden: Brill, 2015), 204–36.

19 Haldon, "Mode of Production," 210, 212; John Haldon, *The State and the Tributary Mode of Production* (London: Verso, 1993), 70–139, esp. 76.

20 Gerald West, "Tracking an Ancient Near Eastern Economic System: The Tributary Mode of Production and the Temple-State," *Old Testament Essays (OTE)* 24, no. 2 (2011): 511–32, at 512.

21 Haldon, *The State and the Tributary Mode of Production,* 54. For a historiographical analysis of the term "Asiatic Mode," see Kimio Shiozawa, "Marx's View of Asian Society and his 'Asiatic Mode of Production'," *The Developing Economies* 4, no. 3 (1966): 299–315, and Joshua A. Fogel, "The Debates over the Asiatic Mode of Production in Soviet Russia, China, and Japan," *The American Historical Review* 93, no. 1 (1988): 56–79.

22 West, "Tracking an Ancient Near Eastern Economic System."

temple is central to the political and economic development of the Kingdom of Israel.

It is important to recognize that the notion of a "temple state" is itself the subject of debate. Benjamin Foster in a study of "the Sumerian Temple State" has stated that "the temple-state hypothesis holds that most or all of the agricultural land in mid-third millennium Sumer belonged to temples which thereby controlled the economy of southern Mesopotamia. Cities and states functioned as theocentric manors in which political leaders derived their authority from management of the gods' households."[23] However, Foster's detailed examination of some of the central documentation for the thesis shows the existence of land which was not in the control of the temples or the state, and he concludes that "the temple-state hypothesis on internal grounds alone must be abandoned or drastically modified; for external reasons it has been shown to be an inadequate and oversimplified reconstruction of Sumerian economy and society."[24]

Clearly an economic model which assumed that the whole of the economy of the immediately post-Roman West was dominated by the Church would equally be in direct conflict with the surviving evidence. As we will see, the Church may have acquired up to a third of the cultivable land of Western Europe between 300 and 750. In other words, it was a major, probably *the* major landowner, but it was by no means the only one. Even so, it is worth keeping the notion of "temple societies" in mind while considering the economic development of the late- and post-Roman world.[25] As Chris Wickham has stressed, modes of production are not exclusive, but in any given period one among them tends to be dominant.[26] Moreover, despite Foster's

---

23 Benjamin Foster, "A New Look at the Sumerian Temple State," *Journal of the Economic and Social History of the Orient* 24, no. 3 (1981): 225–41, at 225–26.

24 Foster, "A New Look at the Sumerian Temple State," 241.

25 Ian Wood, "Creating a 'Temple Society' in the Early Medieval West," *Early Medieval Europe* 29, no. 4 (2021): 462–86.

26 Chris Wickham, "The Other Transition: From the Ancient World to Feudalism," in Chris Wickham, *Land and Power: Studies in Italian and Europe-*

critical approach to the application of the concept of a temple-state to the economy of Sumerian Mesopotamia, other scholars have applied the concept of the temple society not only to ancient Israel, but also to medieval states in southeast Asia, where religious institutions did not constitute the only landowners, and where kings and merchants were major players — as, for instance, in twelfth-century Andhra Pradesh, and more generally in the Hindu world, where "the temple or the religion was used as an integrating force. In other words, the temple became the centrifugal or centripetal force in regulating various cultural entities."[27]

In the early medieval West (and indeed in Byzantium) a large percentage of the land and wealth of the region was directed towards the needs and socio-religious strategies of Christian institutions, which were not exactly those of ordinary landowners. Of course, the Church was not a single institution. Peter Brown has talked of micro-Christendoms,[28] geographical subdivisions of the Christian world, with their own religious character and traditions: "competing regional churches," and "'little Romes' available on their home ground."[29] And not only is there regional variation, but there are distinctions to be drawn between episcopal, local, and proprietary churches, as well as monasteries. Different types of ecclesiastical institutions had different economic concerns. But they all supposedly contributed to the formation of a single *populus Christianus.*[30]

Whereas the central socioeconomic role of the Temple has been much analyzed for southeast Asian and indeed pre-Columbian American societies, the same has not been true of

---

an *Social History, 400–1200* (London: British School at Rome, 1994), 7–42, at 12.

27 P.S. Kanaka Durga and Y.A. Sudhakar Reddy, "Kings, Temples and Legitimation of Autochthonous Communities: A Case Study of a South Indian Temple," *Journal of the Economic and Social History of the Orient* 35, no. 2 (1992): 145–66, at 146.

28 Brown, *The Rise of Western Christendom*, 13–17, 355–79.

29 Ibid., 15.

30 Ian Wood, "The Early Medieval West as a Temple Society," *Rivista di Storia Antica: Periodico trimestrale di antichità classica* 11 (2019): 107–34, at 109.

the churches of the early medieval West. And yet, in each case religious institutions undoubtedly played a central social, economic, and political role. Awareness of the notion of the temple society when considering the post-Roman West has the advantage of alerting the scholar to the fact that Christianity had a socioeconomic and political impact well beyond its obvious religious importance. It also helps us distinguish the post-Roman period from that of the Roman Empire, in which religion played a structurally different role — above all with regard to the accumulation and distribution of wealth.

There is, of course, more than one model for temple society. There are differences between the endowment and functioning of religion institutions in different parts of India, Cambodia, China, and Japan, but in all of them temples were extremely richly funded.[31] However, David Webster, in his discussion of "the fall of the ancient Maya," sets out the characteristics of what he defined as "ancient states": "common (but far from universal) features of early states included complex occupational specialization, widespread trade, market exchange, concentration of physical coercion in the form of professional armies, or police forces, judicial institutions and legal codes, and organised state religion." And he goes on to remark: "All classifications, of course, suppress variety, and not every ancient state exhibited all these organizational characteristics to the same degree."[32] Webster does not define the Maya as a "temple society" here, but he might have done. His warning that classifications suppress variety is, of course, salutary. At the same time, however, the most general classifications can be the most useful in helping us to shift our perspectives. Thus, for all their differences, the Maya will bear some comparison with Anglosaxon England (and other early medieval western societies) in terms of the religious organization of time according to solar and lunar cycles.[33]

---

31 Ibid., 116.

32 David Webster, *The Fall of the Ancient Maya: Solving the Mystery of the Maya Collapse* (London: Thames and Hudson, 2002), 66.

33 Ian Wood, *The Priest, the Temple and the Moon in the Eighth Century,* The Brixworth Lectures, Second Series, no. 7 (Brixworth: Friends of All Saints'

I take as a starting point a definition of temple societies set out by Arjun Appadurai and Carol Appadurai Breckenridge. Although their work has not gone unchallenged,[34] and although more recent and more specific analyses provide additional lines of interpretation, the advantage of the Appadurai/Appadurai Breckenridge model is its simplicity, and therefore its adaptability. Their criteria are as follows:

1) That temple ritual makes little sense unless it is viewed as the expression of homage to the reigning deity who is conceived as a sovereign.

2) That this sovereign figure stands at the center of a set of moral and economic transactions which constitute, in a specific ethno-sociological sense, a redistributive process.

3) That temple endowments provide the organizational framework within which individuals and corporate groups participate in this redistributive process, and acquire distinct autonomous shares in its ritual and economic benefits.

4) That conflicts generated by this process, between various such shareholders, are resolved by an outside agency, whose mandate is to "protect" the temple, thus fulfilling one of the primary requirements for human claims to royal status.[35]

Clearly this model has its limitations, especially when it comes to questions relating to religion and the state in its military capacity, where other studies of temple societies are more sug-

---

Church, 2008).

34 For an overview, see Isabelle Clark-Decès, "Towards an Anthropology of Exchange in Tamil Nadu," *International Journal of Hindu Studies* 22 (2018): 197–215, esp. 200–201, n. 5.

35 Arjun Appadurai and Carol Appadurai Breckenridge, "The South Indian Temple: Authority, Honour and Redistribution," *Contributions to Indian Sociology* 10, no. 2 (1976): 187–211, at 190. See also Wood, "The Early Medieval West as a Temple Society."

gestive.[36] But it provides a very useful starting point. It allows us to de-familiarize the landed Church of the late-antique and early medieval world, and to develop a sharper view of its economic importance. Awareness of anthropology has played a crucial role in the developing understanding of early medieval kinship,[37] dispute settlement,[38] gift-giving,[39] and the workings of the holy;[40] it is of similar value when assessing the early medieval economy. Although this is often assessed without regard for religion, much of the economy came to be geared to the requirements of the Church, which laid down a set of social and economic as well as religious aspirations.

The criteria set out by Appadurai and Appadurai Breckenridge are strikingly applicable to the post-Roman West, where there was certainly recognition of a reigning deity who was regarded as central to a set of moral and economic transactions. Some of those economic transactions (the endowment of the Church and its use of the wealth received) can be described as a redistributive process. The Church amassed vast quantities of wealth, a good proportion of which was then deployed in the service of religious cult and for charitable purposes. And the legislation of emperors and kings certainly paid lip-service to the need to protect the Church, its property, and certain aspects of the distribution of its income.

In talking about the scale of ecclesiastical wealth, I am thinking primarily about landed property and not about moveable goods. The distinction is an important one, as historians of the

---

36 See Chapter 4 in this book.

37 Donald Bullough, "Early Medieval Social Groupings: The Terminology of Kinship," *Past and Present* 45 (1969): 3–18; Karl Leyser, "Maternal Kin in Early Medieval Germany: A Reply," *Past and Present* 49 (1970): 126–34; Alexander C. Murray, *Germanic Kinship Structures: Studies in Law and Society in Antiquity and the Early Middle Ages* (Turnhout: Brepols, 1983).

38 Wendy Davies and Paul Fouracre, eds., *The Settlement of Disputes in Early Medieval Europe* (Cambridge: Cambridge University Press, 1986).

39 Wendy Davies and Paul Fouracre, eds., *The Languages of Gift in the Early Middle Ages* (Cambridge: Cambridge University Press, 2010).

40 Peter Brown, *Society and the Holy in Late Antiquity* (London: Faber and Faber, 1982).

Celtic and Anglosaxon worlds have long noted (and I think primarily of Thomas Charles-Edwards's paper on land and moveable wealth, from 1976).[41] But it has attracted less attention from scholars of the Church of the Mediterranean and the continental West. Most modern comments on the wealth of the late-antique Church have taken together what is known of the donation of treasure and of the donation of land. Although the donation of treasure was often very considerable (as is clear from the record of the *Liber Pontificalis*)[42] and was fundamental to the erection of ecclesiastical buildings (as can also be seen, for instance, throughout Agnellus's *History of the Church of Ravenna*),[43] it differed from the donation of land in that, while a gift of treasure might constitute an economic windfall, unless it was instantly invested in land it did not provide a steady income, something which became increasingly significant as the numbers of clergy and as the social commitments of the Church rose. In addition, there could be a distinction from the donor's point of view — a donation of gold and silver to a church, while preserving control of the estates which had produced the treasure in the first place, allowed the benefactor to retain his or her ability to amass wealth, although there were figures to whom we will return, like Melania and Pinian, who sold their estates in order to provide

---

41 Thomas Charles-Edwards, "The Distinction Between Land and Moveable Wealth in Anglo-Saxon England," in *Medieval Settlement: Continuity and Change,* ed. Peter Sawyer (London: Edward Arnold, 1976), 180–87.

42 Raymond Davis, *The Book of the Pontiffs (Liber Pontificalis): The Ancient Biographies of the First Ninety Roman Bishops to A.D. 715* (Liverpool: Liverpool University Press, 1989), xix–xxvi; Dominic Janes, *God and Gold in Late Antiquity* (Cambridge: Cambridge University Press, 1998), 57; and Ruth Leader-Newby, *Silver and Society in Late Antiquity: Functions and Meanings of Silver Plate in the Fourth to Seventh Centuries* (Aldershot: Ashgate, 2004), 61–66.

43 Agnellus, *Liber Pontificalis ecclesiae Ravennatis,* ed. Deborah Mauskopf Deliyannis, Corpus Christianorum, Continuatio Medievalis 199 (Turnhout: Brepols, 2006); Deborah Mauskopf Deliyannis, trans., *The Book of the Pontiffs of the Church of Ravenna* (Washington, DC: Catholic University of America, 2004).

vast donations of *solidi* to churches.[44] Indeed, there is a cluster of pious aristocrats in the last years of the fourth and early years of the fifth century who deliberately impoverished themselves by selling property and distributing the proceeds. But the transfer of property not only removed the opportunity for the donor to replenish his or her treasure, it also conveyed power, alongside resources, to the Church.

Donation to the Church was seen first and foremost as an insurance for the afterlife: storing up "treasure in heaven," as has been well noted.[45] But of course, the donor of land often expected more than spiritual benefits from giving property to the Church. Donors surely expected their gifts to enhance their standing in the community, as was the case in the temple societies of south India.[46] Scholars have noted the use of property donations in the Early Middle Ages as a method of preserving family wealth and influence, especially through the creation of monasteries, in which leading members of the kin-group might take up positions of authority and from which they could further the interests of their relatives.[47] Moreover, even after alienating an estate a family might continue to have an interest in it, as was also the case in Islam, where the tradition of *waqf* allowed a family to retain interest in a property after it had been permanently transferred to a mosque.[48] But it is striking how rarely one can trace the workings of such a strategy over a period of

---

44 Richard Goodrich, *Contextualizing Cassian: Aristocrats, Asceticism, and Reformation in Fifth-Century Gaul* (Oxford: Oxford University Press, 2007), 157–71.

45 E.g., Brown, *Treasure in Heaven,* and Toneatto, *Les banquiers du Seigneur.*

46 Clark-Decès, "Towards an Anthropology of Exchange in Tamil Nadu," 200. For Chinese parallels, see Simon Yarrow, "Economic Imaginaries of the Global Middle Ages," in *The Global Middle Ages,* ed. Catherine Holmes and Naomi Standen, Past and Present 238, Supplement 13 (Oxford: Oxford University Press, 2018), 214–31, at 224.

47 Yaniv Fox, *Power and Religion in Merovingian Gaul: Columbanian Monasticism and the Frankish Elites* (Cambridge: Cambridge University Press, 2014), 195–218.

48 On the notion of *waqf,* see Alejandro García Sanjuán, *Till God Inherits the Earth: Islamic Pious Endowments in Al-Andalus (9–15th centuries)* (Boston and Leiden: Brill, 2007), 143–48.

more than three generations.[49] Ultimately, the Church (like the mosque) gained more than did the donor's family — and it is with the Church as the recipient of donations of land, rather than donations of treasure, that I am concerned.

Although the early medieval West never became a temple society as defined in the stringent terms laid down by Benjamin Foster, I will suggest that the economy of the sixth and seventh centuries cannot be understood unless one recognizes the centrality of the Church to its mode of production. In what follows, I will first examine the scale of ecclesiastical landholding in the early medieval West, and I will offer some rough estimates of the numbers of ecclesiastics (clerics and monks) at the end of the period with which I am concerned. I then look at the distribution of the Church's income, especially that raised on ecclesiastical property. In the following chapter I examine how the ideals of Christianity impacted upon patterns of the acquisition and distribution of wealth. Thereafter I look at the process by which the Church acquired its property and the chronology of the history of acquisition. How all this related to the State in the sixth and seventh centuries is the subject of the last of the chapters.

---

49 Wood, "The Early Medieval West as a Temple Society," 18–19.

2

Churches, Clergy, and Their Endowments

Although my argument begins chronologically in the fourth century, I take as a point of departure the scale of ecclesiastical landownership in the seventh. Of course, any attempt to estimate that scale can be no more than a guess, but I would suggest that having possessed very little in terms of land in the early fourth century, the Church may have owned as much as a third of the cultivable land of Western Europe by the year 700.[1] This is the figure that was suggested by Paul Roth and Émile Lesne for Merovingian Francia.[2] David Herlihy, who cited the conclusions of Roth and Lesne, however, went on to argue that this scale of landed possession was only achieved in the ninth century, when, in his view, the Church in Italy held twice as much as it had in the eighth.[3] It is, therefore, necessary to set out the reasons for thinking that Church possessions were already massive by 700.

1   Ian Wood, "Entrusting Western Europe to the Church, 400–750," *Transactions of the Royal Historical Society* 23 (2013): 37–73.

2   Paul Roth, *Geschichte des Beneficialwesens von den ältesten Zeiten bis ins 10. Jahrhundert* (Erlangen, 1850), 249; Émile Lesne, *Histoire de la propriété ecclésiastique en France*, vol. 1: *Époques romaine et mérovingienne* (Lille: R. Giard, 1910), 224.

3   David Herlihy, "Church Property on the Continent, 700–1200," *Speculum* 36, no. 1 (1961): 81–105, at 89; also, Thomas S. Brown, *Gentlemen and Offi-*

For Francia, this is a figure that can be calculated very roughly from the evidence of bishops' wills (mainly preserved in diocesan histories written down in the Carolingian period), from
the charter record, and from monastic histories (again, Carolingian in date). With regard to episcopal wills, it is worth noting that there was a widespread view throughout the West that
bishops should leave property to the Church, although some of
our evidence comes from complaints that they were not doing
so. Thus, as early as the mid-fifth century (and, as we shall see,
this is remarkably early for such a complaint) Salvian lamented
that even bishops who had no family did not always give property to the Church.[4] Gregory of Tours relates the fury of a cleric
when in the mid-sixth century Nicetius of Lyon left nothing to
his burial church.[5] In his account of his archiepiscopal namesake who died in 570, Agnellus of Ravenna recorded that the
archbishop left his property to his granddaughter.[6] In a letter to
archbishop Deusdedit of Milan, Gregory the Great noted that
bishops were allowed to dispose freely of what they owned before taking office,[7] but he questioned a grant of land acquired by
Constantius of Milan after his election.[8] He took the same view
of the acquisition of property by abbots.[9] Clearly there was a
notion that bishops ought to leave their property, and more specifically any property acquired after election to the episcopate,

    cers: *Imperial Administration and Aristocratic Power in Byzantine Italy, A.D.
554–800* (Rome: British School at Rome, 1984), 176.

4   Salvian, ep. 9.11, ed. Georges Lagarrigue, *Salvien de Marseille Œuvres,* vol. 1,
Sources Chrétiennes 176 (Paris: Éditions du Cerf, 1971), 126.

5   Gregory of Tours, *Liber Vitae Patrum,* 8.5, ed. Bruno Krusch, Monumenta
Germaniae Historica, Scriptores Rerum Merovingicarum 1.2 (Hanover:
Hahn, 1969 [1885]), 245–46.

6   Agnellus, *Liber Pontificalis ecclesiae Ravennatis,* 85, ed. Deborah Mauskopf
Deliyannis, Corpus Christianorum, Continuatio Medievalis 199 (Turnhout: Brepols, 2006), 252–53.

7   Gregory I, Register, 12.14, in *Registrum Epistularum,* ed. Dag Norberg, Corpus Christianorum, Series Latina 140–140A (Turnhout: Brepols, 1982), 972.

8   See also Gregory I, *Register,* 4.36, 6.1, ed. Norberg, *Registrum Epistularum,*
256–57, 369–70.

9   Gregory I, *Register,* 10.1, ed. Norberg, *Registrum Epistularum,* 825–27.

to their Church, and it is also apparent that this was an expectation frequently honored in its breach. In Spain, however, when the ninth Council of Toledo (655) legislated on the division of property of a *sacerdos* (a term which surely included bishops), it allowed some free disposal of assets, while insisting that the Church should not be defrauded, and that it should receive at least half of what the priest had acquired after his ordination.[10]

We do have some evidence for bishops who left their property to the Church. The best-known example is bishop Bertram of Le Mans, whose will lists 120 units of land donated to the Church in 616.[11] Fernand Cabrol and Henri Leclercq attempted to identify all the estates in question and concluded that they amounted to 300,000 hectares, which is approximately 0.5% of modern France[12] — Margarete Weidemann, who has provided the most recent identification of the properties listed in the will, neither endorses nor questions the figure, so it may stand as a rough estimate. Certainly, this is the most substantial Merovingian will that has survived, and it might be noted that the majority of Bertram's property was acquired in the course of his episcopate, not least in donations from king Chlothar II, whom he had resolutely supported. This, then, was a will that fulfilled ecclesiastical expectations. But it was not the only one. The *Gesta episcoporum Cennomanensium,* which preserves the will of Bertram, also transmits numerous other documents, many of which are thought to be suspect, but the will of his succes-

10 Council of Toledo IX (655), c. 4, ed. Gonzalo Martínez Díez and Félix Rodríguez, *La Colección Canónica Hispana* 5 (Madrid: C.S.I.C., 1992), 496–97.

11 Margarete Weidemann, *Das Testament des Bischofs Berthramn von Le Mans vom 27. März 616* (Mainz: Habelt, 1986).

12 Fernand Cabrol and Henri Leclercq, *Dictionnaire d'archéologie chrétienne et de liturgie,* vol. 10, col. 1495 (Paris: Letouzey et Ané, 1931); Wood, "Entrusting Western Europe to the Church," 43.

sor, Hadoind,[13] is thought to be largely authentic.[14] It lists over twenty properties, some of which were clearly quite extensive. Among other episcopal wills to survive are those of Caesarius of Arles[15] and Remigius of Rheims,[16] both from the first half of the sixth century, but both very much less substantial than that of Bertram. Unfortunately, we lack the wills of other bishops who, like Bertram, were closely associated with the royal court, and who might have made comparable wills: men such as Sulpicius of Bourges or Desiderius of Cahors, although, from the *Vita Desiderii,* which lists the donation of more than ninety estates to various religious institutions, we do learn that the latter gave a considerable amount to his Church,[17] probably leaving it as "the largest landowner of the region," according to Peregrine Horden.[18]

Bertram's will was undoubtedly unusual in its scale — if it were not, given that there were over a hundred Merovingian

13 *Actus Pontificum Cenomannis in urbe degentium,* ed. Margarete Weidemann, *Geschichte des Bistums Le Mans von der Spätantike bis zur Karolingerzeit,* 3 vols. (Mainz: Verlag des Römisch-Germanischen Zentralmuseums, 2002), vol. 2, 193–98, 202–6.

14 See Walter Goffart, *The Le Mans Forgeries: A Chapter from the History of Church Property in the Ninth Century* (Cambridge: Harvard University Press, 1966), 154–55.

15 Adalbert de Vogüé and Joël Courreau, *Césaire d'Arles, Œuves monastiques,* vol. 1: *Œuvres pour les moniales,* Sources Chrétiennes 345 (Paris: Éditions du Cerf, 1988), 360–97.

16 Hincmar, *Vita Remigii,* 32, ed. Bruno Krusch, Monumenta Germaniae Historica, Scriptores Rerum Merovingicarum 3 (Hanover: Hahn, 1896), 336–40; A.H.M. Jones, Philip Grierson, and J. A. Crook, "The Authenticity of the 'Testamentum sancti Remigii'," *Revue belge de Philologie et d'Histoire* 35 (1957): 356–73.

17 *Vita Desiderii Cadurcae urbis,* 34, ed. Bruno Krusch, Monumenta Germaniae Historica, Scriptores Rerum Merovingicarum 4 (Hanover: Hahn, 1902), 591–92. See now *Vita vel actus beati Desiderii,* 30 (9.17), ed. Keith Bate, Élizabeth Carpentier, and Georges Pon, *La Vie de saint Didier évêque de Cahors (630–655),* Hagiologia (Turnhout: Brepols. 2021), vol. 16, 210–19, with full identification of the sites.

18 Peregrine Horden, "Public Health, Hospitals, and Charity" (forthcoming).

dioceses,[19] the Church would have been even wealthier than it was by the end of the seventh century. Perhaps the most sizeable of other donations to episcopal churches was that of the senatorial abbot Aridius of Limoges, who, according to Gregory of Tours, appointed bishops Martin and Hilary as his heirs, that is to say that he gave everything he possessed to the Churches of Tours and Poitiers.[20] Flodoard of Rheims, who transmits highly questionable texts of the wills of bishops Bennadius, Remigius, Romulf, and Sompnantius,[21] also refers to those of queen Suavegotta and her daughter Theudechildis.[22] As royal women, who were among the most notable survivors of the Burgundian royal house, they probably had a good deal to give.

Wills of other non-episcopal Church benefactors have survived.[23] We have the testaments of abbess Burgundofara of Faremoutiers (not, it should be admitted, a major list of donations),[24] the deacon Adalgisel Grimo (who endowed various monasteries and churches in the Verdun region),[25] and an edited version of

---

19 Louis Duchesne, *Fastes épiscopaux de l'ancienne Gaule*, 3 vols. (Paris: Fontemoing, 1894–1915), vol. 1, 1–2, notes around 130 for Gaul, although this includes dioceses in Visigothic Septimania; Robert Godding, *Prêtres en Gaule mérovingienne* (Brussels: Sociétè des Bollandistes, 2001), 209, argues for c. 110.

20 Gregory of Tours, *Decem Libri Historiarum*, 10.29, ed. Bruno Krusch and Wilhelm Levison, Monumenta Germaniae Historica, Scriptores Rerum Merovingicarum 1.1 (Hanover: Hahn, 1951), 525–29.

21 Flodoard, *Historia Remensis Ecclesiae*, 1.9, 18, 2.4, 5, ed. M. Lejeune, *Histoire de l'Église de Reims par Flodoard*, 2 vols. (Reims: Imprimeur de l'Académie, 1854), vol. 1, 53–54, 109–39, 243–45, 240–60.

22 Flodoard, *Historia Remensis Ecclesiae*, 2.1, ed. Lejeune, *Histoire de l'Église de Reims par Flodoard*, vol. 1, 222.

23 Ulrich Nonn, "Merowingische Testamenta: Studien zum Fortleben einer römischen Urkundenform im Frankenreich," *Archiv für Diplomatik* 18 (1972): 1–129.

24 Jean Guérout, "Le testament de sainte Fare: matériaux pour l'étude et l'édition critique de ce document," *Revue d'histoire ecclésiastique* 60, no. 3 (1965): 761–821; Alexander O'Hara and Ian Wood, trans., *Jonas of Bobbio, Life of Columbanus, Life of John of Réomé, and Life of Vedast* (Liverpool: Liverpool University Press, 2017), 311–14.

25 Wilhelm Levison, "Das Testament Diakons Adalgisel-Grimo vom Jahre 634," *Trierer Zeitschrift* 7 (1932): 69–80.

that of Widerad, founder and abbot of Flavigny.[26] The one will to rival that of Bertram is that of the early eighth-century layman Abbo of Provence, much of whose land went to his foundation of Novalesa, in a part of the Italian peninsula which was politically in territory under Frankish control.[27]

For the most part, our evidence for monastic landholding does not come from wills but from the property surveys known as polyptychs and from monastic histories. From the *Gesta* of the abbots of Fontanelle we learn that the monastery of St. Wandrille supposedly held 3,964 *mansi* (although the text talks of 4,264 estates) in the early eighth century.[28] Most of our other figures relate to Charlemagne's reign or later, by which time the scale of the landholding may have grown, as a result of Carolingian bequests. By the early ninth century, St. Germain-des-Près held 8,000 *mansi,* which Benjamin Guérard, who edited the monastery's polyptyque, reckoned amounted to 429,987 hectares,[29] almost 1% of modern France. St. Riquier may have been comparable. By Charlemagne's time Luxeuil held 15,000 hectares.[30] Although the majority of our early evidence is Carolingian, it is clear, however, that this type of documentation belongs to a well-established tradition of estate surveys. Jean Pierre Devroey has shown that the surviving polyptych of St. Victor of Marseille from 813–814 was preceded by a survey from c. 740 that no longer survives.[31] For St. Martin de Tours, we have

26 *Collectio Flaviniacensis,* 8, ed. Karl Zeumer, *Formulae Merowingici et Karolini Aevi,* Monumenta Germaniae Historica, Legum 5 (Hanover: Hahn, 1886), 476–77.

27 Patrick J. Geary, *Aristocracy in Provence: The Rhône Basin at the Dawn of the Carolingian Age* (Stuttgart: Hiersemann, 1985).

28 *Gesta Abbatum Fontanellensium,* 11.3, ed. Pascal Pradié, *Chronique des abbés de Fontenelle* (Paris: Les Belles Lettres, 1999). On the problem of the numbers, Wood, "Entrusting Western Europe to the Church," 40, n. 13.

29 Roth, *Geschichte des Beneficialwesens,* 249–51.

30 Ibid. For Luxeuil's land, see also Adso of Montierender, *Vita Walberti,* 7, ed. Monique Goullet, *Adso Dervensis Opera Hagiographica,* Corpus Christianorum, Continuation Medievalis 198 (Turnhout: Brepols, 2003), 83–84.

31 Jean Pierre Devroey, "Elaboration et usage des polyptyques. Quelques éléments de réflexion à partir de l'exemple des descriptions de l'Église de Marseille (VIIIᵉ–IXᵉ siècles)," in *Akkulturation: Probleme einer germanisch-*

29 sheets of parchment listing dues to the abbey during the days of abbot Agyricus (c. 675),[32] which include around 1,000 personal names, largely of tenants or of those required to pay dues, and 137 place names.[33] These clearly do not cover the full extent of the abbey's holdings, since the chance pattern of discovery of the sheets suggests that there were others that have not survived. The best endowed Merovingian monastery, however, was probably St. Denis, whose wealth is known only from its surviving charters — we have good charter records for the donation of 36 *villae* between 625 and 726, and we know that 46 *loca* were restored by Pippin III in 751. Despite the fragmentary nature of the evidence, it was, without question, richly endowed by royalty.[34]

If we combine the figures for the landholdings of the episcopal churches and for the monasteries of Merovingian Gaul, we are surely looking at a massive amount of ecclesiastical property, although, mindful of Peter Brown's notion of "micro-Christendoms,"[35] we should remember that we are dealing with individual churches, and not a single institutional Church, and we should also bear in mind the distinction between episcopal

romanischen Kultursynthese in Spätantike und frühem Mittelalter, ed. Dieter Hägermann, Wolfgang Haubrichs, and Jörg Jarnut (Berlin: De Gruyter, 2004), 436–72, at 443 and 462. The polyptych of 813–14 (*Descriptio mancipiorum ecclesie Massiliensis*) was edited by M. Guérard, *Cartulaire de l'abbaye de Saint-Victor de Marseille,* vol 2. (Paris: Lahure, 1857), 633–54.

32 Pierre Gasnault, *Documents comptables de Saint-Martin de Tours à l'époque mérovingienne* (Paris: Bibliotheque Nationale, 1975); Pierre Gasnault, "Nouveaux fragments de la comptabilité mérovingienne de Saint-Martin de Tours," *Comptes rendus des séances de l'Académie des Inscriptions et Belles Lettres* 133, no. 2 (1989): 371–72; Pierre Gasnault, "Deux nouveaux documents comptables de l'époque mérovingienne concernant l'abbaye Saint-Martin de Tours," *Bulletin de la Société Nationale des Antiquaires de France* (1989): 164–65; Pierre Gasnault, "Deux nouveaux feuillets de la comptabilité domaniale de l'abbaye Saint-Martin de Tours à l'époque mérovingienne," *Journal des Savants* 2 (1995): 307–9.

33 Shoichi Sato, "The Merovingian Accounting Documents of Tours: Form and Function," *Early Medieval Europe* 9, no. 2 (2000): 143–61.

34 J.M. Wallace-Hadrill, *The Long-haired Kings, and Other Studies in Frankish History* (London: Methuen, 1962), 224–25, 237, 241–42; Wood, "Entrusting Early Medieval Europe to the Church," 40.

35 Brown, *The Rise of Western Christendom,* 355–79.

and monastic churches, which had very different economic and pastoral obligations.

In addition to cathedrals and to those churches whose priests were expected to attend diocesan synods — one may regard them as proto-parish churches — there were private churches established on the estates of the aristocracy, which have been termed "proprietary churches" or *Eigenkirchen*.[36] There were unquestionably significant numbers of these, and they are mentioned in the canons of the Church councils. Aristocrats surely regarded them as integral to their local authority. They are, however, tangential to my argument, which is centered on what we know of diocesan and monastic organization and endowment. Although proprietary churches certainly contributed to the provision of Christian cult and indeed to the spiritual economy, their foundation and endowment is largely separate from that of the diocesan Church, and it was not integral to its social and economic activities, to its provision of cult for the diocese at large, or to its charitable work, even though they may have been involved in all these.

Unfortunately, the ecclesiastical evidence that we have for the rest of the early medieval West is nowhere near so rich as it is for Francia. We can be sure that some Visigothic churches were well endowed. Above all we know that Mérida received a vast bequest from one of the richest senators in Lusitania after bishop Paul had performed surgery to save the man's wife, following

---

36 Susan Wood, *The Proprietary Church in the Medieval West* (Oxford: Oxford University Press, 2006), 9–32; Susan Wood, "Bishops and the Proprietary Church: Diversity of Principle and Practice in Early Medieval Frankish Dominions and in Italy," in *Chiese locali e chiese regionali nell'alto medioevo*, Settimane di Studio del Centro Italiano di studi sull'Alto Medioevo, Spoleto 61 (Spoleto: Fondazione Centro di studi sull'alto medioevo, 2014), 895–912; Odette Pontal, *Die Synoden im Merowingerreich* (Paderborn: Schöningh, 1986), 178–79, 226, 235–36. For Spain, see Damián Fernández, "Property, Social Status, and Church Building in Visigothic Iberia," *Journal of Late Antiquity* 9, no. 2 (2016): 512–41; David Addison, "Property and 'Publicness': Bishops and Lay-founded Churches in Post-Roman Hispania," *Early Medieval Europe* 28, no. 2 (2020): 175–96.

an unsuccessful pregnancy.[37] This is said to have dwarfed all the other donations to the diocese. The author of the *Vitas Patrum Emeretensium* states that as a result "in those days the church of Mérida was so wealthy that no church in the land of Spain was richer." This, however, would seem to imply that other churches had since caught up, and perhaps even overtaken Mérida in wealth by the mid-seventh century; we can guess that these included Toledo and Seville. In terms of the wealth of the monasteries of Visigothic Spain we only have the slightest of hints as to their landholdings, although the recent publication of four early documents from San Martín de Asán shows that already before the conversion of Reccared to Catholicism some monasteries were receiving property over quite a wide territory.[38] But in Visigothic Spain, there were limitations as to how much might be given to the Church, in that a donor who had children or grandchildren was only allowed to donate a fifth of his property to churches.[39] Despite the poverty of the evidence, Pablo Díaz,

37 *Vitas sanctorum Patrum Emeretensium*, 4.2, ed. Antonio Maya Sánchez, Corpus Christianorum, Series Latinorum 116 (Turnhout: Brepols, 1992), 26–30; Andrew T. Fear, trans., *Lives of the Visigothic Fathers* (Liverpool: Liverpool University Press, 1997), 46. Luis García Iglesias, "Las posesiones de la iglesia emeritense en época visigoda," in *Gerión: Estudios sobre la Antigüedad en homenaje al Profesor Santiago Montero Díaz*, Anejos de Gerión 2 (1989): 391–401.

38 Guillermo Tomás-Faci and José Carlos Martín-Iglesias, "Cuatro documentos inéditos del monasterio visigodo de San Martín de Asán (522–586)," *Mittellateinisches Jahrbuch: Internationale Zeitschrift für Mediävistik* 52, no. 2 (2017): 261–86; Guillermo Tomás-Faci, "The Transmission of Visigothic Documents in the Pyrenean Monastery of San Victorián de Asán (6th–12th centuries): Monastic Memory and Episcopal Disputes," *Antiquité tardive* 25 (2017): 303–14. For an additional charter in favor of San Martín de Asán, see Fidel Fita, "Patrología visigótica. Elpidio, Pompeyano, Vicente y Gabino, obispos de Huesca en el siglo VI," *Boletín de la Real Academia de la Historia* 49 (1906): 137–69, at 151–57.

39 *Leges Visigothorum*, 4.3.1, ed. Karl Zeumer, Monumenta Germaniae Historica, Leges Nationum Germanicarum 1 (Hanover: Hahn, 1902), 190. Isabella Velázquez, "Jural Relations as an Indicator of Syncretism from the Law of Inheritance to the Dum Inlicita of Chindaswinth," in *The Visigoths from the Migration Period to the Seventh Century: An Ethnographic Perspective*, ed. Peter Heather (Woodbridge: The Boydell Press, 1999), 225–80, at 245.

following Dietrich Claude, has stated that "the Church in its totality was the largest landowner in the kingdom."[40]

The evidence for Italy is more complicated, not least because of the division of the peninsula between the Lombards and the Empire. For ecclesiastical landholding in the Lombard region before the eighth century we have little to go on. Bobbio was a major landholder by the ninth century, when we have good documentation, which suggests that by the middle of the century the monastery owned 11,605 hectares, and among monastic landowners in northern Italy it was second only to Santa Giulia in Brescia.[41] Santa Giulia was only founded in 753, and so tells us practically nothing about monastic landholding in the Lombard period, but Bobbio certainly had some early endowment, as is clear from the charter record.[42] Most of the other monasteries for which we have evidence are first attested in the reign of Liutprand (712–744), or later.[43] A law of Aistulf (744–756) refers to monasteries with over fifty monks, suggesting that quite large communities were not uncommon by the mid-eighth century.[44]

For the Byzantine-held territory of the Exarchate, we have significant evidence relating both to the papacy and to the diocese of Ravenna.[45] In fact, it is difficult to quantify the scale

---

40 Pablo Díaz, "Visigothic Political Institutions," in *The Visigoths*, ed. Heather, 321–73, at 347.

41 Michael Richter, *Bobbio in the Early Middle Ages: The Abiding Legacy of Columbanus* (Dublin: Four Courts Press, 2008), 134.

42 *Codice diplomatico del monastero di S. Colombano di Bobbio*, vol. 1, ed. Carlo Cipolla, Fonti per la storia d'Italia 52–54 (Rome: Tipografria del Senato, 1918).

43 Gisella Wataghin Cantino, "Monasteri di età longobarda: spunti per una ricerca," in *XXXVI Corso di cultura sull'arte ravennate e bizantina: seminario internazionale di studi sul tema: Ravenna e l'Italia fra Goti e Longobardi: Ravenna, 14–22 aprile 1989* (Ravenna: Girasole, 1989), 73–100; Neil Christie, *The Lombards: the Ancient Langobards* (Oxford: Blackwell, 1995), 195–98.

44 *Ahistulfi leges*, 19, ed. Claudio Assara and Stefano Gasparri, *Le leggi dei Longobardi: Storia, memoria e diritto di un populo germanico* (Rome: Viella, 2005), 282 ff.

45 Merle Eisenberg and Paolo Tedesco, "Seeing the Churches like the State: Taxes and Wealth Redistribution in Late Antique Italy," *Early Medieval Eu-*

of papal landholding. Leaving aside its account of the gifts of Constantine, to which we shall return, the *Liber Pontificalis* is curiously silent about donations of property rather than of treasure, and especially gold and silver liturgical objects.[46] The correspondence of popes Vigilius, Pelagius I, and Gregory the Great, however, has allowed Federico Marazzi to build up a compelling picture of the papal estates in Lazio in the sixth and seventh centuries.[47] In addition, the popes held land in northern Italy, the islands of Sicily, Sardinia, and Corsica, as well as the Cottian Alps, southern Gaul, and Illyricum.[48] In terms of actual figures, we know that the papacy received 2,100 *solidi* from its estates in Picenum under Gelasius (492–496), but that this dropped to 500 *solidi* under Pelagius I (556–561), because of the Gothic Wars.[49] These figures are worth bearing in mind when juxtaposing the evidence for the fifth and the sixth centuries. In some regions of Italy, at least, the economy had collapsed. Under Gregory the Great, the Provençal estates of the bishop of Rome were worth 400 *solidi per annum.*[50]

Our next major piece of evidence is that of Theophanes, concerning the supposed seizure of papal property in southern

---

rope 29, no. 4 (2021): 505–34, at 519–28.

46 For the treasure, Dominic Janes, *God and Gold in Late Antiquity* (Cambridge: Cambridge University Press, 1998), 57–58; Ruth Leader-Newby, *Silver and Society in Late Antiquity: Functions and Meanings of Silver Plate in the Fourth to Seventh Centuries* (Aldershot: Ashgate, 2004), 61–66.

47 Federico Marazzi, *I "patrimonia sanctae Romanae ecclesiae" nel Lazio (secoli IV-X): struttura amministrativa e prassi gestionali*, Nuovi studi storici 37 (Rome: Nella Sede Dell'Istituto Palazzo Borromini, 1998).

48 Jeffrey Richards, *The Popes and the Papacy in the Early Middle Ages, 476–752* (London: Routledge, 1979), 307–22. John R.C. Martyn, *The Letters of Gregory the Great,* 3 vols. (Toronto: Pontifical Institute of Mediaeval Studies, 2004), vol. 1, 162, n. 232, states that seventy-four letters of the pope refer to the patrimony in Sicily: for a list of the Sicilian letters, see the index entry in vol. 3, 950.

49 Philipp Jaffe, *Regesta Pontificum Romanorum,* 2nd edn. (Leipzig: Graz, 1885), 633; Pelagius I, ep. 83, ed. Pius M. Gasso and Columba M. Batlle, *Pelagii Papae epistolae quae supersunt (556–61)* (Montserrat: In Abbatia Montisserati, 1956), 203–4. Richards, *The Popes and the Papacy in the Early Middle Ages,* 307–8.

50 Gregory I, *Register,* 3.33, ed. Norberg, *Registrum Epistularum,* 179.

Italy by the emperor Leo III in 732–733. This talks of landed estates with a yield of either 410,400 or 25,200 *solidi,* depending on which textual reading one accepts.[51] As Vivien Prigent has noted, both of these figures are problematic.[52] The first is almost certainly too high, and the second too low. Agnellus states that the income from just the Sicilian patrimony of Ravenna in the pontificate of Maurus (642–671) was 31,000 *solidi,* of which 16,000 went into the coffers of the Church and 15,000 went to the emperor.[53] Income from the papal estates taken over by agents of the Byzantine emperor was surely greater than this, regardless of the chronological problems in the account given by Theophanes.[54] Ravenna's Sicilian estates also yielded 50,000 *modia* of wheat, reddened hides, purple robes, silk episcopal vestments, and vases of brass and silver for the mother Church.

In addition to its Sicilian estates, Ravenna held land throughout Italy — according to Agnellus, Justinian had granted to its Church "the property of the Goths, not only in the cities, but

---

51 Theophanes, *Chronographia,* AM 6224 *(731/732),* ed. Carl de Boor (Bonn: Teubner, 1883), 410; Cyril Mango and Roger Scott, trans., *The Chronicle of Theophanes the Confessor: Byzantine and Near Eastern History, AD 284–813* (Oxford: Oxford University Press, 1997), 567–69.

52 Vivien Prigent, "Les empereurs isauriens et la confiscation des patrimoines pontificaux d'Italie du Sud," *Mélanges de l'École française de Rome, Moyen Âge* 116, no. 2 (2004): 557–94, at 573–74. For the problems with this passage, see also Wolfram Brandes, "Byzantinischer Bilderstreit, das Papsttum und die Pippinische Schenkung. Neue Forschungen zum Ost-West Verhältnis im 8. Jahrhundert," in *Menschen, Bilder, Spracher, Dinge: Wege der Kommunikation zwischen Byzanz und dem Westen, 2: Menschen und Worte,* ed. Falko Daim, Christian Gastgeber, Dominik Heher, and Claudia Rapp (Mainz: Verlag des Römisch-Germanischen Zentralmuseums, 2018), 63–79, at 64–65; Wolfram Brandes, "Das Schweigen des *Liber pontificalis.* Die 'Enteignung' der päpstlichen Patrimonen Siziliens und Unteritaliens in der 50er Jahren des 8. Jahrhunderts," in *Fontes Minores* 12, ed. Wolfram Brandes, Lars Hoffmann, and Kirill Maksimovič (Frankfurt: Löwenklau-Gesellschaft, 2014), 97–203, at 113.

53 Agnellus, *Liber Pontificalis Ecclesiae Ravennatis,* 111, ed. Mauskopf Deliyannis, 281–82.

54 Brandes, "Das Schweigen des *Liber pontificalis.*"

also in the suburban villas and hamlets."[55] At roughly the same time, archbishop Maximian acquired a large area of woodland in Istria.[56] Clearly these constituted massive acquisitions following Justinian's conquest of Italy. In the late 520s, the income of the Church of Ravenna appears to have been a mere 12,000 *solidi* — not much more than a third of what it received from Sicily alone a century later. The post-Conquest endowments must have been substantial. Jan-Olof Tjäder, who edited the texts, thought that one of the Ravenna papyri, which he dated to 565–570, related to revenue deriving from some of the estates that were given by Justinian.[57] The document, albeit fragmentary, shows the Church paying the *comes patrimonii* 932.5 *solidi* and the prefect 1153.5 *solidi,* and still having revenue left over. In addition to the 31 papyrus documents to survive from the episcopal archive, we also have the tenth-century *Codex Bavarus,* a Breviary of the Church of Ravenna, which covers around 168 land transactions in 8 *territoria* of central Italy up to the late ninth century.[58] Most of the entries refer to leases made by the Church of Ravenna, but 16 donations are also listed,[59] giving an impression of the range of the holdings in the area of the Marche. For the most part, there is no indication of the chronology of acquisition, although one donation is listed as being received in the reign of Heraclius,[60] and another in the episcopate of Damian (689–705).[61] Of the leases, the editor Giuseppi

55 Agnellus, *Liber Pontificalis Ecclesiae Ravennatis,* 85, ed. Mauskopf Deliyannis, 252–53.

56 Agnellus, *Liber Pontificalis Ecclesiae Ravennatis,* 70, ed. Mauskopf Deliyannis, 238–40; trans. Mauskopf Deliyannis, *Book of the Pontiffs,* 184–86.

57 Jan-Olof Tjäder, *Die nichtliterarischen lateinischen Papyri italiens aus der Zeit 445–700,* 2 vols. (Lund: Gleerup, 1955–82), vol. 1, 178–83, n. 2.

58 *Breviarium ecclesiae Ravennatis (Codice Bavaro) secoli VII–X,* ed. Giuseppi Rabotti, Fonti per la Storia d'Italia 110 (Rome: Istituto storico italiano per il Medio Evo, 1985).

59 *Breviarium ecclesiae Ravennatis (Codice Bavaro) secoli VII–X,* 23–92, 48–49, 51–57, 59, 60–61, 93, 152, 155, 156, 174, ed. Rabotti, 23–92.

60 *Breviarium ecclesiae Ravennatis (Codice Bavaro) secoli VII–X,* 174, ed. Rabotti, 92.

61 *Breviarium ecclesiae Ravennatis (Codice Bavaro) secoli VII–X,* 59, ed. Rabotti, 33.

Rabotti dated one to the early seventh century,[62] while a further ten were negotiated in the episcopate of Damian,[63] and thirteen in that of Sergius (744–69).[64] In other words, although the *Breviarium* is primarily a document of the ninth and tenth centuries, it provides some information on Ravenna's landholding in the period of the Exarchate. It therefore illustrates Tom Brown's conclusion, that in the period after Justinian's conquest "most land [...] came to be concentrated in the hands of either the Church or the military commanders."[65]

It would, therefore, seem probable that Herlihy underestimated the scale of ecclesiastical landholding in the seventh century, when he claimed that it was very much lower than it would be two centuries later.[66] It may be that this is in part a reflection of his lack of consideration of the challenge to ecclesiastical property holding that took place across western Europe in the early eighth century, both from the emperor Leo III and from Charles Martel and Pippin III. Herlihy noted the significance of secularization in the late-Carolingian period, but he provided no comment on that of the early Carolingian period, which surely diminished the Church's reserves of property.[67]

As well as the scale of landholding, it is also important to bear in mind the numbers of ecclesiastics, clergy and monks

---

62 *Breviarium ecclesiae Ravennatis (Codice Bavaro) secoli VII–X*, 170, ed. Rabotti, 90–91, xxiii–xxiv.

63 *Breviarium ecclesiae Ravennatis (Codice Bavaro) secoli VII–X*, 23–25, 30, 32, 36–37, 64, 94, 130, ed. Rabotti, 15–17, 19–20, 22, 31, 52, 74.

64 *Breviarium ecclesiae Ravennatis (Codice Bavaro) secoli VII–X*, 27, 33, 34, 41, 63, 65, 70, 80, 129, 132, 134, 158, 177, ed. Rabotti, 12–94.

65 Brown, *Gentlemen and Officers*, 195.

66 Herlihy, "Church Property on the Continent, 700–1200," 89. Gaëlle Calvet-Marcadé, *Assassin des pauvres: l'église et l'inaliénabilité des terres à l'époque carolingienne* (Turnhout: Brepols, 2019), 106–7, has rightly noted that "secularization" is not an adequate term for the re-employment of Church property.

67 But see Paul Fouracre, *The Age of Charles Martel* (Harlow: Longman, 2000), 90–93, 123, 183, for the problematic documentation for the secularization. See also Steffen Patzold and Carine van Rhijn, "The Carolingian Local Ecclesia as a 'Temple Society'?" *Early Medieval Europe* 29, no. 4 (2021): 535–54, at 553–54.

who had to be supported by the yield from Church property. In 600, there were around 1,000 ecclesiastical dioceses in the old Roman West (1,800 is the approximate number for the whole Roman World).[68] Although Louis Duchesne reckoned that 27 Italian sees were abandoned as a result of the Lombard invasions,[69] Sergio Mochi-Onory estimated that there were 250 dioceses in the peninsula in the sixth century.[70] There were approximately 130 bishoprics in Gaul, most of them in the territory later controlled by the Franks, the rest being in Visigothic Septimania.[71] Only 87 dioceses are known in Visigothic Spain, although this may be far lower than the actual number, since there were between 300 and 400 *civitates* in the Roman period.[72] Christian Courtois reckoned that there were some 870 dioceses in Vandal Africa, of which 470 were Catholic.[73] Many of these, however, will have been small and poor.

The numbers of clergy certainly varied from diocese to diocese. Occasionally we have figures. In Rome we hear of at least

---

68 Ian Wood, *The Transformation of the Roman West* (Leeds: ARC Humanities Press, 2018), 58.

69 Louis Duchesne, "Les Évêchés d'Italie et l'invasion lombarde," *Mélanges d'Archéologie et d'Histoire de l'École française de Rome* 23 (1903): 83–116; 25 (1905): 365–99; Brown, *Gentlemen and Officers*, 40.

70 Sergio Mochi Onory, *Vescovi e Citta (sec. IV–VI)* (Bologna: Nicola Zanichelli, 1933), 5–6.

71 Duchesne, *Fastes épiscopaux,* vol. 1, 1–2; Godding, *Prêtres en Gaule mérovingienne,* 209.

72 Laurent Brassous, "Late Roman Spain," in *The Visigothic Kingdom: the Negotiations of Power in Post-Roman Iberia,* ed. Sabine Panzram and Paulo Pachá (Amsterdam: Amsterdam University Press, 2020), 39–55, at 48; J.H.W.G. Liebeschuetz, "Transformation and Decline: Are the Two Really Incompatible?" in *Die Stadt in der Spätantike: Niedergang oder Wandel? Akten des internationalen Kolloquiums in München am 30. und 31. Mai 2003,* ed. Jens-Uwe Krause and Christian Witschel (Stuttgart: Steiner, 2006), 463–83, at 466; Wood, *The Transformation of the Roman West,* 191.

73 Christian Courtois, *Les Vandales et l'Afrique* (Paris: Arts et Métiers Graphiques, 1954), 110.

70 priests in the city in 418,[74] and 67 in 499.[75] Given Justinian's Gothic War, the early sixth century may have marked a high point in clerical numbers in the city. Robert Wiśniewski has argued that there may have been more than 100 priests in Rome in c. 500, but only 40 a century later.[76] 34 priests, together with 7 abbots and 3 deacons, signed the canons of the provincial Synod of Auxerre held between 561 and 605.[77] In a dispute between bishop Ecclesius of Ravenna and his clergy during the pontificate of Felix IV (526–530) 10 priests, 11 deacons, 5 subdeacons, 12 acolytes, 12 lectors, 3 *defensors,* 4 cantors, 1 *orrearius,* and 2 *decani* traveled to Rome.[78] This cannot have been the full complement of Ravenna's clergy. It is unthinkable that the Catholic hierarchy would have left the city at the mercy of the Arians for the three or four weeks that it would have taken to have their case heard. Arnold Pöschl reckoned that the Ravenna clergy at the time must have numbered between 60 and 80.[79] The upper figure looks more likely than the lower. Gregory the Great re-

---

74 *Collectio Avellana,* 17.3, ed. Otto Günther, Corpus Scriptorum Ecclesiasticorum Latinorum 35.1 (Vienna: F. Tempsky, 1895), 64; Robert Wiśniewski, "The Last Shall be Last: The Order of Precedence among Clergy in Late Antiquity," *Sacris Erudiri* 58 (2019): 321–37, at 321. For numbers earlier in the century, see Robert Wiśniewski, "How Numerous and How Busy Were Late-Antique Presbyters?" *Zeitschrift für Antikes Christentum* 25, no. 1 (2021): 3–37, who estimates that there were approximately fifty priests in Rome in c. 400.

75 *Acta synhodi Romani,* a. 499, ed. Theodor Mommsen, *Cassiodorus Variae,* Monumenta Germaniae Historica, Auctores Antiquissimi 12 (Berlin: Weidmann, 1894), 399–415; Wiśniewski, "The Last Shall Be Last," 321.

76 Wiśniewski, "How Numerous and How Busy Were Late-Antique Presbyters?"

77 *Synod of Auxerre,* ed. Brigitte Basdevant, *Les canons des conciles mérovingiens (VIe–VIIe siècles),* 2 vols., Sources Chrétiennes 353–354 (Paris: Éditions du Cerf, 1989), vol. 2, 502–5; Godding, *Prêtres en Gaule mérovingienne,* 209.

78 Agnellus, *Liber Pontificalis ecclesiae Ravennatis,* 60, ed. Mauskopf Deliyannis, 226–31.

79 Arnold Pöschl, *Bischofsgut und mensa episcopalis: Ein Beitrag zur Geschichte des kirchlichen Vermögensrechtes,* 1: *Die Grundlagen* (Bonn: P. Hanstein, 1908), 23.

veals that there were 126 prebendaries in Naples,[80] but, unfortunately, he does not supply figures for the other clergy in the city.

A further indication of clerical numbers may be gained from what we know of the number of churches in individual cities and dioceses. In Rome we know of 8 major basilicas, 28 titular churches, 31 non-titular churches, 14 oratories and chapels, and 11 monasteries and *xenodochia* within the *urbs,* by the end of the seventh century, and an additional 7 major basilicas, 32 smaller churches, and 12 monasteries in the *suburbium.*[81] Some of these churches will have been served by several clerics (as we shall see), while others (particularly among the non-titular churches) may not have had a permanent staff. Tom Brown has noted the existence of 72 churches in Ravenna, as well as 20 monasteries by the eighth century.[82]

Outside the cities we are less well informed, but we do have the evidence of a series of disputes between the bishops of Siena and Arezzo, beginning in c. 650 and stretching to 715 and beyond, over jurisdiction in a number of parishes in Tuscany. This is a dossier that is well known to scholars of the government of Lombard and Carolingian Italy,[83] but it is also of considerable importance for the history of the Church. The initial *intentio* of

---

80 Gregory I, *Register,* 9.22, ed. Norberg, *Registrum Epistularum,* 582.

81 Federico Guidobaldi, "'Topografia ecclesiastica' di Roma (IV–VII) secolo," in *Roma dall'antichita al medioevo: Archeologia e storia,* vol. 1, ed. Maria Stella Arena, Paolo Delogu, Lidia Paroli, Marco Ricci, Lucia Sagui, and Laura Vendittelli (Milan: Electa, 2001), 40–51, at 46–47.

82 Brown, *Gentlemen and Officers,* 176.

83 Stefano Gasparri, "Il regno longobardo in Italia. Struttura e funzionamento di uno stato altomedievale," in *Il regno dei Longobardi in Italia. Archeologia, società e istituzioni,* ed. Stefano Gasparri (Spoleto: Centro italiano di studi sull'Alto Medioevo, 2004), 1–88, at 5–16; Chris Wickham, "Aristocratic Power in Eighth-Century Lombard Italy," in *After Rome's Fall: Narrators and Sources of Early Medieval History,* ed. Alexander C. Murray (Toronto: University of Toronto Press, 1998), 153–70, at 153. Also, Alexandra Chavarria Arnau, "Churches as Assembly Places in Early Medieval Italy," in *Power and Place in Europe in the Early Middle Ages,* ed. Jayne Carroll, Andrew Reynolds, and Barbara Yorke (Oxford: Oxford University Press, 2019), 203–15, at 208, 210–12.

c. 650 deals with 6 parishes,[84] the first *notitia iudicati* of 714 with 16 and 2 monasteries,[85] the *breve de inquisitione* includes a further 6,[86] and the final *iudicium* a total of 22.[87] Exactly how many parishes were involved is unclear because of questions of identification, but certainly more than 20. The bishop of Arezzo, who won the case, claimed that these had belonged to his diocese since Roman times. This was clearly an exaggeration, because a small number of the foundations are explicitly stated to have been recent, but it is probable that most did indeed date to the period before the arrival of the Lombards in 568/569. And this is just the number of churches disputed between the dioceses of Arezzo and Siena — it tells us nothing about the core parishes of either diocese. More than 30 priests testified in the course of the breve of 715.

The evidence for Visigothic Spain is less extensive although for the Suevic kingdom of Galicia, from between 572 and 582, we do have a list of 107 churches to be found in 25 pagi of the dioceses of Bracara (Braga), Portugale (Porto), Lameco, Conimbriga (Coimbra), Viseo, Dumio, Egitania, Luco (Lugo), Auria (Ourense), Asturica (Astorga), Iria, Tude (Tuy), and Britonia.[88]

---

84 *Codice Diplomatico Longobardo, 4 conventio* (c. 650), ed. Luigi Schiaparelli, 3 vols., Fonti per la storia d'Italia 52–54 (Rome: Istituto storico italiano, 1929), vol. 1, 8–11.

85 *Codice Diplomatico Longobardo, 17 notitia iudicati* (714), ed. Schiaparelli, vol. 1, 46–51.

86 *Codice Diplomatico Longobardo, 19 breve de inquisitione* (715), ed. Schiaparelli, vol. 1, 61–77.

87 *Codice Diplomatico Longobardo, 20 iudicatum* (715), ed. Schiaparelli, vol. 1, 77–84.

88 *Parochiale Suevum,* ed. Frater Glorie, *Itineraria et alia Geographica,* Corpus Christianorum, Series Latina 175 (Turnhout: Brepols, 1965), 412–20; José Carlos Sánchez Pardo, "Organización eclesiástica y social en la Galicia tardoantigua. Una perspectiva geográfico-arqueológica del Parroquial suevo," *Hispania Sacra* 66 (2014): 439–80, at 441. See also Jorge López Quiroga, "El I y II Concilios de Braga y el 'Parroquial Suevo'. Élites eclesiásticas y control del territorio en la Gallaecia del siglo VI," in *In tempore Sueborum: el tiempo de los suevos en la Gallaecia (411–585), el primo reino medieval de occidente.* Volumen de estudios, ed. Jorge López Quiroga (Ourense: Deputación Provincial de Ourense, 2018), 139–44.

These are not thought to constitute the total number of churches in the region, but rather to be those to be found in centers of administrative importance.[89]

Turning to Francia, Clare Stancliffe has counted 16 churches, oratories, and monasteries in the diocesan center of Tours, and 42 in the surrounding countryside by c. 600.[90] This is somewhat lower than the 90 noted by Margarete Weidemann for Le Mans.[91] By the eighth century, Metz had 43 churches.[92] One can compare these figures with the 40 churches known from Oxyrhynchus in 535.[93]

Judging from the evidence from Auxerre and Ravenna, most of the churches listed in the western diocesan histories ought to have had at least one senior cleric. From the evidence of cities such as Auxerre, Le Mans, and Metz, we can argue for a figure of around 50 senior clergy (bishop, priests, deacons) on average per diocese, and this may well have been exceeded in such Italian dioceses as Arezzo and Siena. However, the numbers of clerics in the poor rural dioceses of Africa were surely lower than elsewhere. Given the number of dioceses in the post-Roman West, we might be talking of around 40,000 secular clergy at the start of the sixth century. There would, however, have been many more if one adds the lower clerical orders, such as the 126 Neapolitan prebendaries mentioned by Gregory the Great.[94]

---

89 Sánchez Pardo, "Organización eclesiástica y social en la Galicia tardoantigua," 460.
90 Clare Stancliffe, "From Town to Country: The Christianisation of the Touraine, 370–600," in *Studies in Church History* 16: *The Church in Town and Countryside,* ed. Derek Baker (Oxford: Blackwell, 1979), 43–59, at 46–48.
91 Weidemann, *Geschichte des Bistums Le Mans,* vol. 3, 438.
92 Theodor Klauser, "Eine Stationsliste der Metzer Kirche aus dem 8. Jahrhunderts, wahrscheinlich ein Werk Chrodegangs," *Ephemerides Liturgicae* 44 (1930): 162–93; Martin A. Claussen, *The Reform of the Frankish Church. Chrodegang of Metz and the "Regula Canonicorum" in the Eighth Century* (Cambridge: Cambridge University Press, 2004), 276–86.
93 Peter M. Head, "Some Recently Published NT Papyri from Oxyrhynchus: An Overview and Preliminary Assessment," *Tyndale Bulletin* 51 (2000): 1–16, at 4, n. 9, citing Oxyrhynchus Papyrus 1357.
94 Gregory I, *Register,* 11.22, ed. Norberg, *Registrum Epistularum,* 892–93.

Turning to monastic numbers, Jenal identified 100 monasteries in Italy in the sixth century.[95] There were clearly many for which we have no evidence: Cassiodorus talks of monks building monasteries "within the patrimonies of powerful Christians, just as swallows build nests in the cedars of Lebanon."[96] Around 50 monasteries are known from the Lombard regions of Italy, although many of these may have been eighth-century foundations.[97] In what had been the Exarchate, there were 54 in Rome, 20 in Ravenna, and 13 in Naples alone by 819, according to Tom Brown, although some of these, as he notes (like those listed in the documents recording the Arezzo–Siena dispute),[98] were very small.[99] Although Gregory the Great does not provide numbers of monasteries in Rome, he does reveal that there were 3,000 nuns on the census list of the city — and he also tells us that they received 80 lbs. of gold per annum from the coffers of St. Peter's.[100]

The evidence for Spain is distinctly patchy, and only 86 Visigothic monasteries are known.[101] The largest may have been the Suevic monastery of Dumio, although we do hear of a community founded by Donatus, an African abbot, which had 70

95 Georg Jenal, *Italia ascetica atque monastica: das Asketen- und Mönchtum in Italien von den Anfängen bis zur Zeit der Langobarden (ca. 150/250–604)*, 2 vols. (Stuttgart: Hiersemann, 1995).

96 Cassiodorus, *Expositio in Psalterium,* 103, verse 17, Patrologia Latina 70.

97 Wataghin Cantino, "Monasteri di età longobarda: spunti per una ricercar"; Christie, *The Lombards,* 195.

98 *Codice Diplomatico Longobardo,* n. 17, ed. Schiaparelli, vol. 1, 46–51.

99 Brown, *Gentlemen and Officers,* 176.

100 Gregory I, *Register,* 7.23, ed. Norberg, *Registrum Epistularum,* 474–78.

101 Francisco José Moreno Martín, *La arquitectura monástica hispana entre la Tardoantigüedad y la Alta Edad Media,* BAR, International Series 2287 (Oxford: Archaeopress, 2011), 691–92; Wood, "Entrusting Western Europe to the Church," 49; Jorge López Quiroga, "Monasterios altomedievales hispanos: lugares de emplazamiento y ordenación de sus espacios," in *Los monasterios medievales en sus emplazamientos: lugares de memoria de lo sagrado,* ed. José Ángel García de Cortázar and Ramón Teja (Aguilar de Campoo: Fundación Santa María la Real, Centro de Estudios del Románico, 2016), 66–99. Also, Artemio Martínez Tejera, "Monasticism in Late Antique Iberia: Its Origins and Influences," *Visigothic Symposium* 2 (2017–2018): 176–94.

inmates, already in the mid-sixth century.[102] Yet more intriguing is the highly important community of Agali, which was in the neighborhood of Toledo, which produced a number of leading churchmen, including the city's bishops Helladius, Ildefonsus, and perhaps Julian, but whose site remains unidentified and whose scale is hidden from us.[103] And there are additional references to unnamed monasteries, notably to foundations of Fructuosus of Braga, which are said to have attracted so many monks as to cause a crisis in military recruitment.[104]

Our best evidence again comes from Merovingian Francia. Hartmut Atsma calculated that there were around 220 monasteries in the Frankish kingdom by 600, and 550 just over a century later.[105] Some of these had well over 100 inmates: we can reasonably be skeptical of the 800 monks supposedly to be found in Jumièges,[106] but the figure of 220 given for Luxeuil in the *Vita Walarici* is not impossible — especially since Jonas of Bobbio states that Fontaines, a minor offshoot of Luxeuil, boasted 60 monks in the early seventh century.[107] A list preserved in a hagiographical text of the tenth or eleventh century claims that there were 1,335 monks and nuns in 12 monasteries in the city of

---

102 Ildefonsus, *De viris illustribus,* 3, ed. Carmen Codoñer Merino, *Ildefonsi Toletani episcopi Opera,* Corpus Christianorum, Series Latinorum 114A (Turnhout: Brepols, 2007); Martínez Tejera, "Monasticism in Late Antique Iberia," 184–85.

103 Luis García Moreno, "Los monjes y monasterios en las ciudades de las Españas tardorromanas y visigodas," *Habis* 24 (1993): 179–92.

104 *Vita Fructuosi,* 14, ed. Manuel Díaz y Díaz, *La vida de San Fructuoso de Braga* (Braga, 1974), 104–6. Wendy Davies adds, in a personal communication, "Later charters, which attribute foundation of many small monasteries to these centuries, would also suggest many more."

105 Hartmut Atsma, "Les monastères urbains du Nord de la Gaule," *Revue d'Histoire de l'Église de France* 62, no. 168, *La christianisation des pays entre Loire et Rhin (IVᵉ–VIIᵉ siècle)* (1976): 163–87, at 168.

106 Julien Loth, ed., *Histoire de l'abbaye royale de St-Pierre de Jumièges* (Rouen: Société de l'Histoire Normandie, 1882), vol. 1, 22.

107 *Vita Walarici,* 5, ed. Bruno Krusch, Monumenta Germaniae Historica, Scriptores Rerum Merovingicarum 4 (Hanover: Hahn, 1902), 162; Jonas, *Vita Columbani,* I, 17, ed. Bruno Krusch, Monumenta Germaniae Historica, Scriptores Rerum Germanicarum (Hanover: Hahn, 1905), 162.

Vienne.[108] Although the figures have been queried, the numbers for individual communities are not out of line with those collected by Ursmer Berlière.[109] If they are remotely accurate, and I see no reason to doubt them, they may be set alongside the estimated population size of the comparable, and neighboring, city of Lyon, which Tertius Chandler and Gerald Fox calculated as 12,000 inhabitants in the year 800.[110] In other words, monks and nuns may have constituted a tenth of the population of Vienne in the late sixth century!

I leave aside the question of the number of monasteries in Britain and Ireland, where again the evidence is uneven. That monasticism was flourishing in pre-Viking Ireland is clear from the hagiography and from the archaeology.[111] In Anglosaxon England, monastic history, of course, only begins after the conversion of Kent. Thereafter it is reasonably well attested in the charter record and in Bede's narrative, which is, of course, most valuable for the history of Northumbrian monasticism.[112] The Welsh documentation is more problematic, not least because most of the hagiographical material is late in date. But from the Llandaff charters Wendy Davies noted the existence of 35 monasteries in southeast Wales before 700.[113]

Despite the gaps in our evidence, we can reckon that there was a much greater number of monks and nuns to be found

---

108 *Vita Clari* II, in *Acta Sanctorum der Bollandisten, Ökumenisches Heiligen-lexikon,* https://www.heiligenlexikon.de/ASJanuar/Clarus_von_Vienne. html; Ian Wood, *The Transformation of the Roman West* (Leeds: ARC Humanities Press, 2018), 71.

109 Ursmer Berlière, "Le nombre des moines dans les anciens monastères," *Revue Bénédictine* 41 (1929): 231–61; 42 (1930), 19–42.

110 Tertius Chandler and Gerald Fox, *Three Thousand Years of Urban Growth* (New York: Academic Press, 1974), 114.

111 Richard Sharpe, *Medieval Irish Saints' Lives: An Introduction to "Vitae sanctorum Hiberniae"* (Oxford: Clarendon Press, 1991); Dáibhí Ó Cróinín, "Hiberno-Latin literature to 1169," in *A New History of Ireland,* vol. 1: *Prehistoric and Early Ireland,* ed. Dáibhí Ó Cróinín (Oxford: Oxford University Press, 2005), 371–404, at 384–87.

112 Wood, "Entrusting Western Europe to the Church," 52–54.

113 Wendy Davies, *An Early Welsh Microcosm: Studies in the Llandaff Charters* (London: Royal Historical Society, 1978), 121–24, 134–38.

in Western Europe than there were bishops, priests and deacons. We are surely dealing with a total number of clergy and monks in the low hundreds of thousands. In other words, the total number of religious in the seventh century might have approached A.H.M. Jones's estimate of 286,000 soldiers in the fourth-century West.[114] These churchmen had to be provided for, and, although many lived off their own property, others had to be supported from revenues drawn from ecclesiastical landed property, which were also used to fund church buildings, the requirements of Christian cult, and the pastoral work of the Church. In other words, not only was the Church a very considerable landowner, but it was also staffed by a sizeable clerical order, which, although it was a small proportion of the overall population, was a significant consumer of resources. The Church deserves to be treated as an economic entity in its own right, and not just as a segment of the elite.

---

114 A.H.M. Jones, *The Later Roman Empire 284–602* (Oxford: Blackwell, 1964), 679.

3

The Distribution and Redistribution of Church Wealth

Like the soldiers of the Roman army, the clergy and the monks of the late-antique and early medieval world had to be provided for. Unlike the late-Roman army, they were not the recipients of the money raised by imperial or royal taxation, although they often benefitted from exemptions and privileges granted by kings. Above all they were the beneficiaries of gifts, which were regarded as inalienable possessions of the Church, except in certain exceptional circumstances.[1] Monks were supported by the endowments of their monasteries, although, as the letters of Gregory the Great make clear, these were not always adequate. On a number of occasions, the pope provided additional funds for monastic communities, not least for the nuns of Rome.[2] Of

---

1   I deliberately use the phrase coined by Annette Weiner, *Inalienable Possessions: The Paradox of Keeping-While-Giving* (Berkeley: University of California Press, 1992). For its application to the Carolingian world, see Gaëlle Calvet-Marcadé, *Assassin des pauvres: l'église et l'inaliénabilité des terres à l'époque carolingienne* (Turnhout: Brepols, 2019), 105–8. For differing practices with regard to alienation in Gaul and Italy, Merle Eisenberg and Paolo Tedesco, "Seeing the Churches Like the State: Taxes and Wealth Redistribution in Late Antique Italy," *Early Medieval Europe* 29, no. 4 (2021): 505–34, at 515–19.
2   Gregory I, *Register,* 1.23, 2.1, 3.3, 7.23, ed. Dag Norberg, *Registrum Epistularum,* Corpus Christianorum, Series Latina 140–140A (Turnhout: Brepols,

51

course, many of the lower clergy must have earned a living, but we should note the references to provision for priests in the canons of the councils of Epaon (517)[3] and IV Orléans (541),[4] while II Braga (572) stated that no bishop was to dedicate a church unless he had received a charter providing for the lighting of the church and sustenance for the cleric serving there.[5]

Churches and churchmen depended to a large extent on the distribution of funds raised from ecclesiastical property. In addition to the endowments of individual churches, there was the income from the land held by the diocese, as well as various other dues. There is, however, little to indicate that an ecclesiastical tithe was required in this period,[6] although a *decima* is mentioned in the *Vita Severini* by Eugippius,[7] and by Caesarius.[8] The second Council of Mâcon (585) seems to be the first attempt to enforce it.[9] But bishops might claim the *cathedraticum*, a levy of 2 *solidi* from each parish, which is attested in Spain as well as

---

1982), 21, 90, 148–49, 474–78.

3 Council of Epaon (517), c. 5, ed. Brigitte Basdevant, *Les canons des conciles mérovingiens (VIe–VIIe siècles)*, 2 vols., Sources Chrétiennes 353–354 (Paris: Éditions du Cerf, 1989), vol. 1, 104.

4 Council of Orléans IV (541), cc. 7, 18, 26, ed. Basdevant, *Les canons des conciles mérovingiens*, vol. 1, 270, 276, 280.

5 Council of Braga II (572), c. 5, ed. José Vives, *Concilios visigóticos e hispano-romanos* (Madrid: C.S.I.C., 1963), 83. Paul Fouracre, "Lights, Power and the Moral Economy of Early Medieval Europe," *Early Medieval Europe* 28, no. 3 (2020): 367–87, esp. 370–71.

6 Valerio Neri, *I marginali nell'Occidente tardoantico: poveri, "infames" e criminali nella nascente società cristiana*, Munera 12 (Bari: Edipuglia, 1996), 114–15; Robert Godding, *Prêtres en Gaule mérovingienne* (Brussels: Société des Bollandistes, 2001), 346–49.

7 Eugippius, *Vita Severini*, 17–18, ed. Philippe Régerat, Eugippe, *Vie de saint Séverin*, Sources Chrétiennes 374 (Paris: Éditions du Cerf, 1991), 226–31.

8 Caesarius, *Sermons*, 13, 3; 33, 1; 71, 2; 229, 4, ed. Germain Morin, Corpus Christianorum, Series Latina 103–104 (Turnhout: Brepols, 1953); Neri, *I marginali*, 115–16.

9 Council of Mâcon II (585), c. 6, ed. Basdevant, *Les canons des conciles mérovingiens*, vol. 2, 464. A.H.M. Jones, "Church Finance in the Fifth and Sixth Centuries," *Journal of Theological Studies* 11 (1960): 84–94, at 85. Also, Neri, *I marginali*, 113–16.

Italy.[10] The bishops of Ravenna are known to have received 888 hens, 266 chickens, 8,880 eggs, 3,760 pounds (*librae*) of pork (1236.28 kilos) and 3,450 pounds of honey (1124.36 kilos), as well as geese and milk to cover their obligations of hospitality.[11] This may sound considerable, but for his Lenten retreat to the monastery of Île-Barbe the ascetic bishop Eucherius of Lyon ordered 300 *modii* of corn (2,610 liters), 200 of wine (1,740 liters), 200 pounds of cheese (65.76 kilos), and 100 pounds of oil (32.88 kilos).[12] In addition to such renders, churches could also rely on the alms and oblations of the faithful.

For the most part, however, churches must have depended on the income drawn from their own estates. In large areas of western Europe, the majority of ecclesiastical income was redistributed according to the *Quadripartum,* a fourfold division of revenue laid down by a number of authorities, popes, and councils, in the fifth and sixth centuries. The *Quadripartum* is first referred to by pope Simplicius (468–483),[13] and full statements come in three letters and two fragments of letters from Gelasius (492–496), which talk of the *quartae* as *portiones consuetae,*[14] and in the so-called *Responsiones* of Gregory the

---

10 Pelagius I, ep. 25, 32, ed. Pius M. Gasso and Columba M. Batlle, *Pelagii Papae epistolae quae supersunt (556–61)* (Montserrat: In Abbatia Montisserati, 1956), 79–80, 88–89; Jones, "Church Finances in the Fifth and Sixth Centuries," 91; Council of Braga II (572), c. 2 and Council of Toledo VII (646), 4, ed. Vives, *Concilios visigóticos e hispano-romanos,* 81–82 and 254–55.

11 Jan-Olof Tjäder, *Die nichtliterarischen Lateinischen Papyri italiens aus der Zeit 445–700,* 2 vols. (Lund: Gleerup, 1955–1982), vol. 1, 186–88, n. 31; Jones, "Church Finance in the Fifth and Sixth Centuries," 92.

12 Eucherius of Lyon, letter to Philo, ed. Alain Dubreucq, "Les sources textuelles relatives aux monastère de l'Île-Barbe au Haut Moyen Âge" (forthcoming).

13 Simplicius, ep. 1 (475), ed. Andreas Thiel, *Epistolae Romanorum Pontificum Genuinae* (Braunschweig: Brunsbergae, 1868), vol. 1, 176: "de reditibus ecclesiae et oblatione fidelium quod deceat nescienti, nihil licere permittat, sed sola ei ex his quarta portio remittatur. Duas ecclesiasticis fabricis et erogationi peregrinorum et pauperum profuturae […]."

14 Gelasius, ep. 14.27, ed. Thiel, *Epistolae Romanorum Pontificum Genuinae,* vol. 1, 378: "Quatuor autem tam de reditu quam de oblatione fidelium, prout cujuslibet ecclesiae facultas admittit, sicut dudum rationabiliter est decre-

Great (590–604) to Augustine of Canterbury.[15] Other letters of Gregory provide important details on the allocation of Church revenue,[16] and his implementation of the *Quadripartum* is described by John the Deacon in his Life of the pope.[17] It is also referred to in a letter of pope Felix IV (526–530), addressed to bishop Ecclesius of Ravenna[18] — a ruling which was to have significant repercussions for the city's clergy towards the end of the following century, when they claimed that archbishop Theodore (c. 677–c. 691) had stolen their quarter from them.[19] In addition to the papal rulings, we find a similar division of income in the canons of the first Council of Orléans (511).[20]

In all these cases the income of the Church is divided into four, although there is some variation over the recipients of the individual quarters. A classic definition is that given by Gregory the Great, which is essentially the same as the one to be found in the letters of Gelasius: "all money received should be divided into four portions: that is, one for the bishop and his household for the purposes of hospitality and entertainment, a second for the clergy, a third for the poor, and a fourth for the repair of

---

tum, convenit fieri portiones; quarum sit una pontificis, altera clericorum, pauperum tertia, quarta fabricis applicanda."

15 Gregory I, *Register*, 9.36, 39, ed. Norberg, *Registrum Epistularum*, 925–29, 934–36; Bede, *Historia Ecclesiastica Gentis Anglorum*, 1.27, http://www.the-latinlibrary.com/bede.html; Bertram Colgrave and Roger Mynors, trans., *Bede's Ecclesiastical History of the English Nation* (Oxford: Clarendon, 1969), 41–54. The most recent edition of the *Responsiones* is that by Valeria Mattaloni, *Rescriptum beati Gregorii papae ad Augustinum episcopum seu Libellus responsionum* (Florence: Sismel, 2017).

16 Gregory, *Register*, 5.27, 39; 8.7; 9.144; 11.22; 13.45, ed. Norberg, *Registrum Epistularum*, 294, 314–18, 695, 892–93, 1051–52.

17 John the Deacon, *Vita Gregorii*, 2.24, Patrologia Latina 75, cols. 96–97. Jeffrey Richards, *Consul of God: the Life and Times of Gregory the Great* (London: Routledge, 1980), 95.

18 Agnellus, *Liber Pontificalis ecclesiae Ravennatis*, 60, ed. Deborah Mauskopf Deliyannis, Corpus Christianorum, Continuatio Medievalis 199 (Turnhout: Brepols, 2006), 226–31.

19 Agnellus, *Liber Pontificalis ecclesiae Ravennatis*, 117–18, 121, ed. Mauskopf Deliyannis, 288–89, 292–95.

20 Council of Orléans I (511), c. 5, ed. Basdevant, *Les canons des conciles mérovingiens*, vol. 1, 76.

churches."[21] In the canons of the first Council of Orléans, which might only deal with the proceeds from land recently received from Clovis, the quarters were allocated "to the restoration of churches, the alms of clerics (*sacerdotes*), the poor, and the redemption of captives."[22]

The arrangements in Spain were slightly different. The canons from Suevic Gallicia imply that the proper division of Church income was into three. This, oddly enough, was what Theodorus lector, writing in Constantinople in the early sixth century, thought was also the tradition in Rome.[23] Already in the First Council of Braga (561) one finds: "it is agreed that the goods of the Church should be divided into three equal portions: that is, one for the bishop, a second for the clergy, a third for repairs and the lighting of the church, for which part either the archpriest or the archdeacon administering it should render account to the bishop."[24] In an epitome of the council's canons from c. 600 we find a clear reassertion of a tripartite division: "Three portions should be made of the goods of a Church: for the bishop, the church and the clergy."[25] Ten years later, the second Council of

---

21 Bede, *Historia Ecclesiastica Gentis Anglorum*, 1.27.

22 Council of Orléans I (511), c. 5, ed. Basdevant, *Les canons des conciles mérovingiens*, vol. 1, 76.

23 Theodorus lector, *Excerpta ex Historia Ecclesiastica*, 2.55, Patrologia Graeca 86 (1865), cols. 211–12: "Romanae ecclesiae hunc esse morem, ut res immobiles non possideat, sed si forte possessiones obvenerint, confestim eas vendat, et pretium in tres partes distribuat, quarum una tradatur ecclesiae, altera episcopo, tertia clero; idem etiam fit in reliquis rebus, quae non sunt soli."

24 Council of Braga I (561), c. 7, ed. Vives, *Concilios visigóticos e hispano-romanos*, 68: "item placuit ut rebus ecclesiasticis tres aeque fiant portiones, id est una episcopi, alia clericorum, tertia in recuperationem vel in luminariis ecclesiae; de qua parte sive archipresbyter sive archidiaconus illam administrans episcopo faciens rationem."

25 *Ex concilio bracarense*, 7, ed. Gonzalo Martínez Díez, *El Epítome Hispánico. Una colección canónica española del siglo VII. Estudio y texto crítico* (Santander: Universidad Pontificia de Comillas, 1961), 174: "De rebus ecclesiae tres fiant partes: episcopi, ecclesiae et clericorum." My thanks to Dave Addison for supplying me with this reference.

Braga prohibited a bishop from claiming the *tertia* of oblations allocated to the lighting of the churches.[26]

In the Visigothic kingdom, Church income was also subject to a three-fold division. Even prior to the conversion of the Gothic leadership, the Catholic Council of Tarragona (516) forbade a bishop from taking more than a third of the income of a *parrocia*, on account of the poverty of some churches and the ruinous state of their basilicas. And it refers to the arrangement as an ancient tradition.[27] The seventh-century canons specify a division between the bishop, the priests and deacons, and the *primicerius,* who was to distribute the final third among the lower clergy, as appropriate.[28]

In contrast to the pattern of financial distribution laid down by the *Quadraticum,* there is no mention here of any portion allocated to the poor. The fourth Council of Toledo (633) did, however, instruct bishops to protect the poor.[29] But the first canon of V Toledo (636) merely instituted litanies "pro abundante iniquitate et deficiente caritate" ("on account of abundant iniquity and deficient charity").[30] Attached to the canons of the tenth Council of Toledo (656), there is a document condemning the will of bishop Riccimir of Dumio, who had given land to the Church, on condition that the proceeds were distributed to the poor, who he had also supported out of ecclesiastical income. In addition, alongside his own slaves, he had manumitted some which had belonged to the Church, without providing

---

26 Council of Braga II (572), c. 2, ed. Vives, *Concilios visigóticos e hispano-romanos,* 81–82.

27 Council of Tarragona (516), c. 8, ed. Vives, *Concilios visigóticos e hispano-romanos,* 36–37.

28 Council of Mérida (666), cc. 10, 14, ed. Vives, *Concilios visigóticos e hispano-romanos,* 332–33 and 335. E.A. Thompson, *The Goths in Spain* (Oxford: Clarendon, 1969), 298–99. See also Council of Toledo IV (633), c. 33, ed. Vives, *Concilios visigóticos e hispano-romanos,* 204 and Council of Toledo IX (655), c. 6., ed. Vives, *Concilios visigóticos e hispano-romanos,* 301.

29 Council of Toledo IV (633), c. 32, ed. Vives, *Concilios visigóticos e hispano-romanos,* 204.

30 Council of Toledo V (636), c. 1, ed. Vives, *Concilios visigóticos e hispano-romanos,* 226–27.

compensation.[31] The bishops in Council were clearly more concerned with the protection of ecclesiastical property than with providing support for the poor. It would seem that good works were not as institutionalized in Spain as they were elsewhere, although bishop Massona of Mérida did build a *xenodochium* for *peregrini* and the sick.[32] Isidore thought (with the words of Christ in mind) that bishops should care for the poor, feed the hungry, clothe the naked, receive strangers, ransom captives, and care for widows and orphans.[33] And bishops were specifically tasked by Reccared to protect the poor against the unjust exactions of judges,[34] while Recceswinth charged them with opposing inequitable judgements.[35] Isidore also thought that kings had an obligation to look after the poor, and praised Swinthila for so doing,[36] although the king was denigrated by IV Toledo for his oppression.[37] This, however, does not add up to the same

---

31 Council of Toledo X (656), *item aliud decretum,* ed. Vives, *Concilios visigóticos e hispano-romanos,* 322–24. I am indebted to Dave Addison, for drawing my attention to the importance of this document.

32 *Vitas sanctorum Patrum Emeretensium,* 5.3, ed. Antonio Maya Sánchez, Corpus Christianorum, Series Latinorum 116 (Turnhout: Brepols, 1992), 50.

33 Isidore, *De officiis ecclesiasticis,* 2.5, 18–19, ed. Christopher M. Lawson, Corpus Christianorum, Series Latinorum 113 (Turnhout: Brepols, 1989); 56–64, 83–89; Isidore, *Sententiae* 3.48.7–8; 3.49.3; 3.50.4, 6; 3.52.12; 57, ed. Pierre Cazier, Corpus Christianorum, Series Latina 111 (Turnhout: Brepols, 1998), 298, 300–301, 302, 307; Jamie Wood, *Politics of Identity Visigothic Spain: Religion and Power in the Histories of Isidore of Seville,* Brill's Series on the Early Middle Ages (Boston and Leiden: Brill, 2012), 140, 146. On the poor in the *Sententiae,* see also Dolores Castro and Michael J. Kelly, "Isidore's *Sententiae,* the *Liber Iudiciorum,* and Paris BnF Lat. 4667," *Visigothic Symposium* 4 (2020–2021): 144–68, at 155.

34 *Leges Visigothorum,* 1.2., ed. Karl Zeumer, Monumenta Germaniae Historica, Leges Nationum Germanicarum 1 (Hanover: Hahn, 1902), 40–42.

35 *Leges Visigothorum,* 2.1.30, ed. Zeumer, 77–78.

36 Isidore, *Historia Gothorum,* 64, ed. and trans. Cristobal Rodríguez Alonso, *Las Historias de los Godos, los Vandalos y los suevos de Isidoro de Sevilla* (León: Centro de Estudios e Investigación "San Isidoro," 1975), 278–89; Kenneth Baxter Wolf, trans., *Conquerors and Chroniclers of Early Medieval Spain* (Liverpool: Liverpool University Press, 1999), 108.

37 Council of Toledo IV (633), c. 75, ed. Vives, *Concilios visigóticos e hispano-romanos,* 217–22.

pattern of redistribution that we find in papal Italy or Merovingian Francia.

The *tertia* may also have been the norm in the Byzantine East, although it differed from what we can reconstruct of the Spanish system: a threefold division between the poor, the household of the bishop, and the clergy can be deduced from the Apostolic Canons from fourth-century Syria.[38] Some indication of the groups and causes that were to be supported by the Church are also listed in Justinian's Novels.[39] The true complexity of the division of ecclesiastical income, however, is best attested in the rich documentation from Egypt.[40]

The ideal model for the distribution of the *Quadripartum* is set out by John the Deacon in his *Life of Gregory of Great*: the pope translated all the revenues of the papal patrimony into coin, he then summoned the officials of the Church, the palace, the monasteries, the churches, cemeteries, deaconries, and *xenodochia,* and made payments in line with the *polypticum* of Gelasius. And he made the distribution four times a year, at Easter, the Feast of the Apostles, St. Andrew's Day, and the anniversary of his own consecration.[41] The deaconries, or *diaconiae,* were the centers of charitable distribution:[42] in late-antique Rome there were seven of them.[43]

---

38 *Apostolic Canons,* 8.47, 41. https://www.ccel.org/ccel/schaff/anf07/anf07. ix.ix.vi.html. I am indebted to Robert Wiśniewski for the reference.

39 Justinian, *Novellae,* 3.3; 65; 123; 131.9, 11, 13, ed. Rudolf Schöll and Wilhem Kroll, *Corpus Iuris Civilis, Novellae,* 6th edn. (Berlin: Weidemann, 1928), 23–24, 339, 658, 659, 661–62; David J.D. Miller and Peter Sarris, trans., *The Novels of Justinian: A Complete Annotated English Translation* (Cambridge: Cambridge University Press, 2018).

40 Ewa Wipszycka, *Les ressources et les activités économiques des églises en Égypte du IV* au VIII* siècle* (Brussels: Fondation Égyptologique Reine Élisabeth, 1972), 121–53.

41 John the Deacon, *Vita Gregorii,* 2.24; Richards, *Consul of God,* 95.

42 Peter Llewellyn, *Rome in the Dark Ages* (London: Constable, 1971), 137–38.

43 Rosamond McKitterick, *Rome and the Invention of the Papacy: The "Liber Pontificalis"* (Cambridge: Cambridge University Press, 2020), 56–57, 135–36. For the importance of the deacons in Rome see now Conrad Leyser, "Through the Eyes of a Deacon: Lesser Clergy, Major Donors, and Insti-

The precise system by which the clerical portion of the *Quad-ripartum* was distributed in Rome in the time of Gregory can hardly have been the norm for the rest of the Christian West, although Carthage, like Rome, was divided into seven ecclesiastical regions.[44] But, in cities other than Rome, the *diaconiae* did play a crucial role in the distribution of poor relief.[45] Again Gregory provides important information. A letter to a *religiosus*, John, puts him in charge of feeding the poor, which involved the appointment and supervision of deacons, although unfortunately the pope does not specify whether the appointment relates to Rome or to another city.[46] Other letters in the *Register* reveal the existence of a *diaconia* in Pesaro[47] and in Naples.[48] Later sources, including a letter of pope Hadrian (772–795),[49] also note the existence of a *diaconia* in Naples,[50] and there are further references to such institutions in Cremona and Lucca.[51] The institution seems to have been widespread in Italy.

Although it is not explicitly stated that the *quartae* of the *Quadripartum* should be equal, this is surely implied by the Ravenna evidence, and also by Gregory's letter to John of Palermo, which talks of the distribution of the entirety of the clerical *quarta* of the Church's revenues according to the desires and activities of the individual cleric: "that from the Church revenue,

---

tutional Property in Fifth-Century Rome," *Early Medieval Europe* 29, no. 4 (2021): 487–504.

44 Anna Leone, *Changing Townscapes in North Africa from Late Antiquity to the Arab Conquest* (Bari: Edipuglia, 2007), 98–99.

45 On the diaconiae see Neri, *I marginali*, 102–5.

46 Gregory I, *Register*, 11.17, ed. Norberg, *Registrum Epistularum,* 886.

47 Gregory I, *Register*, 5.25, ed. Norberg, *Registrum Epistularum,* 292–93.

48 Gregory I, *Register*, 10.8, ed. Norberg, *Registrum Epistularum,* 834.

49 *Codex Carolinus*, 84, ed. Wilhelm Gundlach, Monumenta Germaniae Historica, Epistolae 3, Merowingici et Karolini Aevi (Berlin: Weidmann, 1892), 619–20. Rosamond McKitterick, Dorine van Espelo, Richard Pollard, and Richard Price, trans., *Codex Epistilaris Carolinus: Letters from the Popes to the Frankish Rulers, 739–891* (Liverpool: Liverpool University Press, 2021), 378–80.

50 Neri, *I marginali*, 104–5.

51 Ibid.,*62*

102, 105

you should provide without any delay a whole quarter share for your church's clergy, according to each one's merit, rank and work [...]"; this was according to established custom: "iuxta pristinam consuetudinem" ("according to the old custom").[52]

There is plenty of evidence that not all bishops actually divided Church revenue as they were supposed to.[53] The best single example of a failure by a bishop to distribute their *quarta* to the clergy is the dispute between bishop Ecclesius of Ravenna and a large section of the clerics of the city, which had to be settled by pope Felix IV.[54] And the issue blew up again in the time of archbishop Theodore, in the late seventh century.[55] Equally illuminating is a set of letters in the *Register* of Gregory the Great. He wrote to bishop Gaudentius of Nola, instructing him to ensure that the clergy of Capua who were living in Naples should receive their *quarta*.[56] He told John of Palermo to distribute the entire *quarta* of the clergy according to their desires.[57] He also wrote to Paschasius of Naples to point out that the bishop's predecessor had made no provision for the clergy or for the poor.[58] So he now instructed Paschasius to set aside 400 *solidi* for the clergy and the poor: 100 *solidi* were to be divided between the clergy as appropriate, 63 *solidi* were to be divided between the 126 prebendaries, a further 50 were to go to priests, deacons and visiting clergy, 150 were to go to the honorable but hard-up (who were to get a *triens* each — in other words, there were 450 of them), and 36 *solidi* were to go to the ordinary poor. In fact, it

---

52 Gregory I, *Register*, 13.45, ed. Norberg, *Registrum Epistularum*, 1051–52: "de reditibus ecclesiae quartam in integro portionem ecclesiae tuae clericis secundum meritum vel officium sive laborem suum"; John R.C. Martyn, trans., *The Letters of Gregory the Great*, 3 vols. (Toronto: Pontifical Institute of Mediaeval Studies, 2004), vol. 3, 859.

53 Gregory I, *Register*, 8.7, 9.144, ed. Norberg, *Registrum Epistularum*, 524, 695.

54 Agnellus, *Liber Pontificalis ecclesiae Ravennatis*, 60, ed. Mauskopf Deliyannis, 226–31.

55 Agnellus, *Liber Pontificalis ecclesiae Ravennatis*, 117–18, 121, ed. Mauskopf Deliyannis, 288–89, 292–95.

56 Gregory I, *Register*, 5.27, ed. Norberg, *Registrum Epistularum*, 294.

57 Gregory I, *Register*, 13.45, ed. Norberg, *Registrum Epistularum*, 1051–52.

58 Gregory I, *Register*, 11.22, ed. Norberg, *Registrum Epistularum*, 892–93.

appears that Paschasius went on to squander the Church's revenues in building boats — the pope fumed that he had enjoyed going down to the sea every day.[59]

There is evidence from elsewhere of a failure to divide ecclesiastical income in accordance with the norms. The Council of Mérida (666) condemned bishops for taking the *tertia* of the parochial churches.[60] And the sixteenth Council of Toledo (693) reaffirmed the legislation.[61] In the canons of the Council of Carpentras in 527, we find a statement that in some dioceses the bishop had kept all the offerings made by the faithful of the *parrochiae,* passing nothing on to the churches, either for their clergy or for the upkeep of the basilicas.[62] The Fourth Council of Toledo inveighed against bishops taking more than the *tertia oblationum* — their avarice had left parishes impoverished, with their basilicas falling into ruin.[63]

We should be aware of a distinction between the distribution of the Church's income from its property, and that of the alms and oblations of the faithful — and the Councils of Carpentras and IV Toledo refer to oblations, not to the revenue derived from property. According to Gregory the Great, such donations ought also to be allocated according to a division into quarters.[64] But, although the first Council of Orléans (511) suggests a fourfold division of the revenue from lands given to the Church by Clovis, it allocates half of the offerings placed on the altar (perhaps of the cathedral church) to the bishop and the other half to the remainder of the clergy, while only a third of

59 Gregory I, *Register,* 13.27, ed. Norberg, *Registrum Epistularum,* 1028–29.

60 Council of Mérida (666), c. 16, ed. Vives, *Concilios visigóticos e hispano-romanos,* 336–37.

61 Council of Toledo XVI (693), c. 5, ed. Vives, *Concilios visigóticos e hispano-romanos,* 501–2.

62 Council of Carpentras (527), c. 1, ed. Basdevant, *Les canons des conciles mérovingiens,* vol. 1, 146.

63 Council of Toledo IV (633), c. 33, ed. Vives, *Concilios visigóticos e hispano-romanos,* 204.

64 Gregory I, *Register,* 13.45, ed. Norberg, *Registrum Epistularum,* 1051–52. See also Neri, *I marginali,* 97.

the offerings in rural parishes (*parrochiae*) went to the bishop.[65] The third Council of Orléans (538), on the other hand, gives the bishop discretion over the division of oblations offered in the urban basilicas, while leaving the allocation of offerings made in parishes (*parrochiae*) and rural basilicas to established tradition.[66] There are several references to the distribution of offerings in the works of Gregory of Tours.[67] In Spain, the second Council of Braga refers to the *tertia* of oblations allocated to the lighting of the churches.[68]

Despite the clear variation, it would seem that the income of a considerable proportion of western Europe, together with other dues and bequests, was divided between the bishop, the clergy, the upkeep of ecclesiastical buildings, and the poor — alongside whom, at various moments, there were captives, whose ransom could also be a matter of ecclesiastical concern.[69] We have already noted the numbers of clergy who were supported by the revenues of the Church, and of the numbers of churches. It is worth pausing on the allocation of funds to the poor, the captives, and, first, to the provisions made for the performance

65 Council of Orléans I (511), c. 14, 15, ed. Basdevant, *Les canons des conciles mérovingiens*, vol. 1, 80.

66 Council of Orléans III (538), c. 5, ed. Basdevant, *Les canons des conciles mérovingiens*, vol. 1, 234.

67 Gregory of Tours, *Decem Libri Historiarum*, 4.32, 7.29, ed. Bruno Krusch and Wilhelm Levison, Monumenta Germaniae Historica, Scriptores Rerum Merovingicarum 1.1 (Hanover: Hahn, 1951), 166, 346–49; *Liber de virtutibus sancti Martini*, 1.31; 2.22, 46, ed. Bruno Krusch, Monumenta Germaniae Historica, Scriptores Rerum Merovingicarum 1.2 (Hanover: Hahn, 1885), 153, 166, 175; *Liber de virtutibus sancti Juliani*, 9, 12, 38, ed. Bruno Krusch, Monumenta Germaniae Historica, Scriptores Rerum Merovingicarum 1.2 (Hanover: Hahn, 1885), 118–19, 119, 130; Neri, *I marginali*, 98–102.

68 Council of Braga II (572), c. 2, ed. Vives, *Concilios visigóticos e hispano-romanos*, 81–82.

69 William Klingshirn, "Charity and Power: Caesarius of Arles and the Ransoming of Captives in Sub-Roman Gaul," *Journal of Roman Studies* 75 (1983): 183–203; Pauline Allen and Bronwen Neil, *Crisis Management in Late Antiquity (410–590 CE): A Survey of the Evidence from Episcopal Letters*, Vigiliae Christianae Supplement 121 (Boston and Leiden: Brill, 2013), 39–43; Bronwen Neil, "Crisis and Wealth in Byzantine Italy: The *Libri Pontificales* of Rome and Ravenna," *Byzantion* 82 (2012): 279–303.

of the liturgy, which went beyond the mere upkeep of church buildings. The demands on ecclesiastical revenue made by the State will concern us in the final chapter.

The performance of cult depended on the provision of liturgical vessels, many of which were costly, as can be seen most obviously in the lists of donations to be found in the *Liber Pontificalis*.[70] In addition, there was a need for gospel and liturgical books (potentially a huge expense — think of the 1525 animal skins needed for the three Pandects of the Bible produced for Ceolfrith at Monkwearmouth-Jarrow, although these codices were exceptional).[71] And, of course, there were festal days to be catered for. Gregory the Great allocated 10 *solidi* for the poor, 30 amphorae of wine, 200 sacks of corn, 2 large jars of olive oil, 12 rams, and 100 chickens for the dedication feast of a simple oratory of the Virgin, because abbot Marinianus and his community were too poor to pay for the celebration.[72]

Liturgical vessels, manuscripts, and dedication feasts, however, did not require regular expenditure, unlike the lighting of a church, which was often the object of specifically allocated funding. The oil or wax needed for lighting churches was a very considerable expense, as has been shown in recent work by Stefan Esders and Paul Fouracre.[73] The allocation of funds for

---

70 Ruth Leader-Newby, *Silver and Society in Late Antiquity: Functions and Meanings of Silver Plate in the Fourth to Seventh Centuries* (Aldershot: Ashgate, 2004), 61–66.

71 Rupert Bruce-Mitford, "The Art of the *Codex Amiatinus*," *Journal of the British Archaeological Association*, 3rd ser., 32 (1969): 1–25 and plates, and Jarrow Lecture (1967).

72 Gregory I, *Register,* 1.54, ed. Norberg, *Registrum Epistularum,* 67.

73 Paul Fouracre, "Eternal Light and Earthly Needs: Practical Aspects of the Development of Frankish Immunities," in *Property and Power in the Early Middle Ages,* ed. Wendy Davies and Paul Fouracre (Cambridge: Cambridge University Press, 1995), 53–81; Paul Fouracre, "Framing and Lighting: Another Angle on Transition," in *Italy and Early Medieval Europe,* ed. Ross Balzaretti, Julia Barrow, and Patricia Skinner (Oxford: Oxford University Press, 2018), 305–14; Paul Fouracre, "Lights, Power and the Moral Economy"; Joanna Story, "Lands and Lights in Early Medieval Rome," in *Italy and Early Medieval Europe,* ed. Balzaretti, Barrow, and Skinner, 315–38: Stefan Esders, *Die Formierung der Zensualität* (Ostfildern: Thorbecke, 2010); Paul Foura-

lights (*luminaria*) could be remarkably precise. In a grant to the monastery of Corbie issued in 716, Chilperic II confirmed the concession issued by his uncle Chlothar II and his grandmother Balthild of toll income (*telloneum*) at the southern port of Fos. The monastery was to receive the toll taken on 10,000 pounds of oil, 30 *modii* of garum, 30 pounds of pepper, 150 pounds of cumin, 2 pounds of cloves, 1 pound of cinnamon, 2 pounds of nard, 30 pounds of bitter root, 50 pounds of dates, 100 pounds of figs, 100 pounds of almonds, 30 pounds of pistachios, 100 pounds of olives, 50 pounds of water pots(?), 150 pounds of chickpeas, 20 pounds of rice, 10 pounds of gold pigment, 10 jeweled skins, 10 Cordoban skins, and 50 quires of papyrus.[74]

As Paul Fouracre has noted, the monastery of St. Denis had an annual grant of 300 *solidi* for lights in 695.[75] The first Council of Braga allocated one *tertia* for the upkeep and lighting of churches.[76] This pales into insignificance when one remembers the 7 estates, yielding 4,390 *solidi* a year, supposedly given by Constantine to the Lateran for its lighting[77] — I do not doubt the number of estates in papal hands by the sixth century, but I will come back to the problem of the chronology of some of

---

cre, *Eternal Light and Earthly Concerns: Belief and the Shaping of Medieval Society* (Manchester: Manchester University Press, 2021), 57, 60, 62, 68.

74 *Diplomata Merowingica*, 171, ed. Theo Kölzer, *Die Urkunden der Merowinger*, 2 vols., Monumenta Germaniae Historica (Hanover, 2001), vol. 1, 424–26. The value of the charter has been questioned by Simon Loseby, "Marseille and the Pirenne Thesis II: Ville Morte," in *The Long Eighth Century: Production, Distribution and Demand*, ed. Inge Lise Hansen and Chris Wickham (Boston and Leiden: Brill, 2000), 167–93, at 187. Certainly, it does not provide evidence for goods reaching Corbie, but it surely does provide evidence for goods being taxed in Marseille.

75 Fouracre, "Eternal Light and Earthly Needs," 70.

76 Council of Braga I (561), c. 7, ed. Vives, *Concilios visigóticos e hispano-romanos*, 68.

77 *Liber Pontificalis*, 34.14–15, ed. Louis Duchesne, *"Liber Pontificalis": Texte, Introduction et Commentaire*, 2 vols. (Paris, 1886–1892), vol. 1, 174–75; Raymond Davis, trans., *The Book of Pontiffs: The Ancient Biographies of the First Ninety Roman Bishops to AD 715*, rev. edn. (Liverpool: Liverpool University Press, 2000), 17–18.

the emperor's supposed donations. The provision of lights, one might add, is a significant issue in the temple societies of India.[78]

As for Church provision for the poor, one needs to begin by stressing the point that has been made frequently by modern scholars, that it differed from the official corn dole of the Roman Empire, the *annona civica,* which was not intended for paupers. Jean-Michel Carrié has shown that those eligible for the *frumentatio* in Rome were native male citizens who had achieved age of majority.[79] It was a privilege that was available to registered adult men not only in Rome, but also in other centers such as Constantinople, Alexandria, and Antioch. It was also available in smaller centers, as is apparent from the Oxyrhynchus papyri. John Rea, in his study of the Oxyrhynchus evidence, stated: "It is very clearly confirmed [...] that the doles were not a provision for the very poor, but the perquisite for the already privileged middle class of the cities, as in Rome."[80] Whether the Oxyrhynchus evidence can be taken as illustrating arrangements in smaller cities throughout the Empire is, however, unclear. But while the Roman State was concerned with providing for citizens, including citizens who had fallen on hard times, it had little time for beggars.[81]

As Michele Salzman, following Peter Brown, has argued, Christian concern for the poor marked a new departure in a number of respects[82] — although both of them, like Bronwen

---

78 P.S. Kanaka Durga and Y.A. Sudhakar Reddy, "Kings, Temples and Legitimation of Autochthonous Communities: A Case Study of a South Indian Temple," *Journal of the Economic and Social History of the Orient* 35 (1992): 145–66, at 155–57.

79 Jean-Michel Carrié, "Les distributions alimentaires dans les cités de l'empire romain tardif," *Mélanges de l'École française de Rome* 87 (1975): 995–1101, at 1012, 1030–32.

80 John Rowland Rea, ed., *The Oxyrhynchus Papyri,* XL (London: The Egypt Exploration Society, 1972), 8.

81 *Codex Theodosianus,* 14.18, https://droitromain.univ-grenoble-alpes.fr/.

82 Michèle Renée Salzman, "From a Classical to a Christian City: Civic Evergetism and Charity in Late Antique Rome," *Studies in Late Antiquity* 1 (2017): 65–85.

Neil,[83] have stressed the extent to which civic societal relations survived well into the fifth century. This was in part because the emperors themselves began to legislate in terms that reflected Christian values. Thus, Valentinian I authorized the distribution of the *annona civica* according to the needs of citizens, and not automatically to those who claimed citizenship.[84] Salzman, following Jean-Michel Carrié, has noted that the *annona civica* continued into the sixth century, although Justinian charged the pope, Vigilius, not the City Prefect, with its distribution.[85]

But Christian charity was directed much more towards the economic poor than towards the citizens who could claim the right to the dole — although Gregory the Great certainly did show concern for "distressed gentlefolk," to use Peter Brown's favored expression for those who had fallen on hard times.[86] Already in the fourth century the pagan emperor Julian the Apostate seems to have noted and approved of the attention paid to the poor by Jews and Christians. In a letter to Arsacius, high priest of Galatia, he stated:

> I have given directions that 30,000 *modii* of corn shall be assigned every year for the whole of Galatia, and 60,000 pints of wine. I order that one-fifth of this be used for the poor who serve the priests, and the remainder be distributed by us to strangers and beggars. For it is disgraceful that, when no Jew

83 Bronwen Neil, "Imperial Benefactions to the Fifth-century Roman Church," in *Basileia: Essays on Imperium and Culture in Honour of E.M. and M.J. Jeffreys*, ed. Geoffrey Nathan and Lynda Garland (Sydney: University of New South Wales, 2011), 55–66.

84 *Codex Theodosianus*, 14.17.5, https://droitromain.univ-grenoble-alpes.fr/. Salzman, "From a Classical to a Christian City," 72.

85 Justinian, *Pragmatic Sanction, Novellae Appendix constitutionum dispersarum*, 7, ed. Schöll and Kroll, 799–802; Salzman, "From a Classical to a Christian City," 77.

86 Gregory I, *Register*, 1.37, 57 (on members of the senatorial class); 1.65; 2.18, 21; 4.28; 8.35; 9.110, 137, ed. Norberg, *Registrum Epistularum*, 44, 69, 74–75, 104–5, 108, 400–401, 662, 688. Peter Brown, *Poverty and Leadership in the Late Roman Empire* (Lebanon: University Press of New England, 2002), 59; Gary B. Ferngren, *Medicine and Health Care in Early Christianity* (Baltimore: Johns Hopkins University Press, 2009), 132.

ever has to beg, and the impious Galilaeans support not only their own poor but ours as well, all men see that our people lack aid from us. Teach those of the Hellenic faith to contribute to public service of this sort, and the Hellenic villages to offer their first fruits to the gods; and accustom those who love the Hellenic religion to these good works by teaching them that this was our practice of old.[87]

Significantly, when he illustrates what he regards as the traditional practices of the pagans, he does so with a citation from Homer and not with an illustration from any more recent history. Julian, of course, was writing a full century before the first reference to the *Quadripartum,* but institutionalized concern for the "distressed" on the part of the Christians is already attested in 251, when pope Cornelius claimed that there were "more than 1500 widows and distressed persons" on the books of the Church of Rome.[88]

We have a good deal of evidence on distribution to the poor in Gregory the Great's letters. Some of the poor are very definitely distressed gentlefolk; Gregory's own aunt Pateria is given 20 *solidi* a year, and her children 40, as "shoe-money" ("ad calcarium suorum") and 300 *modii* of wheat, while two other noble ladies, Palatina and Viviana, were allocated 20 *solidi* and an equal amount of grain.[89] Shortly after, Palatina's allowance was raised to 30 *solidi.*[90] The one-time governor of Samnium, Sisinnius, who had fallen on hard times, was given 20 *modii* of wheat and 4 *solidi* annually, because he was now poor.[91] Among others facing financial hardship, the palace officials of Rome were to

---

87 Julian, ep. 22, trans. Wilmer Cave Wright, *The Works of the Emperor Julian,* 3 vols. (New York: Putnam, 1923), 69–71.

88 Eusebius, *Historia Ecclesiastica,* 6.43.11, ed. T.E. Page et al., trans. J.E.L. Oulton, Loeb Classics, 2 vols. (Cambridge: Harvard University Press, 1942), 119.

89 Gregory I, *Register,* 1.37, ed. Norberg, *Registrum Epistularum,* 44. For Gregory's information on poor relief, Neri, *I marginali,* 94–109.

90 Gregory I, *Register,* 1.57, ed. Norberg, *Registrum Epistularum,* 69.

91 Gregory I, *Register,* 1.50, ed. Norberg, *Registrum Epistularum,* 63–64.

be provided with corn,[92] and the *religiosus* Anastasius and the mother of Urbicus with 6 *solidi* each.[93] Other beneficiaries were Theodore,[94] the children of Urbicus,[95] the blind Pastor, who received a regular supply of beans and corn,[96] Albinus, also with impaired vision (who was to receive 2 *tremisses* a year),[97] and the scholar Mateus (12 *solidi*).[98]

In some of these cases, we may not be dealing with the funds of the *Quadripartum*. In a letter to John of Palermo, Gregory makes it quite clear that there was a distinction between the distribution of the revenue from Church property and the distribution of money that had been offered as alms and oblations by the pious. The donations were to be put on one side, and then added to the income of the Church, the whole of which was to be supervised by a manager.[99]

Perhaps better known than the information provided by Gregory the Great is that to be found in the *Histories* and *Miracula* of Gregory of Tours, not least because those on the poor lists of Francia, the *matricularii,* attracted the attention of Arnold Pöschl,[100] and more recently of Valerio Neri[101] and Peter Brown.[102] We find references to those involved in the distribution of the *matricula* in Candes and Brioude. A woman with a withered arm, who helped in the distribution of the *matricula* at Candes, was cured as a result of her good works,[103]

92 Gregory I, *Register,* 9.110, ed. Norberg, *Registrum Epistularum,* 662.

93 Gregory I, *Register,* 2.50, ed. Norberg, *Registrum Epistularum,* 141–45.

94 Gregory I, *Register,* 3.18, ed. Norberg, *Registrum Epistularum,* 164–65.

95 Gregory I, *Register,* 3.21, ed. Norberg, *Registrum Epistularum,* 166–67.

96 Gregory I, *Register,* 1.65, ed. Norberg, *Registrum Epistularum,* 74–75.

97 Gregory I, *Register,* 4.28, ed. Norberg, *Registrum Epistularum,* 247.

98 Gregory I, *Register,* 9.137, ed. Norberg, *Registrum Epistularum,* 668.

99 Gregory I, *Register,* 13.45, ed. Norberg, *Registrum Epistularum,* 1051–52.

100 Arnold Pöschl, *Bischofsgut und mensa episcopalis: Ein Beitrag zur Geschichte des kirchlichen Vermögensrechtes* 1: *Die Grundlagen* (Bonn: P. Hanstein, 1908), 105–10.

101 Neri, *I marginali,* 97–101.

102 Peter Brown, *Through the Eye of a Needle: Wealth, the Fall of Rome, and the Making of Christianity in the West, 350–550 AD* (Princeton: Princeton University Press, 2012), 510, 513, 516.

103 Gregory of Tours, *Liber de virtutibus sancti Martini,* 2.22, ed. Krusch, 166.

while the blind girl, whose father supported the *matricula* at Brioude, gained her sight.[104] There is a reference to the *matricula* of Rheims in the will of Remigius, preserved by Hincmar, where we hear that the bishop left 2 *solidi* to each of those on the list.[105] And the statement in the Second Council of Tours (567) that each *civitas*, as well as *presbyteri* and *cives* should provide for its *pauperes* and *egenos* as best they could, which implies a reference to the *matricula*.[106] But in some instances, it seems that we are dealing with the distribution of alms rather than the *Quadripartum*. Gregory provides numerous references to those hanging around the shrines of the saints, expecting support and hoping for a cure, not least the lame and the deformed.[107] These could form a significant force in support of their local church, as did the *matricularii* and *pauperes* of St. Martin's following the sacrilege perpetrated in the course of the murder of Eberulf in the holy precinct.[108] As Valerio Neri has noted, we seem to have two categories of people in this story: the official *matricularii*, registered on the poor list, and other *pauperes*, who were waiting for the distribution of alms.[109] These other *pauperes* seem to be the subject of a further anecdote in Gregory: in the *atrium* at Tours a *custos* was given a gold coin to donate to the poor, but he pocketed it, substituting a silver piece, and promptly died.[110] In Spain, there may also be a distinction between the revenue that came from property and the oblations of the people.[111]

---

104 Gregory of Tours, *Liber de virtutibus sancti Juliani,* 38, ed. Krusch, 130.

105 Hincmar, *Vita Remigii,* 32, ed. Bruno Krusch, Monumenta Germaniae Historica, Scriptores Rerum Merovingicarum 3 (Hanover: Hahn, 1896), 336–40; Neri, *I marginali,* 100.

106 Council of Tours (567), c. 5, ed. Basdevant, *Les canons des conciles mérovingiens,* vol. 2, 354.

107 Gregory of Tours, *Decem Libri Historiarum,* 4.32, 7.29, ed. Krusch and Levison, 166, 346–49; *Liber de virtutibus sancti Martini,* 2.46, ed. Krusch, 175; *Liber de virtutibus sancti Juliani,* 9, 12, ed. Krusch, 118–19, 119.

108 Gregory of Tours, *Decem Libri Historiarum,* 7.29, ed. Krusch and Levison, 346–49.

109 Neri, *I marginali,* 97–102.

110 Gregory of Tours, *Liber de virtutibus sancti Martini,* 1.31, ed. Krusch, 153.

111 Oblations are mentioned in the Council of Braga II (572), c. 2 and the Council of Toledo IV (633), c. 33, but not in Council of Mérida (666), c. 16, ed.

Alongside care for the poor one can note that for the sick. The notion of the hospital seems to emerge in fourth-century Anatolia.[112] There are examples in Rome around 400, and in Gaul from the days of Caesarius of Arles.[113] There may have been 34 hospitals in Merovingian Francia, while 282 have been identified for the late- and post-Roman World.[114] They clearly catered primarily to the poor as well as the diseased. Gregory of Tours talks of *hospitiola pauperum* in Tours,[115] as well as a leper house in Chalon-sur-Saône.[116] How well-endowed they were is unclear, but in the case of the *xenodochium* founded in Lyon by king Childebert and his queen Ostrogotha we may guess that the endowment was substantial. And the foundation, like the others of which we hear, was a religious one — in the case of the Lyon *xenodochium,* its establishment was the key point in the canons of the fifth Council of Orléans (549). [117]

"You have the poor among you always" (Matthew 26:11) — and they are a pretty constant feature of references to the *Quadripartum.* Captives, by contrast, are not. Only one version of the *Quadripartum,* that to be found in the first Council of Orléans (511), allocates a *quarta* for the ransom of those taken prisoner.[118] But ecclesiastical involvement in the ransoming of captives is documented not just in the *Quadripartum.* A law of Honorius and Theodosius II from 408 charges clergy with ensuring the

---

Vives, *Concilios visigóticos e hispano-romanos,* 81–82, 204, 336–37.

112 See Peregrine Horden, "Public Health, Hospitals, and Charity" (forthcoming).

113 Cyprian of Toulon, et al., *Vita Caesarii,* 1.20, ed. Bruno Krusch, Monumenta Germaniae Historica, Scriptores Rerum Merovingicarum 3 (Hanover: Hahn, 1896), 464; William Klingshirn, trans., *Caesarius of Arles, Life, Testament, Letters* (Liverpool: Liverpool University Press, 1994).

114 Mark Alan Anderson, "Hospitals, Hospices, and Shelters for the Poor in Late Antiquity," PhD diss., Yale University, 2012.

115 Gregory of Tours, *Liber de virtutibus sancti Martini,* 2.27, ed. Krusch, 169.

116 Gregory of Tours, *Decem Libri Historiarum,* 5.45, ed. Krusch and Levison, 254–46.

117 Council of Orléans V (549), ed. Basdevant, *Les canons des conciles mérovingiens,* vol. 1, 300–27.

118 Council of Orléans I (511), c. 5, ed. Basdevant, *Les canons des conciles mérovingiens,* vol. 1, 76.

return of freed captives to their homes.[119] It is also a regular issue in ecclesiastical literature. Ambrose had to defend himself
for having melted down liturgical vessels to ransom captives.[120]
Bill Klingshirn has traced the influence of Ambrose's actions in
ransoming captives on Augustine, Hilary of Arles, Deogratias of
Carthage, Caesarius of Arles, and Maroveus of Poitiers, and has
noted that Patrick regarded the transfer of thousands of *solidi* to
the Franks for the redemption of captives as a custom (*consuetu-
do*) of Roman and Gallic Christians.[121] For both Justinian[122] and
the Merovingian bishops at the Council of Clichy (626–627),[123]
the ransom of captives was the one circumstance in which the
melting down of liturgical plate was justified. And Gregory the
Great was firmly of the same opinion.[124] It was, nevertheless, a
questionable action: the Council of Agde noted the significance
of the initial donation.[125] Clearly, from the Church's point of

---

119 *Codex Theodosianus,* 6.2, https://droitromain.univ-grenoble-alpes.fr/.

120 Ambrose, *De Officiis,* 2.15, 28, ed. Ivor J. Davidson, 2 vols. (Oxford: Oxford University Press, 2002), vol. 2, 276, 284. See also Allen and Neil, *Crisis
Management in Late Antiquity,* 40–41; Neil, "Crisis and Wealth in Byzantine
Italy"; Michèle Renée Salzman, "The Religious Economics of Crisis: The Papal Use of Liturgical Vessels as Symbolic Capital in Late Antiquity," *Religion
in the Roman Empire* 5, no. 1: *Transformations of Value: Lived Religion and
the Economy* (2019): 125–41, at 132; Neri, *I marginali,* 112, n. 115, for a fuller
list. See also Robert Wiśniewski, "Clerical Hagiography in Late Antiquity,"
in *The Hagiographical Experiment: Developing Discourses of Sainthood,* ed.
Christa Gray and James Corke-Webster (Boston and Leiden: Brill, 2020),
93–118, at 108–9.

121 Klingshirn, "Caesarius of Arles and the Ransoming of Captives," 186.

122 *Codex Iustinianus,* 1.2.21 (529), https://droitromain.univ-grenoble-alpes.fr/;
Justinian, *Novellae,* 65; 108; 115; 120.10 (544); 123.37; 131.11, 13, ed. Schöll and
Kroll, 339, 513–14, 589–91, 620–21, 659–60, 661–62.

123 Council of Clichy (626–627), c. 25, ed. Basdevant, *Les canons des conciles
mérovingiens,* vol. 2, 542.

124 Gregory I, *Register,* 7.13, 35, ed. Norberg, *Registrum Epistularum,* 462–63,
499–98.

125 Council of Agde (506), c. 7, ed. Charles Munier, *Concilia Galliae, c. 314–c.
506,* Corpus Christianorum, Series Latina 148 (Turnhout: Brepols, 1963),
195–96. Salzman, "The Religious Economics of Crisis," 132, cites the Council
of Arles (314), c. 14, ed. Munier, but this surely relates to the *traditio* of sacred objects in the course of the previous period of persecution.

view, it was better to draw on funds that were set aside as a matter of course, than to melt down liturgical vessels.

To judge by the distribution of our evidence, there were periods when the fate of captives was more pressing than at others. Klingshirn has stressed the significance in ransoming captives in the activities of Caesarius of Arles.[126] There is an impressive cluster of evidence on either side of 500 for similar activity. Avitus of Vienne played a key role in ransoming captives taken by Gundobad in the course of the Burgundian raid on Liguria in c. 490.[127] In the *Liber Pontificalis,* pope Symmachus (498–514) is remembered for his ransoming prisoners "throughout the Ligurias, Milan and various provinces."[128] As we have already noted, the ransom of captives is specifically provided for in the version of the *Quadripartum* to be found in Orléans I in 511.

In addition to the evidence for the ransoming of captives in the decades on either side of 500, we have a substantial body of evidence for the activity in the late sixth and early seventh centuries in the letters of Gregory the Great. We hear, for instance, of the priest Tribunus, who was ransomed for 12 *solidi,* but was unable to repay the sum.[129] The pope thanked Theoctista and Andrew for their gift of 30 *solidi,* half of which was spent on ransoming people from Cotrone who had been seized by the Lombards.[130] This, one might note, was something of a bargain, given that a priest had to raise 12 *solidi,* while Faustinus was faced with a demand for 130 *solidi* to secure the freedom of his daughters.[131] The value of a captive varied according the status of the individual, and those who took prisoners clearly understood as much. The cost of the Lombard threat was something that Gregory emphasized in his correspondence with the empress

---

126 Klingshirn, "Caesarius of Arles and the Ransoming of Captives," 186.

127 Ennodius, *Vita Epifani,* 171–81, ed. Frideric Vogel, Monumenta Germaniae Historica, Auctores Antiquissimi 7 (Berlin: Weidmann, 1885), 105–7.

128 *Liber Pontificalis,* 53.11, ed. Duchesne, vol. 1, 263; Neil, "Crisis and Wealth in Byzantine Italy," 289–90.

129 Gregory I, *Register,* 4.17, ed. Norberg, *Registrum Epistularum,* 235–36.

130 Gregory I, *Register,* 7.23, ed. Norberg, *Registrum Epistularum,* 477–78.

131 Gregory I, *Register,* 7.35, ed. Norberg, *Registrum Epistularum,* 498–99.

Constantina, wife of Maurice.[132] And references to ransom are to be found in other letters preserved in the pope's *Register*.[133]

Prisoners, it would seem, were more of a feature of the period after the establishment of the Successor States, when rival kingdoms were plundering their neighbors, than they were of the period of the barbarian settlements — no doubt slaves were more useful to settled barbarians than they were to migratory peoples. At such moments they placed huge demands on the resources of the Church, alongside the other demands to be found in the *Quadripartum*.

As has been noted by numerous scholars, the act of almsgiving came to be envisaged as something which might help secure the salvation of the donor. Salzman has pointed to the centrality of the contribution of pope Leo the Great, noting that forty out of his surviving 96 sermons are concerned with charity — in sermon 78, for instance, he insisted on the need to provide food for the poor, help for the lame, and ransom for captives, all actions that would increase a donor's piety, and aid his or her salvation.[134] Christian charity, as Leo's sermons make plain, occupied a central place in what Brown and others have called the spiritual economy. Acts of charity were part of a set of negotiations in which a man or woman might store up treasure in heaven for the future. The economic metaphor has been most fully explored by Valentina Toneatto in *Les banquiers du Seigneur*, in which the bankers of the Lord are the bishops and monks of the fourth to ninth centuries.[135]

But it is important to note the financial realities that lay behind the metaphors of a Christian economy. The acquisition of

---

132 Gregory I, *Register,* 5.39, ed. Norberg, *Registrum Epistularum,* 314–18.

133 Gregory I, *Register,* 3.40, 55; 4.32, ed. Norberg, *Registrum Epistularum,* 185–86, 204, 251–52.

134 Leo, sermon 78, ed. Antonius Chavasse, *Leo Magnus Tractatus,* Corpus Christianorum, Series Latinorum 138 (Turnhout: Brepols, 1978); Salzman, "From a Classical to a Christian City," 67–68, 74–75.

135 Valentina Toneatto, *Les banquiers du Seigneur: Évêques et moines face à la richesse (IVᵉ–début IXᵉ siècle)* (Rennes: Presses universitaires de Rennes, 2012).

land and treasure by the Church, and the allocation of diocesan revenues according to the formula of the *Quadripartum,*
amounts to a very considerable "redistributive process," to re-
call the definition of temple societies given by Appadurai and
Appadurai Breckenridge; not only did the Church amass vast
amounts of land, but dioceses also distributed the revenues
from that land (as well as the income from other payments and
from the oblations of the pious) according to predetermined
formulae, while monasteries employed their revenues to provide for monks and nuns, and for the performance of religious
cult. And it is worth bearing in mind how much it cost to per-
form the liturgy.

This Christian economy was not a substitute for an earlier
pagan one. Anyone familiar with the archaeological sites of the
Classical World might instinctively assume that the model of a
temple society could more reasonably be applied to the Roman
Empire of the pagan period than to the Christian Empire that
followed. In the next chapter we will look a little more closely
at the funding of paganism, but for the present we should note
that Roman religion did not, apparently, depend on large-scale
property endowments — although the temples of the Pharaohs
and of the cities of the Hellenistic Levant seem to have done
so before the Roman conquest of the eastern Mediterranean.
Thereafter temples clearly did own some land, but apparently
not a great deal; the majority of donations to temples seems
to have taken the form of treasure, for which we have the evidence of inscriptions, like that from the temple of Isis at Nemi.[136]
Most priesthoods, however, seem to have been honorific; pagan
priests continued to live in their own properties, and draw on
their own income, and their cultic duties were rarely such as
to occupy large periods of time, unlike those of monks, nuns,
or some members of the Christian clergy. In other words, the

---

[136] Paolo Liverani, "Osservazioni sul *Libellus* delle donazioni Costantiniane
nel *Liber Pontificalis,*" *Athenaeum* 107 (2019): 169–217, at 183–84. See the
general comments of Dominic Janes, *God and Gold in Late Antiquity* (Cambridge: Cambridge University Press, 1998), 44.

funding of the latter and of church buildings differed substantially from the funding of religion in the period before Constantine. Julian clearly understood that the structure of the Church was different from that of paganism, and he wished to introduce what he saw as the merits of Christian organization into revivified pagan cult.[137]

Christian churches, as is clear from the *Quadripartum* and from the Visigothic *Tertia,* were usually expected to support their congregations economically as well as spiritually — there was provision for cult, for the poor, and for captives. Pagan temples in some cases, to judge from the evidence of inscriptions in Lydia and Phrygia, provided some care for their communities, especially with the occasional provision of feasts.[138] However, there are better precedents for the distribution of Church revenue to support the poor and to ransom captives in imperial legislation than in our evidence for pagan religious behavior. The late-Roman State did show some concern for captives, although increasingly there was a recognition that bishops might be involved in their ransom, even allowing for the sale of Church property and goods to raise funds.[139]

An impressive array of scholarship has explored the spiritual economy of Late Antiquity as a metaphor within the quest for salvation. The spiritual economy was, however, a matter of real economics, which involved a major process of redistribution, hence my emphasis not only on the scale of the transfer of property to the Church, but also on the ensuing redistribution of wealth, which is most sharply characterized by the injunctions of the *Quadripartum* and the *Tertia.*

---

137 Julian, ep. 20, trans. Cave Wright, 55–61.

138 Marijana Ricl, "Society and Economy of Sanctuaries in Roman Lydia and Phrygia," *Epigraphica Anatolica* 35 (2003): 77–101.

139 *Codex Justinianus,* 1.2.21, https://droitromain.univ-grenoble-alpes.fr/; Justinian, *Novellae,* 65; 120, 10, ed. Schöll and G. Kroll, 339, 589. See in general, Klingshirn, "Charity and Power," 184–87; Claudia Rapp, *Holy Bishops in Late Antiquity: The Nature of Christian Leadership in an Age of Transition* (Berkeley: University of California Press, 2005), 224–31; Salzman, "The Religious Economics of Crisis," 138–39.

Certainly, economic historians have noted the existence of Church property. For instance, Jairus Banaji has commented on the transfer of land to the Church, especially in Egypt[140] and Asia Minor,[141] but he portrays the Church as simply an extension of the aristocracy: "the increased weight of institutional land-holders such as the Church and the monasteries (the only other groups of any significance) also suggests that the countryside of late Byzantine Egypt was now firmly under the control of the most powerful landholders (above all the aristocracy)."[142] There is nothing here to suggest that the Church was involved in a redistributive process that differed from that of the secular aris-tocracy. So too, Tom Brown, while noting that churchmen and soldiers ended up as the major landowners in Italy, concentrates his attention on gentlemen and officers, and not on clergy.[143]

Of course, the socio-economic structure of the seventh-century West, especially in the area of the Exarchate, where the demands of the Empire and the army were unlike anything to be found in Francia and Spain, involved very much more than the redistribution of wealth to and by the Church. Indeed, the sur-vival of the tax system in Byzantine Italy had significant implica-tions for church finances in the peninsula.[144] But I would argue that this redistributive process was a, if not the, dominant mode of distribution in the late-sixth- and seventh-century West, and not only in Francia.[145]

---

140 Jairus Banaji, *Agrarian Change in Late Antiquity: Gold, Labour, and Aristo-cratic Dominance* (Oxford: Oxford University Press, 2001), 118, 128.

141 Ibid., 173, 182.

142 Ibid., 128.

143 Thomas S. Brown, *Gentlemen and Officers: Imperial Administration and Aristocratic Power in Byzantine Italy, A.D. 554–800* (Rome: British School at Rome, 1984), 195.

144 The differences are well brought out in Eisenberg and Tedesco, "Seeing the Churches Like the State," 509–19.

145 For other patterns of distribution, see, for example, Banaji, *Agrarian Change in Late Antiquity*; Jairus Banaji, *Exploring the Economy of Late Antiquity: Selected Essays* (Cambridge: Cambridge University Press, 2016); Jean-Pierre Devroey, *Économie rurale et société dans l'Europe franque (VIᵉ–IXᵉ siècles)*, 1: *Fondements matériels, échanges et lien social* (Paris: Belin, 2003); Jean Durliat, *De l'Antiquité au Moyen Âge: L'Occident de 313–800* (Lyon: Ellipses,

In other words, I would argue that what Peter Brown and other students of spirituality, including Valentina Toneatto, have presented in terms of spiritual ideology — "Treasure in Heaven" — can actually be envisaged as an economic model, and one that differs fundamentally from that of the Empire in the early fourth century. It involved the transfer of very large quantities of wealth, both treasure and, more significantly, land, which was conveyed to the Church, the proceeds of which were then redistributed to churchmen, the poor, the captives, and to the provision of cult. In the terms set out by Appadurai and Appadurai Breckenridge, this is a redistributive process. But if the temple society of the sixth and seventh centuries has little in common with the religious economy of the late pagan period, we need to ask how and when the new mode of distribution was established, and this is the question that will take up much of the next two chapters.

2002); Elisabeth Magnou-Nortier, *Aux origines de la fiscalité moderne: le système fiscal et sa gestion dans le royaume des Francs à l'épreuve des sources (V^e–XIe siècles)* (Geneve: Droz, 2012); Michael McCormick, *Origins of the European Economy: Communications and Commerce AD 300–900* (Cambridge: Cambridge University Press, 2001); Chris Wickham, *Framing the Early Middle Ages: Europe and the Mediterranean 400–800* (Oxford: Oxford University Press, 2005).

4

Personal Renunciation, Communal Possession, and Institutional Funds

By the end of the seventh century the Church owned a very sizeable proportion of the land of western Europe. This property-holding, moreover, can be seen as being at the heart of a "redistributive process," which has parallels in the temple societies of southern India, where "the reigning deity" is "at the centre of a set of moral and economic transactions," and "temple endowments provide the organizational framework within which individuals and corporate groups participate in this redistributive process."[1] Donors contributed wealth to the Church, which redistributed that wealth to support the performance of cult (through the funding of church building, and provision for priests and liturgy), and to carry out the charitable functions (support for the poor and ransom for captives) that were at the heart of the Christian message — a system that is most neatly illustrated in the division of Church income known as the *Quadripartum* — although in Spain the standard division was into thirds, and it did not include a specific allocation for charitable work. This redistributive process seems to have had no exact

---

1   Arjun Appadurai and Carol Appadurai Breckenridge, "The South Indian Temple: Authority, Honour and Redistribution," *Contributions to Indian Sociology* 10, no. 2 (1976): 187–211, at 190.

precedent in the religious structures of the pagan Roman Empire prior to the conversion of Constantine, although, as several scholars have shown, there was some overlap with the classical notion of evergetism.[2] It is important to understand quite how unusual and tortuous was the formation of the landed Church which came to underpin this process of redistribution. I will begin by looking at the endowment of pagan temples in the Roman Empire, before turning to the models provided by Judaism and the Old and New Testaments.

As I have noted, although some pagan temples unquestionably had vast reserves of treasure, they do not seem to have been great landowners. That some temples owned property is clear enough from the legislation relating to its confiscation in the second half of the fourth and first half of the fifth century. Thus, in 364 Valentinian and Valens ordered that all "parcels of land and all landed estates which are now property of temples and which have been sold or donated by various emperors shall be reclaimed and added to our private patrimony."[3] In fact, it would seem from legislation of 408 included in the Sirmondian Constitutions that numerous temples had been established on imperial land.[4] A law of 385, from Gratian, Valentinian II, and

---

2   For the transformation of classical evergetism, Évelyne Patlagean, *Pauvreté économique et pauvreté sociale à Byzance (IVᵉ–VIIᵉ siècle)* (Paris: Mouton, 1977), 9–35; Peter Brown, *Poverty and Leadership in the Late Roman Empire* (Lebanon: University Press of New England, 2002), 4–8; Bronwen Neil, "Imperial Benefactions to the Fifth-century Roman Church," in *Basileia: Essays on Imperium and Culture in Honour of E.M. and M.J. Jeffreys*, ed. Geoffrey Nathan and Lynda Garland (Sydney: University of New South Wales Press, 2011), 55–66.

3   *Codex Theodosianus*, 10.1.8, trans. Clyde Pharr, *The Theodosian Code* (Princeton: Princeton University Press, 1952), 268, http://thelatinlibrary. com/theodosius/theod10.shtml: "universa loca vel praedia, quae nunc in iure templorum sunt, quaeque a diversis principibus vendita vel donata sunt retracta, et patrimonio, quod privatum nostrum est, placuit adgregari."

4   *Sirmondian Constitution*, 12, in *Theodosiani libri XVI cum constitutionibus Sirmondianis et Leges novellae ad Theodosianum pertinentes*, ed. Theodor Mommsen and Paul M. Meyer (Berlin: Weismann, 1905), 916–17, https:// droitromain.univ-grenoble-alpes.fr/.

Theodosius refers to farms (*fundi*) held by temples.[5] One issued by Arcadius and Honorius in 400 refers to edifices, buildings, and gardens in their ownership.[6] Further laws of 405 from Arcadius, Honorius, and Theodosius, and of 425 from Theodosius II and Valentinian III refer to *possessiones*,[7] and a law of 430 from Theodosius II refers to the *iuga* and *capita* of temples.[8] For the most part, however, this property would seem to have consisted of the land on which the temple stood, together with other small farms or parcels of territory, which are implied by a law of 415, which refers to "all places that were possessed by the *Frediani* [sacred porters?[9]], by the *Dendrophori* [carpenters associated with pagan cult[10]], or by various names and pagan professions, and that were assigned to their feasts and expenditures."[11]

In the case of the Vestal Virgins, we hear of the properties which they held within the city of Rome itself in a law of Valentinian and Valens from 368: "As many chief physicians shall be appointed as there are districts of the City, except in the districts of Portus Xystus and in the areas belonging to the Vestal Virgins. Such physicians, knowing that their subsistence allowances are paid from the taxes of the people, shall prefer to minister to the poor honorably rather than to serve the rich shamefully."[12] The income of the Vestals and of priests of the imperial cult is also at

---

5   *Codex Theodosianus*, 10. 3.4, https://droitromain.univ-grenoble-alpes.fr/.

6   *Codex Theodosianus*, 10.3.5.

7   *Codex Theodosianus*, 10.10.16.

8   *Codex Theodosianus*, 11.20.6.

9   Jean-Marie Salmito, "Les dendrophores dans l'Empire chrétien à propos de Code Théodosien, XIV, 8, 1, et XVI, 10, 20, 2," *Mélanges de l'école française de Rome* 99, no.2 (1987): 991–1018, at 1009–10.

10 Salmito, "Les dendrophores dans l'Empire chrétien."

11 *Codex Theodosianus*, 16.10.20.2, trans. Pharr, *The Theodosian Code*, 475: "ita ut omnis expensa illius temporis ad superstitionem pertinens, quae iure damnata est, omniaque loca, quae frediani, quae dendrophori, quae singula quaeque nomina et professiones gentiliciae tenuerunt epulis vel sumptibus deputata, possint hoc errore submoto compendia nostrae domus sublevare."

12 *Codex Theodosianus*, 13.3.8.pr., trans. Pharr, *The Theodosian Code*, 388: "Idem aaa. ad praetextatum praefectum urbi. exceptis portus xysti virginumque vestalium quot regiones urbis sunt, totidem constituantur archiatri.

issue in the argument between Ambrose and Symmachus over the Altar of Victory, although here we are dealing mainly with the allocation of tax revenue and with privileges granted to the virgins.[13]

In the pre-Roman period, temples in the eastern Mediterranean had been richly endowed. The temple of Karnak, for instance, is said to have been the third richest landowner in Egypt. In documents of the New Kingdom we hear that it owned 65 cities, 276,400 hectares of agricultural land, 421,000 head of cattle, 83 ships, and had 81,000 people working for it.[14] But such extensive property-holding seems to have ended with the Roman conquest.[15]

We do have some evidence for temple property in the Roman period outside of that to be found in the documentation for the dismantling of pagan cult. As Marijana Ricl has shown from an examination of surviving inscriptions, rural sanctuaries in Lydia and Phrygia had landholdings, which provided support for their local communities and for the religious feasts associated with the shrines. These were indeed small-scale temple societies. In Ricl's words "sanctuaries, big and small, possessed lands which were their territory and the essential base of their patrimony."[16] The use of their revenues for the provision of festivals fits with the reference to feasts that we have noted in a law

---

qui scientes annonaria sibi commoda a populi commodis ministrari honeste obsequi tenuioribus malint quam turpiter servire divitibus."

13   Ambrose, epp. 72.14; (Symmachus) 72A.7, 15; 73.3, 11, trans. J.H.W.G. Liebeschuetz, *Ambrose of Milan: Political Letters and Speeches* (Liverpool: Liverpool University Press, 2005), 68, 73, 76, 81, 84.

14   Roman Herzog, *Staaten der Frühzeit: Ursprünge und Heerschaftsformen* (Munich: Beck, 1998), 172. See also Richard Holton Pierce, "Land Use, Social Organisation and Temple Economy," *RAIN* 15 (1976): 15–17; Anthony Spalinger, "Some Revisions of Temple Endowments in the New Kingdom," *Journal of the American Research Center in Egypt* 28 (1991): 21–39.

15   Alan Bowman, *Egypt after the Pharaohs 332 BC–AD 642* (London: British Museum, 1986), 96.

16   Marijana Ricl, "Society and Economy of Sanctuaries in Roman Lydia and Phrygia," *Epigraphica Anatolica* 35 (2003): 77–101.

of 415.[17] But there is nothing to suggest that the landholdings were large, or that they extended over vast areas.

In fact, Roman law discouraged donations to the gods: the early third-century jurist Ulpian stated that men were not to make the gods their heirs except in specific cases allowed by a *senatus consultum* — and he named Tarpeian Jove, Apollo of Didyma, Mars in Gaul, Minerva of Ilion, Hercules of Cadiz, Diana of Ephesus, the Magnesian mother of the gods, Nemesis of Smyrna, and Carthaginian Salinensis (or Astarte) as the only acceptable divine recipients of donations.[18] The Church in acquiring huge reserves of property over wide areas of land was not, therefore, replicating any standard model of late-Roman cult, although at the level of the individual shrine there may have been some similarity between the possessions of a pagan sanctuary before the Christianization of the Empire and those of a church or chapel after conversion to Christianity.

If we turn to the pagan priesthood, we can instantly see why there was little need for large-scale landholding. It was rare that a temple boasted numerous personnel who had to be supported economically. Ricl notes the existence of sizeable priestly communities at Didyma, Lagina, Ephesus, Nysa, and Pergamon,[19] but this was clearly unusual. The Vestals did constitute a community, and like priests of the imperial cult in Rome, they received some wages from the State — Symmachus calls it a modest living.[20] Ambrose, of course, felt that they did not deserve their income, and that true virginity was its own reward.[21] But the Vestals were not numerous: initially, according to Plutarch, Numa consecrated two, subsequently increasing the number

---

17 *Codex Theodosianus*, 16.20.2.

18 *Domitii Ulpiani Fragmenta*, 22.6, ed. Edward Böcking (Bonn: Marcus, 1831), 33.

19 Ricl, "Society and Economy of Sanctuaries in Roman Lydia and Phrygia," 80.

20 Ambrose, ep. 72A.15, trans. Liebeschuetz, *Political Letters and Speeches*, 76.

21 Ambrose, epp. 72.14, 73.11, trans. Liebeschuetz, *Political Letters and Speeches*, 68, 84.

to four, and a further two were added by Servius[22] — a number which had grown to seven by the time of Ambrose.[23]

Most priesthoods were honorary and short-term — even the Vestals were consecrated for a limited time period, as Ambrose was keen to point out, noting a difference between them and Christian virgins.[24] Moreover, priests would seem to have normally lived at home in their private residences — at least if one takes as representative an anecdote at the start of Varro's *De Re Rustica,* where a group of friends meet at the temple of Tellus on the invitation of the *aedituus* (temple custodian).[25] The *aedituus,* however, had been summoned by the *aedile* who was in charge of the temple, but had left a message for them to wait for his return. They settled down on a bench and discussed matters of agriculture, until the freedman of the *aedituus* rushed up to say that his master had been stabbed to death, and that his body had been taken to his house. As John Stambaugh has noted, the fact that the group of friends had to wait outside suggests that some temples were kept locked except during a festival, and it is clear from the anecdote that the keeper did not live on the site, nor did the *aedile.*

Of course, most individual churches had a very small clerical staff, usually no more than a single priest, who might well have lived in his own property and have supported himself through some form of non-clerical work.[26] But some of the larger churches boasted very large numbers of clergy. From the Novels of Jus-

22 Plutarch, *Life of Numa,* 10, ed. Bernadotte Perrin, *Plutarch, "Parallel Lives"* (Cambridge: Harvard University Press, 1914), vol. 1, 341.

23 Ambrose, ep. 73.11, trans. Liebeschuetz, *Political Letters and Speeches,* 84.

24 Ibid.

25 Varro, *De re rustica,* 1.2, 69, ed. William D. Hooper and Harrison B. Ash (Cambridge: Harvard University Press, 1934), 166–67, 302–3. John E. Stambaugh, "The Functions of Roman Temples," *Aufstieg und Niedergang der römischen Welt: Geschichte und Kultur Roms im Spiegel der neueren Forschung,* second series, vol. 2, Principat, ed. Hildegard Temporini and Wolfgang Haase (Berlin: de Gruyter, 1978), 554–608, at 575.

26 *Statuta Ecclesiae Antiqua,* 29, ed. Charles Munier, *Concilia Galliae, c. 314–c. 506,* Corpus Christianorum, Series Latinorum 148 (Turnhout: Brepols, 1968), 171.

tinian, we learn that in Constantinople in 535 the Great Church, or Hagia Sophia, alone had over 60 priests, 100 deacons, 40 deaconesses, 90 subdeacons, 110 readers, 25 singers, and 100 doorkeepers.[27] By 612, according to a Novel of Heraclius, those numbers had risen to 80 priests, 150 deacons, and 160 readers; the number of deaconesses and singers had remained the same, but the number of subdeacons had dropped to 70 and doorkeepers to 75. For the church of the Blachernae we hear of 12 priests, 18 deacons, 6 deaconesses, 8 subdeacons, 20 readers, 4 singers, and 6 doorkeepers.[28] We do not have equivalent figures for any of the major churches in Rome, but we do know that as early as the time of pope Cornelius (251–253) the Church of Rome as a whole supported 46 presbyters, 7 deacons, 7 sub-deacons, 42 acolytes, readers and doorkeepers, and more than 1500 widows and distressed persons.[29] Not surprisingly, the number of priests had risen by 418, when around 70 local clergy confirmed the election of pope Boniface,[30] and 67 were present at a council in Rome in 499.[31] Moreover, the clergy of individual churches were

27 Justinian, *Novellae*, 3.1, ed. Rudolf Schöll and Wilhelm Kroll, *Corpus Iuris Civilis, Novellae*, 6th edn. (Berlin: Weidmann, 1928), 20–21; David J.D. Miller and Peter Sarris, trans., *The Novels of Justinian: A Complete Annotated English Translation* (Cambridge: Cambridge University Press, 2018); Michael McCormick, *Charlemagne's Survey of the Holy Land: Wealth, Personnel, and Buildings of a Mediterranean Church between Antiquity and the Middle Ages* (Washington, DC: Dumbarton Oaks Research Library and Collection, 2011), 24.

28 Heraclius, *Novellae*, 1.64–8, ed. Iohannes Konidaris, "Die Novellen des Kaiser Herakleios," in *Fontes Minores* 5, ed. Dieter Simon, *Forschungen zum byzantinischen Rechtsgeschichte* 8 (Frankfurt am Main: Löwenklau Gesellschaft, 1982), 33–106. McCormick, *Charlemagne's Survey of the Holy Land*, 24–25.

29 Peter Brown, *Treasure in Heaven: the Holy Poor in Early Christianity* (Charlottesville: University of Virginia Press, 2016), 26.

30 *Collectio Avellana*, 17.3, ed. Otto Günther, Corpus Scriptorum Ecclesiasticorum Latinorum 3 (Vienna: Tempsky, 1895), 64; Robert Wiśniewski, "The Last Shall Be Last: The Order of Precedence among Clergy in Late Antiquity," *Sacris Erudiri* 58 (2019): 321–37, at 321.

31 *Acta synodi Romani*, a. 499, ed. Theodor Mommsen, *Cassiodorus Variae*, Monumenta Germaniae Historica, Auctores Antiquissimi 12 (Berlin: Weidmann, 1894), 399–415; Wiśniewski, "The Last Shall Be Last," 321.

also part of the ecclesiastical establishment of the diocese, and beyond that of the metropolitan province. There was an overarching structure to the Christian Church, which was absent from Roman paganism as a whole, at least until Julian instituted regional high-priesthoods, like that of Galatia, under the supervision of Arsacius.[32]

Pagan temples and their priests did not, therefore, provide the Christians with a model for a Church that depended on its landed properties for the support of its religious functionaries and the performance of its charitable duties. Nor did Judaism, despite the centrality of the Temple of Jerusalem in the funding of the early Jewish State[33] — even though, as described in the Old Testament, it provided a crucial metaphor for the Christian community, as is most obvious from Bede's *De Templo,* written shortly before 731.[34] Synagogues, as is still the case, belonged to the community that ran them, and which nominated the "Shamash" (equivalent to the *aeditui* of the pagan temples, or Christian sacristans), who took care of the place, without any expectation of reward: the community also chose the rabbi (who lived off donations).[35] Inscriptions provide evidence for the funding raised or donated for the building and repair of a synagogue,[36] and the *Theodosian Code* provides plenty of evi-

---

32 Julian, ep. 22, ed. Wilmer C. Wright, *The Works of the Emperor Julian,* 3 vols: III *Letters. Epigrams. Against the Galilaeans. Fragments,* Loeb Classical Library 157 (London: William Heinemann, 1923), 66–73.

33 West, "Tracking an Ancient Near Eastern Economic System."

34 Bede, *De templo,* ed. David Hurst, *Opera exegetica* 2A, Corpus Christianorum, Series Latina 119A (Turnhout: Brepols, 1969).

35 I am indebted to Yitzhak Hen for information on the organization of the synagogue. Krystyna Stebnicka, *Identity of the Diaspora: Jews in Asia Minor in the Imperial period,* Journal of Juristic Papyrology Supplements 26 (Warsaw: Faculty of Law and Administration of the University of Warsaw, the Institute of Archaeology of the University of Warsaw, and Fundacja im. Rafała Taubenschlaga, 2015), 62–67, follows the evidence provided by the New Testament.

36 See Floyd V. Filson, "Ancient Greek Synagogue Inscriptions," *The Biblical Archaeologist* 32 (1969): 41–46, commenting on Baruch Lifshitz, *Donateurs et fondateurs dans les synagogues juives: répertoire des dédicaces grecques relatives à la construction et à la réfection des synagogues* (Paris: Gabalda,

dence for the building and protection of synagogues,[37] but says nothing about any associated property. The meeting places of the early Church may have been based on this model, but as A.H.M. Jones noted, churches already possessed property before the conversion of Constantine:[38] as we have seen, by the seventh century they were major landowners.

Probably more influential than the synagogue as a model for Christians was the Jewish priesthood. As set down in the Old Testament, the Levites constituted a priestly tribe, which was supported by the members of the other tribes of Israelites. Thus, in the Book of Numbers 18:20, we find the divine injunction: "The Lord said to Aaron: 'You shall have no patrimony in the land of Israel, no holding among them: I am your holding in Israel, I am your patrimony.'" This is reiterated in Deuteronomy 10:9: "the Levites have no holding or patrimony with their kinsmen; the Lord is their patrimony, as he promised them." And the idea is repeated in Deuteronomy 18:1–2: "The levitical priests, the whole tribe of Levi, shall have no holding or patrimony in Israel: they shall eat the food-offerings of the Lord, their patrimony. They shall have no patrimony among their fellow-countrymen: the Lord is their patrimony, as he promised them." In fact, we know that these rulings were not followed to the letter: even in the Old Testament (Jeremiah 32:6–15) there are references to priests and prophets who held land, and in Acts 4:36–37 we meet a landowning Levite from Cyprus called Joseph, known as Barnabas, who sold a field and gave the money raised to the Jerusalem community. In theory, however, the Lev-

---

1967). Rachel Hachlili, *Ancient Synagogues — Archaeology and Art: New Discoveries and Current Research* (Boston and Leiden: Brill, 2013) provides a full survey of the evidence from Israel; Stebnicka, *Identity of the Diaspora,* 283–317, lists the synagogues known in Asia Minor.

37 *Codex Theodosianus,* 7.8.2, 16.8, Theodosius II, *Novellae,* 3.1, trans. Pharr, *The Theodosian Code,* 488–90.

38 A.H.M. Jones, *The Later Roman Empire 284–602* (Oxford: Blackwell, 1964), 904; Julia Hillner, "Families, Patronage, and the Titular Churches of Rome, c. 300–c.600," in *Religion, Dynasty and Patronage in Early Christian Rome, 300–900,* ed. Kate Cooper and Julia Hillner (Cambridge: Cambridge, University Press, 2007), 225–61, at 228–47.

ites held no property, but they were supported by members of the other tribes.

The injunctions in the Books of Numbers and Deuteronomy do not seem to have attracted much comment in Late Antiquity, although Paulinus of Milan cites Deuteronomy 18:1–2 in his account of Ambrose's grief over the prevalence of avarice, especially in his last days.[39] But the idea that clergy should not own property was certainly current. Here, of course, there were also New Testament injunctions to lay alongside those of the Old Testament. In Matthew 19:21, for instance, we find: "If you wish to go the whole way, go, sell your possessions, and give to the poor, and then you will have riches in heaven."[40] And in Luke 12:33 we find a quotation seized on by Salvian: "Sell your possessions, and give in charity. Provide for yourselves purses that do not wear out, and never-failing treasure in heaven, where no thief can get near it, no moth destroy it."[41]

The idea that ecclesiastics should divest themselves of property was certainly thought appropriate for the senior clergy, and for monks and nuns — although for the secular clergy this was an ideal rather than a requirement. That priests had little need for property is stated by Ambrose in his attack on Symmachus over the Altar of Victory. Not every Christian felt the same, but, unsurprisingly, this was an idea that was adopted by Augustine: he did, after all, commission Paulinus to write the *Life of Ambrose,* where we find the reference to the lack of property enjoined on the Levites. Augustine's own views are clear from two extraordinary sermons, 355 and 356, dealing with the ecclesiastical community in Hippo, which circulated as a tract under the title *De vita et moribus clericorum suorum* ("On the life and customs of his clergy") and subsequently under that of *De*

---

39 Paulinus of Milan, *Vita Ambrosii,* 41, Paolino di Milano, *Vita di S. Ambrogio,* ed. Michele Pellegrino (Rome, 1961), 110–11.

40 Valentina Toneatto, *Les banquiers du Seigneur: Évêques et moines face à la richesse (IVe–début IXe siècle)* (Rennes: Presses universitaires de Rennes, 2012), 171.

41 Salvian, *Ad Ecclesiam,* 3.1–5, ed. Georges Lagarrigue, Salvien de Marseille, *Œuvres,* vol. 1 (Paris: Éditions du Cerf, 1971), 240–43.

gradibus ecclesiasticis ("On ecclesiastical grades").[42] For Augustine, as for several other leading ecclesiastics, the ideal model was the Jerusalem community described in the Book of Acts (4:32), where everything was held in common.[43] He therefore determined that no priest in the small clerical community that he gathered round himself in Hippo should have any personal landed possessions. When he discovered that one member of the group had not followed this ideal, he was so aggravated that he enquired about the property holdings of all the other members and was relieved to find that they either held nothing or were about to relinquish the property that they did own (none of which seems to have been very sizeable).[44] In reality, one may guess that they were forced to do so by Augustine.

---

42 Conrad Leyser, *Authority and Asceticism from Augustine to Gregory the Great* (Oxford: Oxford University Press, 2000), 23–24; Conrad Leyser, "Homo pauper, de pauperibus natum: Augustine, Church Property, and the Cult of Stephen," *Augustinian Studies* 36 (2005): 229–37; Conrad Leyser, "Augustine in the Latin West, 430–c.900," in *A Companion to Augustine,* ed. Mark Vessey (Oxford: Oxford University Press, 2012), 450–64, at 456–60; Neil B. McLynn, "Administrator: Augustine in His Diocese," in *A Companion to Augustine,* ed. Vessey, 310–22; Przemysław Nehring, "Literary Sources for Everyday Life of the Early Monastic Communities in North Africa," in *La vie quotidienne des moines en Orient et en Occident (IVᵉ–Xᵉ siècle),* vol. 1: *L'état des sources,* ed. Olivier Delouis and Maria Mossakowska-Gaubert (Paris: Institut français d'archéologie orientale, 2015), 325–35, at 332–33. See also Peter Brown, *Through the Eye of a Needle: Wealth, the Fall of Rome, and the Making of Christianity in the West, 350–550 AD* (Princeton: Princeton University Press, 2012), 483–85. I am indebted to Conrad Leyser for drawing my attention to this material.

43 See also Augustine, *Praeceptum,* 1.3, ed. Luc Verheijen, *La règle de saint Augustin* (Paris: Études augustiniennes, 1967), vol. 1, 417–37; Nehring, "Literary Sources," 331; David Ganz, "The Ideology of Sharing: Apostolic Community and Ecclesiastical Property in the Early Middle Ages," in *Property and Power in the Early Middle Ages,* ed. Wendy Davies and Paul Fouracre (Cambridge: Cambridge University Press, 1995), 17–30.

44 Przemysław Nehring, "Disposal of Private Property: Theory and Practice in the Earliest Augustinian Monastic Communities," in *La vie quotidienne des moines en Orient et en Occident (IVᵉ–Xᵉ siècle),* vol. 2: *Questions transversales,* ed. Olivier Delouis and Maria Mossakowska-Gaubert (Paris: Institut français d'archéologie orientale, 2019), 393–411.

The Augustinian ideal was certainly not the norm: the bishop of Hippo was effectively creating a monastic community for his cathedral clergy. Even so, similar ideas are also set out by late fifth-century African émigré, Julianus Pomerius, who was a key influence on Caesarius of Arles, whose sermons and monastic rules, alongside the canons of the councils over which he presided, constitute the most extensive statement of a religious program to have survived from sixth-century Gaul.[45] Pomerius addresses the question of the personal property of clergy directly in Book 2, chapter 9 of the *De vita contemplativa* ("On the contemplative life"), which is entitled, "Priests should have nothing of their own and should receive the possessions of the Church as common goods of which they are to render an account to God."[46] As examples of men who followed this pattern of life he cites Paulinus of Nola and Hilary of Arles.

Of course, despite the ideal that a bishop or cleric should dispose of his property, we have plenty of evidence that they continued to have possessions — and indeed this was allowed by canon law. The Council of Antioch in 330/341 had merely insisted on there being a distinction between the property of the Church and the personal property of the bishop.[47] An African council, which Jones dated to 409, allowed a bishop to leave property to a relative or to the Church, but not to a pagan or a heretic.[48] Clearly there was an awareness that the bishop was likely to have property to dispose of. The wills of Merovingian

---

45 William Klingshirn, *Caesarius of Arles: The Making of a Christian Community in Late Antique Gaul* (Cambridge: Cambridge University Press, 1994).

46 Pomerius, *De vita contemplativa*, 2.9, Patrologia Latina 59, cols. 453–54; Sister Mary Josephine Suelzer, trans., *Julianus Pomerius, the Contemplative Life* (Westminster: Newman Press, 1947), 72. On Pomerius, see Brown, *Through the Eye of a Needle*, 485–86; Leyser, *Authority and Asceticism*, 65–80; Leyser, "Augustine in the Latin West, 430–c.900," 459.

47 Council of Antioch (330/341), c. 24, ed. Giovanni Domenico Mansi, *Sacrorum Conciliorum nova et amplissima collectio*, vol. 2 (Florence: n.p., 1759), cols. 1305–50.

48 *Concilia Africana sec. trad. coll. Hispanae*, c. 81, ed. Charles Munier, *Concilia Africae 345–525*, Corpus Christianorum, Series Latina 149 (Turnhout: Brepols, 1974), 538: Jones, *The Later Roman Empire*, 1371–72, n. 56.

bishops show how extensive the private estates of a cleric might be. We have already noted the 120 estates in the possession of Bertram of Le Mans. And when Agnellus of Ravenna attacked the testamentary provisions of his namesake, bishop Agnellus, it was not because he owned land, but rather because he left it to his granddaughter.[49] In Spain, the ideal of a poor bishop seems to have been largely ignored: Isidore stated in the *Sententiae* that many wanted to become bishops to gain wealth and honor.[50] On the other hand, there was considerable canonical legislation to ensure that the property of the Church did not pass into the hands of a bishop's relatives when he died.[51]

The abandonment of property was much more common for ascetics and especially monks and nuns. The disposal of wealth by those entering the monastic life is, of course, well known, though one should note that this is very much a Judeo-Christian tradition — one that is attested at least as early as Philo's first-century account of the Jewish *Therapeutae,* an account that was drawn on by Eusebius.[52] It is worth noting that not all ascetic traditions promote the abandonment of property. In an article which takes full cognizance of the writings of Basil and Bene-

49 Agnellus, *Liber Pontificalis ecclesiae Ravennatis,* 60, ed. Deborah Mauskopf Deliyannis, Corpus Christianorum, Continuatio Medievalis 199 (Turnhout: Brepols, 2006), 226–31; Deborah Mauskopf Deliyannis, trans., *The Book of the Pontiffs of the Church of Ravenna* (Washington, DC.: The Catholic University of America Press, 2004), 84.

50 Isidore, *Sententiae,* 3.34.5, ed. Pierre Cazier, Corpus Christianorum, Series Latina 111 (Turnhout: Brepols, 1998), 275. E.A. Thompson, *The Goths in Spain* (Oxford: Clarendon, 1969), 298, n. 2. See also David Addison, "Property and 'Publicness': Bishops and Lay-founded Churches in Post-Roman Hispania," *Early Medieval Europe* 28 (2020): 175–96.

51 Council of Lérida (546), c. 16; Council of Valencia (549), c. 3; Council of Toledo IX (655), c. 7, ed. José Vives, *Concilios visigóticos e hispano-romanos* (Madrid: C.S.I.C., 1963), 59–60, 62–63, 301; Pedro Castillo Maldonado, "In hora mortis: deceso, duelo, rapiña y legado en la muerte del obispo visigótico," *Hispania Sacra* 64 (2012): 7–28, at 17–25.

52 Eusebius, *Historia Ecclesiastica,* 2.16–17, ed. T.E. Page et al., trans. J.E.L. Oulton, Loeb Classics, 2 vols. (Cambridge: Harvard University Press, 1942), 145–57. Sabrina Inowlocki, "Eusebius of Caesarea's *Interpretatio Christiana* of Philo's *De vita contemplativa,*" *Harvard Theological Review* 97 (2004): 305–28.

dict, Gregory Schopen concluded that some Buddhist writings "unequivocally and explicitly acknowledged and supported the continuing right of Buddhist monks to inherit family property and to have absolute possession of such property to be used 'in whatever way one wishes.'"[53] Already for Eusebius, by contrast, the renunciation of property was a hallmark of the Jerusalem community, along with a rejection of marriage and childbearing.[54] Renunciation is also to be found in Basil, who, interestingly, insisted that on entering a monastery a monk remained liable for his unpaid taxes[55] — a clear indication of his appreciation of the Roman State. Gregory the Great was also aware of the State's demands. In a letter to the emperor Maurice, where he accepted that a public administrator should not be allowed to take up ecclesiastical office, he questioned the applicability of the ruling on those who wanted to enter a monastery, even when the community could repay their debts.[56] According to Paulinus of Nola, Sulpicius Severus refused inherited wealth, much to his father's fury — though he did continue to live on the property of his mother-in-law, regarding it as something for which he was only an administrator.[57] In the *Vita Martini*, Sulpicius claimed that Paulinus sold all his property and distributed the proceeds to the poor.[58]

Cassian, who claimed to represent Egyptian tradition, was stricter. For him the ascetic piety of the likes of Sulpicius Sever-

---

53 Gregory Schopen, "Monastic Law Meets the Real World: A Monk's Continuing Right to Inherit Family Property in Classical India," *History of Religions* 35 (1995): 101–23, at 123.

54 Eusebius, *Historiae Ecclesiastica,* 2.17, ed. Page et al., trans. Oulton, 147–57.

55 Schopen, "Monastic Law," 103.

56 Gregory I, *Register,* 3.61, ed. Dag Norberg, *Registrum Epistularum,* Corpus Christianorum, Series Latina, 140–140A (Turnhout: Brepols, 1982), 209–11.

57 Paulinus of Nola, *Epistulae,* 5.6, ed. Wilhelm Hartel, Corpus Scriptorum Ecclesiasticorum Latinorum 29 (Vienna: F. Tempsky, 1894), 28–29; Richard Goodrich, *Contextualizing Cassian: Aristocrats, Asceticism, and Reformation in Fifth-Century Gaul* (Oxford: Oxford University Press, 2007), 160, 165.

58 Sulpicius Severus, *Vita Martini,* 25, ed. Jacques Fontaine, *Sulpice Sévère, Vie de saint Martin,* Sources Chrétiennes 133–34 (Paris: Éditions du Cerf, 1967), 311.

us was totally inadequate. He insisted on a complete rejection of wealth even before a postulant entered a monastic community. He or she should be in no position to be benefactors, and thus to have undue influence over the institution just joined.[59] Caesarius, in his *Rule for Nuns,* stated that any widow entering a community should dispose of her wealth by sale or gift: as for those who were too young to dispose of any wealth, they were to do so on reaching the legal age.[60] Perhaps aware of the concerns of Cassian, he noted that those who had been wealthy and had handed property over to the abbess might see themselves as superior to those who had not, and warned against such attitudes.[61] Benedict also forbade all private property, stating that everything should be held in common.[62] Unlike Cassian, but like Caesarius, he did not forbid a monk from conveying his property on the monastery he joined. The notion that a monk should have no possessions is also to be found in secular law: it is a requirement stated in Justinian's Novel 133, issued in the consulship of Ario in 539, where we find that monks "should not have separate places to live, nor amass property, nor have an unwitnessed life."[63]

Despite the fact that Augustine, in his Rule, stated that postulants should hand over their wealth and property to the monastery on entry,[64] and that monks should hand over any property they received from their relatives,[65] he did not require his own

---

59 Cassian, *Institutiones,* passim, but esp. 2.2.1, 4.3.2, ed. Jean Claude Guy, *Jean Cassien, Institutions cénobitiques,* Sources Chrétiennes 109 (Paris: Éditions du Cerf, 1965), 58, 126. Goodrich, *Contextualizing Cassian,* 157, 167–70.

60 Caesarius, *Statuta sanctarum virginum,* 5–6, 52, ed. Adalbert de Vogüé and Joël Courreau, *Césaire d'Arles, Œuvres monastiques,* vol. 1: *Œuvres pour les moniales,* Sources Chrétiennes 345 (Paris: Éditions du Cerf, 1988), 182–86, 238–40.

61 Caesarius, *Statuta sanctarum virginum,* 21, ed. Vogüé and Courreau 194–96.

62 Benedict, *Regula,* 33, ed. Adalbert de Vogüé and Jean Neufville, *La règle de saint Benoît,* Sources Chrétiennes 182 (Paris: Éditions du Cerf, 1972), 562.

63 Justinian, *Novellae,* 133.13, trans. Miller and Sarris, *The Novels of Justinian,* 881.

64 Augustine, *Regula,* 1.7, ed. Verheijen, *La règle de saint Augustin.*

65 Augustine, *Regula,* 5.3, ed. Verheijen, *La règle de saint Augustin.*

clergy to donate their property to the Church, as we can see from sermons 355 and 356. Indeed, he insisted that the first financial concern for anyone joining his community should be for the well-being of his family, and he noted approvingly that the clergy in his community had made provision for relatives rather than transferring their property to the Church.[66] Augustine was apparently deeply committed to the notion that family had the first claim on property. According to his biographer, Possidius, the bishop thought that donation to the Church should be secondary to donation to family.[67]

The emphasis on donation to the family had Biblical justification in Paul's first letter to Timothy (Timothy 5:8), where we find: "But if anyone does not make provision for his relations, and especially for members of his own household, he has denied the faith, and is worse than an unbeliever." This was an idea that was upheld not only by Augustine, but also by Ambrose and Jerome. In Paulinus's *Life of Ambrose,* for instance, we hear that "on the occasion of his consecration as bishop he gave away to the Church or to the poor all the gold and silver that was at his disposal. He also presented his estates to the Church, after arranging for his sister to retain the use of them."[68] In Pomerius's *De vita contemplativa,* Hilary gave some of his property to relatives, and sold the rest, giving the money to the poor.[69] In other words, on becoming a monk, or on taking ecclesiastical orders, a man should ideally dispose of his property, but before the year 500 there was no expectation that the property should go to the Church. Even in the sixth and seventh centuries, when there was an expectation that bishops should endow their churches, this was with any property acquired in the course of their episcopate — the disposal of inherited property was not subject to the same rulings.

66 Augustine, sermons 355, 356, Patrologia Latina 39, cols. 1569–81.

67 Possidius, *Vita Augustini,* 24, ed. Wilhelm Geerlings (Paderborn: Schöningh, 2005).

68 Paulinus, *Vita Ambrosii,* 38, trans. Frederick R. Hoare, *The Western Fathers* (New York: Sheed and Ward, 1954), 177.

69 Pomerius, *De vita contemplativa,* 2.9, Patrologia Latina 59, cols. 453–54.

The idea that a priest, ecclesiastic, or ascetic should have only a minimum amount of property, and that he should dispose of the rest within the family is also to be found in civil law. Thus, in 390 Valentinian II, Theodosius I, and Arcadius stated that deaconesses (who had to be over 60 years of age) should leave their property to their children and other relatives,[70] although the law was revoked almost immediately.[71] In 434, Theodosius II and Valentinian III ruled that the property of intestate bishops, priests, deacons, deaconesses, subdeacons, or any cleric with no kin should go to the Church: the implication being that any surviving kin would normally have a prior claim.[72] This law was retained in the *Breviary of Alaric*[73] and it was repeated in the *Edictum Theodorici*.[74] The *Codex Euricianus* is explicit that the property of clerics, monks, and nuns should only pass to the Church if they had no kin up to the seventh degree,[75] and this was repeated by Recceswinth.[76] In a Novel of 439, Valentinian III ordered that a decurion, on entering the Church, should divide his property among his relatives, retaining only a third to provide necessary subsistence.[77] Late Roman Christian law, therefore, showed the same concern for provision for the priest's rela-

---

70 *Codex Theodosianus,* 16.2.27.

71 *Codex Theodosianus,* 16.2.28.

72 *Codex Theodosianus,* 5.3.1, https://www.thelatinlibrary.com/theodosius/ theod5.shtml (434) = Justinian, *Codex,* 1.3.20, http://thelatinlibrary.com/ justinian/codex1.shtml.

73 *Breviary of Alaric,* 5.3.1, ed. Gustav Haenel, *Lex Romana Visigothorum* (Leipzig: Teubner, 1848), 140–42.

74 *Edictum Theodorici,* 26, ed. Ingemar König, *Edictum Theodorici regis: Das "Gesetzbuch" des Ostgotenkönigs Theoderich des Großen* (Darmstadt: Wissenschaftliche Buchgesellschaft, 2018).

75 *Codex Euricianus,* 335, ed. Karl Zeumer, *Leges Visigothorum,* Monumenta Germaniae Historica, Leges Nationum Germanicarum 1 (Hanover: Hahn, 1902), 1–32.

76 *Leges Visigothorum,* 4.2.12, ed. Zeumer, 177–78; see also 4.5.1 (195–98) where Chindaswinth, and later Erwig, only allows a donor with children or grandchildren to grant up to a fifth of his or her estate to the Church; 4.5.2 (198–99), where Chindaswinth allows a woman with children or grandchildren to grant up to a quarter of her dowry to the Church.

77 Valentinian III, *Novellae,* 3.1–2, trans. Pharr, *The Theodosian Code,* 518, https://droitromain.univ-grenoble-alpes.fr/.

tives that we have seen in Augustine's sermons and in Pomerius's reference to the actions of Hilary. Of course, emperors were more concerned with the implications for taxation and the performance of *munera* than they were with the well-being of families. Even so, in the case of Valentinian's legislation of 439 the emperor glosses the ruling with a moralizing statement: "For it is seemly that a person who desires to hold fast in the sacred mysteries shall be proved rich in faith rather than in property."

However, there were pious men and women who deliberately challenged the tradition that one should give pride of place to relatives when disposing of one's property. Salvian explicitly rejected the idea in Book 3 of the *Ad Ecclesiam*,[78] and although he was unusual among theologians, there were those whose actions were intended to exclude their relatives from any inheritance. Melania the Elder set about distributing her wealth so as to ensure that there should be nothing left at her death.[79] And Paula did much the same.[80] The question of endowing one's family occurs dramatically in a little-known hagiographical text, the *Vita Vasii,* which was probably written originally before the mid-sixth century (perhaps before 506, since it presents Alaric II in a very favorable light), and then revised later in the Merovingian period (when prefatory remarks on Visigothic Arianism, and concluding remarks on Clovis were added).[81] According to the *Life,* Vasius (or Vaise of Saintes), who was of senatorial origin, inherited considerable wealth from his parents. However, on hearing the words of Paul to Timothy (1:6, 9), "Those who want to be rich fall into temptations and snares and many foolish harmful desires which plunge men into ruin and perdition,"

---

78 Salvian, *Ad Ecclesiam*, 3, ed. Lagarrigue, *Œuvres*, 240–309.

79 Palladius, *Historia Lausiaca*, 61.2, ed. Adelheid Hübner, *Historia Lausiaca: Geschichten aus dem frühen Mönchtum* (Freiburg: Herder, 2016), 307; Goodrich, *Contextualizing Cassian*, 164.

80 Jerome, *Epistulae*, 108.15–16, ed. Isidore Hilberg, *Sancti Eusebii Hieronymi Epistolae*, Corpus Scriptorum Ecclesiasticorum Latinorum 55 (Vienna: Tempsky, 1912), 325–28; Goodrich, *Contextualizing Cassian,* 162.

81 Christian Stadermann, *Gothus: Konstruktion und Rezeption von Gotenbildern in narrativen Schriften des merowingischen Gallien* (Stuttgart: Franz Steiner, 2017), 109, 507–8.

he decided to get rid of all his possessions, freeing his household, and distributing all his property to the poor.[82] His neighbor Proculus, who was clearly a relative, pointed out to his son Naumancius that Vasius was stupidly giving everything to the poor and keeping nothing for his heirs. Vasius said that he could do as he pleased with his wealth, because Proculus had already received his part of the family inheritance, and he announced that he had made God his heir. In reply, Naumancius said that the law allowed him to eject Vasius from the *hereditas* of his fathers. The saint appealed to the Visigothic king, Alaric II, who ruled in his favor. Proculus then incited Naumancius to kill the saint. The *Vita Vasii* is an extraordinary text in many respects. Above all, it brings home the significance of the depletion of family wealth. Proculus and Naumancius claimed to have the law on their side: Naumancius announced to Vasius that he would drive him from his inheritance, according to the law: "I have the law on my side, and in accordance with the law today I eject you from the inheritance of my forefathers."[83] As we have just noted, there is legislation favoring the rights of the family over the donation of land even in the case of a man or woman entering the Church. Remarkably, this is overruled by Alaric, who in this text is on the side of the saint.

If we turn from the question of the property of an individual cleric to that of the Church as an institution, we should note from the start that Christ advocated the dispensing of treasure, but said nothing about the accumulation of landed property, which is scarcely surprising, given the nature of his ministry and his early following. For the initial institution of the Church, we can turn to the description of the Jerusalem community, to which we have already referred, to be found in Acts 4:34–35: "for all who had property in land or houses sold it, brought the proceeds of the sale, and laid the money at the feet of the apostles;

---

82 *Vita Vasii*, Acta Sanctorum, https://www.heiligenlexikon.de/ActaSanctorum/16.April.html.

83 *Vita Vasii*, 2, https://www.heiligenlexikon.de/ActaSanctorum/16.April.html: "Et legem habeo, et secundum legem hodie te ejiciam de hereditate patrum meorum."

and it was distributed to any who stood in need."[84] This, one might note, is a central text for early monasticism. The terrible fate of Ananias and Sapphira, who retained part of the purchase price they had gained from selling a property, was a warning to those who tried to cheat.[85]

The notion that one should support religious institutions with gifts of moveable wealth rather than landed property is well illustrated by the history of Melania and Pinian. When they left Italy for Africa, they sold estates and began to donate the proceeds to various churches. According to the *Life of Melania,* Augustine intervened, explaining to the pious couple that it would be better to transfer estates to individual churches, thus providing a permanent income, instead of giving a one-off windfall that would soon be spent.[86] In Africa, Melania and Pinian did indeed do as Augustine suggested, but when they moved on to the Holy Land they reverted to their old practices, selling property and distributing 45,000 *solidi* to the poor, 10,000 to the Church of Palestine, and 15,000 to the Church of Antioch.[87] Despite the financial wisdom of Augustine's advice, Melania and Pinian clearly preferred to follow the injunctions of Christ and the model of the early Jerusalem community, and to donate treasure rather than land to the Church. But as we have al-

---

84 Toneatto, *Les banquiers du Seigneur,* 154–55, 235–38, 278, 280, 339.

85 Ibid., 116–19.

86 Gerontius, *Vita Melaniae (Βίος τῆς Ὁσίας Μελάνης),* 20–21, ed. Denys Gorce, *Vie de sainte Mélanie,* Sources Chrétiennes 90 (Paris: Éditions du Cerf, 1962), 169–73; Brown, *Through the Eye of a Needle,* 366.

87 Palladius, *Historia Lausiaca,* 16, ed. Hübner, 136–41; Claire Sotinel, "The Christian Gift and Its Economic Impact in Late Antiquity," in Claire Sotinel, *Church and Society in Late Antique Italy and Beyond* (London: Aldershot, 2010), 1–23, at 7–8; Andrea Giardina, "Carità eversiva. Le donazioni di Melania la Giovane et gli equilibri della società tardoromana," *Studi storici* 29 (1988): 127–42; Andrea Giardina, "Carità eversiva. Le donazioni di Melania la Giovane e gli equilibri della società tardoantica," in *Hestiasis: Studi di tarda antichità offerti a Salvatore Calderone* (Messina: Sicania, 1986), 77–102; Chris Wickham, *Framing the Early Middle Ages: Europe and the Mediterranean 400–800* (Oxford: Oxford University Press, 2005), 162, n. 22, notes the stupidity of large-scale land sales, citing John Lydus, *On Powers,* 3.48, ed. Anastasius C. Bandy (Philadelphia: American Philosophical Society, 1983).

ready noted, there is a considerable difference between land and moveable wealth. Essentially, in selling property to distribute the cash to the poor Melania was doing much the same as her grandmother and namesake, Melania the Elder, had done. We find a similar picture in Jerome's account of Paula.[88] With regard to his own estates, however, he merely sold them, but retained the profits to support himself in Bethlehem.[89]

The Bible provided no model for the notion of a landed Church: rather, the community was to be sustained by financial oblations, derived from the sale of property. Interestingly, this model was still in the mind of the scribes who drew up two sixth-century charters conveying land to the monastery of San Martín de Asán in the south-central Pyrenees. In 522, on becoming a monk, Gaudiosus donated to the monastery a *villa* in Tierrantona, two *casellae* in Barbastro, a *domus* in Osicierda, a *fundus* in Llerida, a *castellum* in Guisona, a *colonica* and a *domus* in Osona, a *domus* in Orrit, a *casa* in Aneu, and another in Aquense. This is clearly landed property, but the charter begins with the words of Christ, "Sell everything you have and distribute to the poor […] and come, follow me," together with the description of the early community in Jerusalem from Acts, where the believers sold the property and brought the proceeds to the apostles.[90] Equally, in 576 bishop Aquilinus of Narbonne gave San Martín de Asán a *domus* in Tierrantona and another in Barbastro. This time the charter is prefaced with what are supposed to be the words of Christ: "unless a man renounces all that he has, and gives his property to the most humble poor, he cannot be my disciple." In fact, as the editors have noted, this is

---

88 Jerome, ep. 108, ed. Hilberg, *Sancti Eusebii Hieronymi Epistolae,* Corpus Scriptorum Ecclesiasticorum Latinorum 55 (Vienna: Tempsky, 1912), 306–51; Goodrich, *Contextualizing Cassian,* 162–63.

89 Jerome, ep. 66.14, ed. Hilberg, *Sancti Eusebii Hieronymi Epistolae,* Corpus Scriptorum Ecclesiasticorum Latinorum 54 (Vienna: Tempsky, 1910), 665; Goodrich, *Contextualizing Cassian,* 163–64.

90 Guillermo Tomás-Faci and José Carlos Martín-Iglesias, "Cuatro documentos inéditos des monasterio visigodo de San Martín de Asán (522–586)," *Mittellateinisches Jahrbuch* 52 (2017): 261–86, at 277.

an amalgamation of Christ's words (Luke 14:33), "none of you can be a disciple of mine without parting with his possessions," and (Luke 18:22), "Sell everything that you have and distribute to the poor."[91] The scribe, in other words, had no Biblical model for land donation, but only for giving money and treasure to the Church.

The model for the Church provided by Acts was of a community that did not depend on land, or on the income from land, but on the donation of treasure or coin. The members of that community, and especially its leaders, were expected to sell their own possessions and give the proceeds to the Church. Of course, that did not prevent an individual clergyman from having a profession. Indeed, even in the fifth century a cleric might be expected to support himself through his profession, as is stated in the *Statuta Ecclesiasticae Antiqua,* a compilation possibly put together by Gennadius of Marseille between 476 and 485.[92] Pomerius, in the *De vita contemplativa,* assumed that most clergy would have "the wherewithal of life," and that they would be self-sufficient.[93] And certainly Augustine arranged for clergy to manage individual estates, in order to support themselves or pay off their debts.[94]

This model, however, was inadequate once the Church was staffed by clerics, some of whom (especially those in the larger cities) had duties (whether with regard to cult, pastoral care, or to charity) that prevented them from pursuing another profession at the same time. Gregory the Great provided a church for one cleric to reduce his financial needs,[95] but he tended to order the provision of coin for impoverished clergy.[96] Moreover, the charitable duties — in particular support for the poor and

---

91 Tomás-Faci and Martín-Iglesias, "Cuatro documentos," 279–80.

92 *Statuta Ecclesiae Antiqua,* 29, ed. Munier, *Concilia Galliae,* 171.

93 Pomerius, *De vita contemplativa,* 2.10.2, trans. Suelzer, *Julianus Pomerius, the Contemplative Life,* 74–75.

94 Augustine, sermon 356, Patrologia Latina 39, cols. 1569–81.

95 Gregory I, *Register,* 8.1, ed. Norberg, *Registrum Epistularum,* 513–14.

96 Gregory I, *Register,* 1.23; 2.1; 3.3, 53; 5.27; 9.109, 144, ed. Norberg, *Registrum Epistularum,* 21, 90, 148–49, 199–200, 294, 661–62, 695.

the ransom of captives — themselves involved considerable economic outlay. So too did the building,[97] upkeep, and lighting of churches. The needs of the Church became such that reliance on donations and oblations was no longer satisfactory. This holds true for the monastic as for the secular Church. The charters for San Martín de Asán kept the rhetoric of a world when gifts of treasure were apposite, but they applied it to the transfer of estates.

Increasingly the Church needed a regular income, and that income was best assured through the possession of property. This is clearly the lesson to be learned from Augustine's dealings with Melania and Pinian. By the end of the century, it was obvious to Pomerius that a bishop should have no personal property, but that at the same time he should be the administrator of his Church's estates: "whoever has given away or sold all that he owns and become a despiser of his own property, when he has been put in charge of a church, becomes steward of all the church possesses."[98]

Although, as we have seen, Pomerius's notion of episcopal poverty was an ideal, the fact that bishops should act as administrators naturally implied that the Church was understood to have a juridical personality, and that it was itself the owner of the property. This had effectively been established by Constantine in 321 when he stated that "every person shall have the liberty to leave at his death any property that he wishes to the most holy and venerable council of the Catholic Church."[99] Although Constantine's wording is slightly obscure, the idea that the Church had a juridical personality is implicit in Justinian's

---

97 Alexandra Chavarría Arnau, "¿Quanto costaba construir una iglesia tardo-antigua?," in *Academica Libertas: Essais en l'honneur du Professeur Javier Arce*, ed. Dominic Moreau and Raúl González Salinero (Turnhout: Brepols, 2020), 345–52.

98 Pomerius, *De vita contemplativa*, 2.9, trans. Sueltzer, *Julianus Pomerius, the Contemplative Life*, 72.

99 *Codex Theodosianus*, 16.2.4; Hillner, "Families, Patronage, and the Titular Churches of Rome, c.300–c.600," 238.

legislation.[100] Emile Lesne thought that this meant that churches and monasteries were equivalent to earlier *collegia, corpora,* and *universitates,*[101] and Julia Hillner has shown that there were already Christian *collegia* in the fourth century.[102] The notion that a church or collegium might be the legal owner of land may well have been modeled on established practice relating to pagan temples. That a temple might be a possessor is clearly set out in a ruling of Scaevola preserved in the Digest, where he stated in response to Attius, who had named a priest, custodian, and freedman attached to a temple in his act of donation, that "although the officers had been mentioned, the legacy was bequeathed to the temple."[103]

Through the course of the fifth century we find a growing emphasis on the administration of church estates.[104] Already, at the Council of Antioch in 330 the bishop is presented as the administrator of the Church's property.[105] By the time of the Council of Chalcedon this aspect of a bishop's duties had become so onerous that there was an injunction that an administrator (*oeconomos*) should be employed.[106] Perhaps in line with this, the theologian Claudianus Mamertus acted as *procurator in negotiis* and *vilicus in praediis* for his brother, bishop Mamertus of

100 Justinian, *Codex,* 2.25 (26) (530), and 3.45 (46) (530); Justinian, *Novellae,* 123 (38) (546), ed. Schöll and Kroll, 636–46.

101 Emile Lesne, *Histoire de la propriété ecclésiastique en France,* vol. 1: *Époques romaine et mérovingienne* (Lille: R. Giard, 1910), 258–60. For the development of the idea, Susan Wood, *The Proprietary Church in the Medieval West* (Oxford: Oxford University Press, 2006), 729–39.

102 Hillner, "Families, Patronage, and the Titular Churches of Rome, c.300–c.600," 239.

103 Justinian, *Digest,* 33.1.20, ed. Theodor Mommsen and Paul Krüger, *Corpus Iuris Civilis,* vol. 1: *Institutiones. Digesta* (Berlin: Weidmann, 1895), 459.

104 Toneatto, *Les banquiers du Seigneur,* 187–89.

105 Council of Antioch (330/341), c. 24, ed. Mansi, *Sacrorum Conciliorum nova et amplissima collection,* cols. 1305–50.

106 Council of Chalcedon, c. 26. *The Acts of the Council of Chalcedon,* trans. Richard M. Price and Michael Gaddis, 3 vols., Translated Texts for Historians 45 (Liverpool: Liverpool University Press, 2007), vol. 3, 102.

Vienne, in the following decades[107] — although one might also note that a later bishop of the same city, Avitus, assumed that bishops had to take charge of agricultural land.[108] The Merovingian Councils of Orléans in 511, 538, and 541, and that of Paris in 614, present the bishop as the administrator of the Church's patrimony.[109]

The Visigothic Councils were also concerned with the administration of ecclesiastical property, and the Fourth Council of Toledo (633) cites Chalcedon: "those whom the Greeks call *oeconomos,* that is those who deal with *res ecclesiasticas* in the place of the bishop, as laid down by the Council of Chalcedon, all bishops should appoint such men from among their clergy, for the administration of the churches. He who fails to do so will be held guilty by the great council."[110] Not surprisingly, the need for a diocesan administrator is something that recurs in the letters of Gregory the Great: he urges bishop Cyricus of Palermo to appoint a manager to deal with financial issues[111] and he insists on the drawing up of inventories of Church property and plate.[112] The finances of the church of Bevagna are put under the control of the priest Honoratus, because of the losses it has

---

107 Sidonius Apollinaris, ep. 4.11.13, ed. André Loyen, *Sidoine Apollinaire,* 3 vols. (Paris: Les Belles Lettres, 1960–1970); Jill Harries, *Sidonius Apollinaris and the Fall of Rome, AD 407–485* (Oxford: Oxford University Press, 1994), 218.

108 Avitus of Vienne, ep. 90, ed. Rudolf Peiper, *Alcimi Ecdicii Aviti Viennensis episcopi Opera quae supersunt,* Monumenta Germaniae Historica, Auctores Antiquissimi 6.2 (Berlin: Weidmann, 1883), 98; see Gregory Halfond, *Bishops and the Politics of Patronage in Merovingian Gaul* (Ithaca: Cornell University Press, 2019), 1.

109 Councils of Orléans I (511) 14, 15, 17; III Orléans (538) 5, 13, 20, 21, 25, 26; IV Orléans (541) 9, 11, 12, 18, 33–36; V Paris (614) 8, ed. Brigitte Basdevant, *Les canons des conciles mérovingiens (VIᵉ–VIIᵉ siècles),* 2 vols., Sources Chrétiennes 353–354 (Paris: Éditions du Cerf, 1989), 80–83, 234–35, 242–43, 246–48, 250–53, 270–73, 276–77, 284–87, 512–13.

110 Council of Toledo IV (633), c. 48, ed. Vives, *Concilios visigóticos e hispanoromanos,* 208.

111 Gregory I, *Register,* 13.45, ed. Norberg, *Registrum Epistularum,* 1051–52.

112 Gregory I, *Register,* 3.41, ed. Norberg, *Registrum Epistularum,* 186.

sustained.[113] And the administration of the papal patrimony was a matter of considerable concern.[114] Peter Brown has talked of the "managerial bishop."[115]

Valentina Toneatto has examined the application of financial metaphors to descriptions of the episcopate: the bishops were "les banquiers du Seigneur," "the Lord's bankers."[116] Although the phrase is symbolic, the duties of a bishop and his agents included hard matters of finance. Bishops, or their agents, were indeed the bankers of the property that had been donated to the Lord. Jean-Michel Carrié has rightly insisted on the reality of the impact of Christian discourse on everyday economic life.[117]

To return to the model of the redistributive process of temple societies, the ecclesiastical ideal that the clergy and the inmates of monasteries should personally be poor meant that they had to be supported by the Church itself, or by the faithful. This had not been the case for most pagan priesthoods, although it was in line with statements from the Old and New Testaments. On the other hand, unlike the Levites and the leaders of the Apostolic community in Jerusalem, the scale of the Christian priesthood and its growing obligations meant that funding in terms of donations of treasure or coin was increasingly inadequate. As a result, landed endowment became increasingly necessary. Churches, apparently unlike synagogues, thus came to possess land. Here there were precedents in paganism, where, as we have seen, the temple itself did have a legal personality and a right of possession, although in the imperial period temples seem not to have owned property on anything like the scale of the estates of episcopal churches and some monasteries. That the Church, in acquiring landed property rather than treasure, was responding

---

113 Gregory I, *Register*, 1.78, ed. Norberg, *Registrum Epistularum*, 86.

114 Gregory I, *Register*, 1.80; 3.22, 33, ed. Norberg, *Registrum Epistularum*, 87–88, 167–69, 179. Robert Markus, *Gregory the Great and His World* (Cambridge: Cambridge University Press, 1997), 112–24.

115 Brown, *Through the Eye of a Needle*, 496–97.

116 Toneatto, *Les banquiers du Seigneur.*

117 Jean-Michel Carrié, "Pratique et idéologie chrétiennes de l'économique (IVe–VIe siècles)," *Antiquité Tardive* 14 (2006): 17–26, at 17.

to necessity (and not just the necessity of providing for priests, but also of carrying out charitable obligations), brings us to the question of the chronology of the acquisition of estates. When and how the Church became a great landowner is an issue of some importance.

5

The Chronology and the Causes of the Acquisition of Church Property

The Church's acquisition of landed property is sometimes presented as a relatively straightforward development.[1] However, religious institutions in the Roman period relied less on land than on gifts of treasure. This posed little problem for most pagan priests, whose position was not onerous and was largely ritualized and honorary, and who, moreover, had their own property to support them. It was more of a problem for a Church, several of whose leading apologists were advocating personal poverty for its priesthood, and which at the same time was undertaking major charitable work as well as carrying out its religious and ritual obligations. A landed Church was a solution to this dilemma, but this meant a change in attitudes towards the financial support of religion. This raises the question of the chronology of the acquisition of land.

A.H.M. Jones, while noting that there is evidence for some churches holding property before the reign of Constantine, stated that ecclesiastical landholding grew rapidly and steadily after the emperor's conversion. He illustrated this statement with a comment on Constantine's legalization of bequests to the

---

1   E.g., A.H.M. Jones, *The Later Roman Empire 284–602* (Oxford: Blackwell, 1964), 895.

Church in 321, the emperor's own donations, the gifts of members of the senatorial aristocracy, exemplified by Melania, as well as the evidence of papyri from Ravenna and from Egypt.[2] Although this may seem to be a reasonable body of evidence, it relates to two and a half centuries, and for the West the papyrus evidence for Church endowment, apart from one fragmentary charter of 491,[3] almost all dates from the later sixth or seventh century.[4] Moreover, for the most part the evidence of the papyri concerns relatively small donations. In other words, Jones claimed that there was a rapid growth of ecclesiastical landholding after the conversion of Constantine, and he illustrated his claim with the gifts supposedly presented by the emperor to the Church of Rome, and by one block of substantial senatorial donations just under a century later, and little more. This can scarcely be said to support the statement "that the property of the churches grew rapidly and steadily after 312," and we have, to my mind, good reason to think that the statement is misleading. Certainly for the fourth century the evidence is less strong than one might deduce from Jones's statement. As Kate Cooper has noted, "[o]ur understanding of the property arrangements underlying Christian congregations even in the fourth century is surprisingly weak."[5]

Lellia Cracco Ruggini, who was much more sensitive than Jones to the chronology of the Ravenna documents, saw the expansion of Church property in Italy as taking place in the course of the fifth and sixth centuries: "Above all thanks to the large number of donations, and the tendency of large properties

---

2 Ibid., 1371, n. 55.

3 Jan-Olof Tjäder, *Die nichtliterarischen lateinischen Papyri Italiens aus der Zeit 445–700*, 2 vols. (Lund: Gleerup, 1955–1982), vol. 1, doc. 12, 294–99.

4 Merle Eisenberg and Paolo Tedesco, "Seeing the Churches Like the State: Taxes and Wealth Redistribution in Late Antique Italy," *Early Medieval Europe* 29, no. 4 (2021): 505–34, at 525–28. Earlier documents relate to estates that were subsequently acquired by the Church.

5 Kate Cooper, "Property, Power, and Conflict: Rethinking the Constantinian Revolution," in *Making Early Medieval Societies: Conflict and Belonging in the Latin West, 300–1200*, ed. Kate Cooper and Conrad Leyser (Cambridge: Cambridge University Press, 2016), 16–32, at 27.

to absorb the smaller ones, ecclesiastical land patrimony had in fact expanded enormously during the fifth and sixth centuries."[6] Writing of Gaul, Émile Lesne placed the expansion of Church property after 500. In a couple of florid sentences, he remarked: "Born in the Roman period, ecclesiastical property in France reached adulthood in the Merovingian period. The roots that had sunk into the land of the Gauls in the fifth century allowed the growth of the tree that already had a superb crown in the sixth and seventh centuries."[7] It is a view echoed by Jean Gaudemet: "In Gaul the institution of ecclesiastical inheritance did not appear before the end of the fifth century."[8] These views would seem to be rather more accurate than those of Jones.

Most scholars would accept that Constantine's grants to the Church of Rome constitute a reasonable starting point for a history of ecclesiastical landholding, and they may be right to do so, but we need to exercise caution when considering the evidence.[9] If we restrict ourselves to the Constantinian donations to the Lateran, St. Peter's, St. Paul's, Santa Croce, Sta. Agnese, San Lorenzo, and SS. Marcellino e Pietro, the *Liber Pontificalis* lists over 69 properties that it claims were given by Constantine to Roman churches in the pontificate of Silvester, and a further

---

6　Lellia Cracco Ruggini, *Economia e socièta nell' "Italia annonaria": Rapporti fra agricoltura e commercio dal IV al VI secolo d.C.* (Milan: A. Giuffre, 1961), 458: "Soprattutto in grazia al grande numero di donazioni, e per la tendenza della grande proprietà a riassorbire quella più piccola, il patrimonio fondiario ecclesiastico si era andato di fatto estendendo in maniera ingentissima nel corso del V e VI secolo."

7　Émile Lesne, *Histoire de la propriété ecclésiastique en France*, vol. 1: *Époques romaine et mérovingienne* (Lille: R. Giard, 1910), vol. 1, 143: "Née à l'époque romaine, la propriété ecclésiastique attent en France l'âge adulte au temps des Mérovingiens. Les radicelles qui s'enfoncèrent, dès le Vᵉ siècle, en la terre des Gaules, preparaient la croissance de l'arbre qui, aux VIᵉ et VIIᵉ siècles, dresse une cime déjà superbe."

8　Jean Gaudemet, *L'Église dans l'empire romain (IVᵉ-Vᵉ siècles)* (Paris: Sirey, 1958), 296: "En Gaule, l'institution d'héritier au profit d'une église n'apparaît pas avant la fin du Vᵉ siècle."

9　Federico Montinaro, "Les fausses donations de Constantin dans le *Liber Pontificalis*," *Millennium* 12 (2015): 203–30.

four in that of Mark, Silvester's successor as bishop of Rome.[10] Together they provided a revenue of 27,269 *solidi,* allocated to specific foundations.[11] In addition, there are the problematic *tituli* of Equitius and Silvester, two adjacent foundations, whose endowment as described in the *Liber Pontificalis* is not entirely clear.[12] The first was endowed with 5 farms, 2 houses, and a garden, with a revenue of 428 *solidi* and 1 *tremissis,* and the second with 9 farms and 1 property, yielding 476 *solidi* and 1 *tremissis.*[13] Outside the city itself, SS. Pietro, Paolo e Giovanni in Ostia was given an island and 4 properties, with a revenue of 463 *solidi,*[14] while a church in Monte Albano received 11 properties worth 1,400 *solidi,*[15] one in Capua 6 properties worth 710 *solidi,*[16] and finally a church in Naples 6 properties worth 673 *solidi.*[17] The estates varied widely in value: the highest providing a yield of 2,300 *solidi,* the lowest 10. The list has, of course, been carefully

---

10 *Liber Pontificalis,* 35.3–4, ed. Louis Duchesne, *"Liber Pontificalis": Texte, Introduction et Commentaire,* 2 vols. (Paris, 1886–1892), vol. 1, 202. See Montinaro, "Les fausses donations de Constantin dans le *Liber Pontificalis,*" 206–7, 225–28; Rosamond McKitterick, *Rome and the Invention of the Papacy: The "Liber Pontificalis"* (Cambridge: Cambridge University Press, 2020), 101–16.

11 *Liber Pontificalis,* 34.9, 12, 13–16, 19–23, 25–27, ed. Duchesne, vol. 1, 173–87. My figures differ slightly from those provided by Montinaro, "Les fausses donations de Constantin dans le *Liber Pontificalis,*" 206–7, 225–28; perhaps we have included or excluded certain estates. The ball-park figures, however, are similar. See now Eisenberg and Tedesco, "Seeing the Churches Like the State," 519–25.

12 Michael Mulryan, "A Few Thoughts on the *tituli* of Equitius and Sylvester in the Late Antique and Early Medieval Subura in Rome," in *Religious Practices and the Christianisation of the Late Antique City (4th–7th century),* ed. Aude Busine (Boston and Leiden: Brill, 2015), 166–78; Julia Hillner, "Families, Patronage, and the Titular Churches of Rome, c. 300–c. 600," in *Religion, Dynasty and Patronage in Early Christian Rome,* ed. Kate Cooper and Julia Hillner (Cambridge: Cambridge University Press, 2007), 225–61, at 230.

13 *Liber Pontificalis,* 34.3, 33, ed. Duchesne, vol. 1, 170–71, 187.

14 *Liber Pontificalis,* 34.28–29, ed. Duchesne, vol. 1, 183–84.

15 *Liber Pontificalis,* 34.30, ed. Duchesne, vol. 1, 184–85.

16 *Liber Pontificalis,* 34.31, ed. Duchesne, vol. 1, 185–86.

17 *Liber Pontificalis,* 34.32, ed. Duchesne, vol. 1, 186–87.

examined, not least by Federico Marazzi.[18] Charles Pietri essentially accepted the authenticity of the evidence of the *Liber Pontificalis*,[19] and Paolo Liverani has argued compellingly that the information (especially that dealing with gifts of treasure) was drawn from archival records.[20] Raymond Davis suggested that the evidence was gathered together in the time of Constantius II, noting that some of the original information may have referred to the younger emperor, whose name even occurs in some manuscripts alongside that of his father.[21] Federico Montinaro, however, has pointed out that the system of accounting used in the donation lists of the *Liber Pontificalis* is not appropriate for the days of Constantine, and has also noted that at least one property donated to the Lateran baptistery is likely to have been given after the Justinianic reconquest of North Africa. In addition, by comparing the lists in the *Liber Pontificalis* itself and those in the Felician and Cononian epitomes of the text, he has concluded that the donation lists were modified up until the end of the sixth century.[22] Richard Westall has also noted anachronisms in the list of donations to St. Peter's, and has concluded that they contain material from the 350s.[23] According to both

---

18 Federico Marazzi, *I "patrimonia sanctae Romanae ecclesiae" nel Lazio (secoli IV-X): struttura amministrativa e prassi gestionali*, Nuovi studi storici 37 (Rome: Nella Sede Dell'Istituto Palazzo Borromini, 1998), 25–47.

19 Charles Pietri, *Roma Christiana: recherches sur l'Église de Rome, son organisation, sa politique, son idéologie de Miltiade à Sixte III (311–440)*, 2 vols. (Paris and Rome: École française de Rome, 1976), 79. Also, Charles Pietri, "Évergétisme et richesses ecclésiastiques dans l'Italie du IVe à la fin du Ve siècle: l'exemple romain," *Ktèma: civilisations de l'Orient, de la Grèce et de Rome antiques* 3 (1978): 317–37, reprinted in Charles Pietri, *Christiana respublica: Éléments d'une enquête sur le christianisme antique* (Paris and Rome: École française de Rome, 1997), 813–33.

20 Paolo Liverani, "Osservazioni sul Libellus delle donazioni Costantiniane nel *Liber Pontificalis*," *Athenaeum* 107 (2019): 169–217.

21 Raymond Davis, *The Book of the Pontiffs (Liber Pontificalis): The Ancient Biographies of the First Ninety Roman Bishops to A.D. 715* (Liverpool: Liverpool University Press, 1989), xxix–xxxvi; McKitterick, *Rome and the Invention of the Papacy*, 111.

22 Montinaro, "Les fausses donations de Constantin dans le *Liber Pontificalis*."

23 Richard Westall, "Constantius II and the Basilica of St. Peter in the Vatican," *Historia* 64, no. 2 (2015): 205–42, at 207, 230–31.

Marco Maiuro[24] and Paolo Tedesco,[25] the vocabulary of the lists suggests that some of them cannot be earlier than the 380s.

With these doubts over the veracity of the lists in mind, it is worth revisiting the "Constantinian" gifts. The scale of the land donations is substantial, but not massive — although I have only listed the landed property, not the gifts of gold and silver (which are genuinely breathtaking).[26] It is not, therefore, immediately suspect in terms of its size. As a point of comparison, one might note Olympiodorus's statement that the annual income of a Roman aristocratic family might amount to 3,000 pounds of gold — equivalent to around 375,000 *solidi*:[27] in other words, well over ten times the value of the estates supposedly granted to all the Roman churches by Constantine. David Hunt noted that the supposed Constantinian donations listed in the *Liber Pontificalis* were the equivalent of c. 400 pounds of gold, which was only a quarter of Melania's annual income.[28] And he compared the situation in Antioch, where the wealth of the Church "matched

---

24 Marco Maiuro, "Archivi, amministrazione del patrimonio e proprietà imperiali nel *Liber Pontificalis*. La redazione del *Libellus* imperiale copiato nell *Vita Silvestri*," in *La proprietà imperiale nell'Italia romana: Economia, produzione, amministrazione,* ed. Daniela Pupillo (Florence: Le lettere, 2007), 235–58.

25 Paolo Tedesco, "Economia monetaria e fiscalità tardoantica: una sintesi," *Annali dell'Istituto Italiano di Numismatica* 62 (2016): 107–49, at 122–24.

26 Davis, *The Book of the Pontiffs (to A.D. 715),* xix–xxvi; Dominic Janes, *God and Gold in Late Antiquity* (Cambridge: Cambridge University Press, 1998), 57–58. For the likelihood that the lists of donations of treasure do relate to gifts made by Constantine, Liverani, "Osservazioni sul *Libellus* delle donazioni Costantiniane nel *Liber Pontificalis*," esp. 181–86.

27 Olympiodorus, frag., 41.2, ed. Roger C. Blockley, *The Fragmentary Classicising Historians of the Later Roman Empire,* vol. 2 (Liverpool: Cairns, 1983), 204–6; Chris Wickham, *Framing the Early Middle Ages: Europe and the Mediterranean 400–800* (Oxford: Oxford University Press, 2005), 162. Of course Olympiodorus may exaggerate.

28 David Hunt, "The Church as a Public Institution," in *The Late Empire A.D. 337–425,* ed. Averil Cameron and Peter Garnsey, The Cambridge Ancient History 13 (Cambridge: Cambridge University Press, 1998), 238–76, at 261. See also Jacob A. Latham, "From Literal to Spiritual Soldiers of Christ: Disputed Episcopal Elections and the Advent of Christian Processions in Late Antique Rome," *Church History* 81 (2012): 298–327, at 302–3.

one of the city's wealthier — but not the wealthiest — residents"
in the days of John Chrysostom, at the end of the century.[29]

But while the supposed Constantinian donations may not be
stratospherically large, they do mark a departure in terms of the
funding of religion, given what we have seen of the endowment
of Roman temples, although it looks less exceptional if one turns
to the Pharaonic or Hellenistic evidence.[30] Constantine was perhaps endowing churches much as a pagan emperor might endow
any individual temple. If so, that would raise the question of the
type of donation that was involved, since it would seem from the
later reversion of temple land to the *res privata* that emperors
had retained an interest in estates on which they had allowed the
erection of religious monuments.[31] Because we do not have the
texts of the deeds of donation, we do not know exactly what was
conceded, but Montinaro has noted that the evidence that we
have for imperial donations to churches in the sixth and seventh
centuries suggests that emperors tended to grant income from
estates rather than the estates themselves.[32] And it is the annual
rental value of estates that is listed in the *Liber Pontificalis*. The
sixth-century compiler (or compilers) of the Constantinian section of the papal biographies[33] was (or were) not interested in
any legal niceties. By then there was a growing canonical tradition that ecclesiastical property was inalienable without the
general consent of the clergy.[34] There were, however, those who

---

29 Hunt, "The Church as a Public Institution," 261.

30 See above.

31 *Codex Theodosianus,* 10.1.8; also, 5.13.3, https://droitromain.univ-grenoble-
alpes.fr/.

32 Montinaro, "Les fausses donations de Constantin dans le *Liber Pontificalis*,"
217.

33 For the chronology of composition, see McKitterick, *Rome and the Invention of the Papacy,* 25–35, with the modifications required by Montinaro,
"Les fausses donations de Constantin dans le *Liber Pontificalis*," 221–29.

34 Council of Ancyra (314), c. 15, ed. Giovanni Domenico Mansi, *Sacrorum
Conciliorum nova et amplissima collectio (Florence, 1759),* vol. 2, cols. 513–
39; Council of Carthage (419), c. 26, ed. Charles Munier, *Concilia Africae
345–525,* Corpus Christianorum, Series Latina 144 (Turnhout: Brepols,
1974), 109; Council of Chalcedon, cc. 3, 24, 26, https://www.newadvent.org/
fathers/3811.htm; *Statuta Ecclesiae Antiqua,* c. 50, ed. Charles Munier, *Con-*

thought that the Church received its land from the ruler. Avitus of Vienne remarked to Gundobad: "Whatever my small Church has, nay all of our Churches, is yours in its substance, since up to now you have either guarded it or given it."[35] Justinian was of the view that Church land ultimately came from the emperor: "all the wealth and subsistence of the most holy churches is forever bestowed on them by acts of sovereign munificence."[36] This was an idea that would receive more attention in the ninth century.[37]

We should not only note the novelty of Constantine's supposed donations. We should also remember that one of the authors of the *Liber Pontificalis* peddled a complete falsehood in stating that Silvester baptized Constantine, an assertion made in the opening paragraph of the *Life* of the pope,[38] and thus clearly intended to influence one's interpretation of the imperial gifts. Whether the confusion was deliberate or not, the author subsequently states that Eusebius, the homoean bishop of Nicomedia,

cilia Galliae, c. 314–c. 506, Corpus Christianorum, Series Latinorum 148 (Turnhout: Brepols, 1968), 174; *Apostolic Canons,* c. 39, https://www.ccel. org/ccel/schaff/anf07/anf07.ix.ix.vi.html. For legislation on the inalienable nature of Church land, see also Stefan Esders, "'Because their Patron Never Dies': Ecclesiastical Freedmen under the Aegis of 'Church Property' in the Early Medieval West (6th–11th centuries)," *Early Medieval Europe* 29, no. 4 (2021): 565–68.

35 Avitus, ep. 44, ed. Rudolf Peiper, *Alcimi Ecdicii Aviti Viennensis episcopi Opera quae supersunt,* Monumenta Germaniae Historica, Auctores Antiquissimi 6.2 (Berlin: Weidmann, 1883), 73–74: "Quicquid habet ecclesiola mea, immo omnes ecclesiae nostrae, vestrum est de substantia, quam vel servastis hactenus vel donastis"; Danuta Shanzer and Ian Wood, trans., *Avitus of Vienne: Letters and Selected Prose* (Liverpool: Liverpool University Press, 2002), 218.

36 Justinian, Nov 7.2.1, ed. Rudolf Schöll and Wilhem Kroll, *Corpus Iuris Civilis, Novellae,* 6th edn. (Berlin: Weidemann, 1928), 52, https://droitromain. univ-grenoble-alpes.fr/; David J.D. Miller and Peter Sarris, trans., *The Novels of Justinian: A Complete Annotated English Translation* (Cambridge: Cambridge University Press, 2018), 781, 117: "et et sacrae res a communibus et publicis, quando omnis sanctissimis ecclesiis abundantia et status ex imperialibus munificentiis perpetuo praebetur." See Esders, "'Because Their Patron Never Dies,'" 565–68.

37 Gaëlle Calvet-Marcadé, *Assassin des pauvres: l'église et l'inaliénabilité des terres à l'époque carolingienne* (Turnhout: Brepols, 2019), 195–96.

38 *Liber Pontificalis,* 34.1, ed. Duchesne, vol. 1, 170.

rebaptized Constantius, and places the information in its account of the pontificate of Felix II[39] — it was, of course, Eusebius, and not Silvester, who baptized Constantine (not Constantius). Moreover, although sickness led to Constantine being baptized in Nicomedia, his intention had not been to return to Rome for the ceremony, but rather to go to the river Jordan, in imitation of Christ.[40] Bearing in mind the false statement about the emperor's baptism, we may want to question whether the very considerable donations to the Lateran Baptistery, which are implicitly linked with the baptism, were actually Constantinian. Its 21 estates, with an annual yield of 10,736 *solidi,* dwarfs the property of every other church, including the Lateran itself, at 7 estates, worth 4,390 *solidi,* and St. Peter's at 16 estates, worth 3,708 *solidi* and 1 *tremissis.* Constantine was surely responsible for the building of the Lateran basilica, but so lavish an endowment for the baptistery in his day seems questionable.[41] And, indeed, as we have noted, Montinaro has argued that one of the donations was probably made after Justinian's reconquest of Africa.[42]

By the late sixth century, the Church of Rome obviously did lay claim to all the properties listed as gifts of Constantine. One of the authors of the *Liber Pontificalis* is honest enough to state that an estate supposedly acquired by Innocent I was under dispute,[43] which implies that other estates were not in question. But it would seem that some gifts ascribed to Constantine came from later emperors, [44] some from emperors who were subsequently regarded as Arian. Constantius II is particularly likely to have been involved in the initial endowment of San Paolo fuori le Mura, and indeed he is associated with the founda-

---

39 *Liber Pontificalis,* 38.1, ed. Duchesne, vol. 1, 211.

40 Eusebius, *Life of Constantine,* 4.61–62, trans. Averil Cameron and Stuart Hall (Oxford: Clarendon, 1999), 177–78, with commentary on 340–41.

41 For the building, Hugo Brandenburg, *Ancient Churches of Rome from the Fourth to the Seventh Century* (Turnhout: Brepols, 2004), 37–54.

42 Montinaro, "Les fausses donations de Constantin dans le *Liber Pontificalis,*" 218–21.

43 *Liber Pontificalis,* 42.6, ed. Duchesne, vol. 1, 221–22: the property on the Clivus Patricius.

44 Montinaro, "Les fausses donations de Constantin dans le *Liber Pontificalis.*"

tion in some manuscripts of the *Liber Pontificalis*.[45] In addition, Richard Westall has provided a conclusive case for seeing Constantius as being involved in the construction of St. Peter's, the building of which he has dated firmly to 357–359.[46] And he has noted that the landed endowment listed in the *Liber Pontificalis*, all of which was to be found in the East, dates to that period. Ammianus commented on Constantius's erection of an obelisk in the Circus Maximus[47] — but the emperor also made a significant contribution to the Christian skyline.

With this in mind, it is perhaps worth asking whether Constantius rather than Constantine was responsible for the building, or at least the main endowment of the Lateran baptistery. As noted above, the *Liber Pontificalis* places its account of the rebaptism of Constantius by Eusebius of Nicomedia under the pontificate of Felix II. This we can certainly reject. Felix was pope between 355 and 358 (although he lived on until 365),[48] while Eusebius died in 341.[49] Moreover, in all probability Constantius was baptized in Antioch, shortly before his death in 361, by bishop Euzoius.[50] Even so, it is worth asking why the *Liber*

---

45 Davis, *The Book of the Pontiffs (to A.D. 715)*, xxix–xxx; McKitterick, *Rome and the Invention of the Papacy*, 111

46 Westall, "Constantius II and the Basilica of St. Peter in the Vatican." See also John Curran, *Pagan City and Christian Capital: Rome in the Fourth Century* (Oxford: Clarendon, 2000), 113–14.

47 Ammianus Marcellinus, *Res gestae*, 16.10, 17; 17.4. http://thelatinlibrary.com/ammianus.html. On Constantius in Rome, Mark Humphries, "Emperors, Usurpers, and the City of Rome: Performing Power from Diocletian to Theodosius," in *Contested Monarchy: Integrating the Roman Empire in the Fourth Century AD*, ed. Johannes Wienand (Oxford: Oxford University Press, 2015), 151–68, at 158–60; Mark Humphries, "Narrative and Subversion: Exemplary Rome and Imperial Misrule in Ammianus Marcellinus," in *Some Organic Readings in Narrative: Ancient and Modern*, ed. Ian Redpath and Fritz-Gregor Hermann (Groningen: Eelde & Barkhuis, 2019), 233–54.

48 For Felix II, see Curran, *Pagan City and Christian Capital*, 129–37, which notes the importance of the period of the schism between Felix and Liberius for church building.

49 *Liber Pontificalis*, 38, ed. Duchesne, vol. 1, 211.

50 Socrates Scholasticus, *Historia Ecclesiastica*, 2.47, ed. Günther C. Hansen, *Die griechischen christlichen Schriftsteller* (Berlin: Akademie, 1995), 186;

Pontificalis placed a reference to the baptism of Constantius during the pontificate of Felix.

The *Liber Pontificalis* claims that when pope Liberius was driven out of Rome by Constantius in 355, the exiled pope appointed Felix in his place. Subsequently, Liberius came to terms with the emperor, and was reinstated, initially holding the bishopric of Rome jointly with Felix, before the latter was forced into retirement, and subsequently executed on the emperor's orders.[51] There is a rather different take on events in the account provided by Athanasius of Alexandria, in his *Historia Arianorum*, where we find that Felix was an imperial appointee and was installed in the Lateran by Constantius.[52] Athanasius provides no mention of the fate of Felix, who is simply portrayed as a heretic — and surely if he had been executed Athanasius would have used the fact as further illustration of the emperor's wickedness. Almost as damning of the account in the *Liber Pontificalis* is the first document in the collection of papal documents known as the *Collectio Avellana,* where Felix is portrayed as a perjurer who accepted papal office despite having sworn that there should be no pope other than Liberius. When Constantius visited Rome in 357, two years after the consecration of Felix as pope, the emperor was induced to allow Liberius back to the city, and a year later than that Felix was driven out by the senate and people of Rome.[53] In the *De viris illustribus* Jerome provides the additional information that Felix was appointed by Constantius at the in-

---

Philostorgius, *Historia Ecclesiastica,* 6.5, Patrologia Graeca 65, cols. 459–638, at col. 535.

51 *Liber Pontificalis,* 37–38, ed. Duchesne, vol. 1, 207–11.

52 Athanasius, *Historia Arianorum,* 75.3–7, ed. Hans-George Opitz, *Athanasius Werke* 2.1 (Berlin: De Gruyter, 1935), 225; Richard Flower, trans., *Imperial Invectives against Constantius II, Athanasius of Alexandria, Hilary of Poitiers and Lucifer of Cagliari* (Liverpool: Liverpool University Press, 2016). Timothy Barnes, *Athanasius and Constantius: Theology and Politics in the Constantinian Empire* (Cambridge: Harvard University Press, 1993), 118. Also, Mark Humphries, "*In nomine Patris*: Constantine the Great and Constantius II in Christological Polemic," *Historia* 46 (1997): 448–64, at 454–57.

53 *Collectio Avellana,* 1.1–3, ed. Otto Günther, Corpus Scriptorum Ecclesiasticorum Latinorum 35.1 (Vienna: F. Tempsky, 1895), 1–2.

stigation of the leading Arian apologist Acacius of Caesarea.[54] In other words, despite the *Liber Pontificalis,* Felix would seem to have been Constantius's man, and Socrates is explicit that the emperor was unwilling to see him removed from office.[55] Moreover, although the ecclesiastical historians of the later fourth and fifth centuries largely accepted him as being orthodox, he was consistently regarded as having consorted with the Arians.[56]

The connections between Felix and Constantius surely provide the context for the emperor's building work at St. Peter's, and his endowment of the basilica. And one may wonder whether this was also the context for the foundation and endowment of the Lateran baptistery, which was perhaps intended to be the site of the emperor's own baptism. The silence of the *Liber Pontificalis* would simply be part of the *abolitio memoriae* of Constantius, noted by Westall in his discussion of the building of St. Peter's.[57]

The sheer oddity of the account of Constantine's gifts to be found in the *Liber Pontificalis* becomes yet more apparent when one considers how little attention is paid to the donation of land (as opposed to liturgical vessels and other gifts of treasure) elsewhere in the text. We hear of Felix II buying an estate,[58] and of Damasus (366–384) giving 3 properties, which provided a revenue of 405 *solidi* and 1 tremissis.[59] We learn that pope Innocent I (401/2–417) established the *titulus Vestinae,* dedicated to SS. Gervasius and Protasius, which had an endowment of units of property, including 2 baths, a bakery, and 3 *unciae,* that provided an income of 1,033 *solidi,* 1 *tremissis,* and 3 *siliquae.* It is unclear from the text how much of this was provided by the senatorial

---

54 Jerome, *De viris illustribus,* 98, Patrologia Latina 23, cols. 181–206.

55 Socrates Scholasticus, *Historia Ecclesiastica,* 2.37, ed. Hansen, *Die griechischen christlichen Schriftsteller,* 152–63.

56 Rufinus, *Historia Ecclesiastica,* 10.23, Patrologia Latina 21; Theodoret, *Historia Ecclesiastica,* 2.17.3, Patrologia Graeca 82, cols. 883–84; Sozomen, *Historia Ecclesiastica,* 4.11, Patrologia Graeca 67, cols. 143–45. Barnes, *Athanasius and Constantius,* 276, n. 60, prefers to emphasize his orthodoxy.

57 Westall, "Constantius II and the Basilica of St. Peter in the Vatican," 242.

58 *Liber Pontificalis,* 38, ed. Duchesne, vol. 1, 211.

59 *Liber Pontificalis,* 39.1, ed. Duchesne, vol. 1, 212.

lady Vestina, whose will certainly instructed that the church of SS. Gervasius and Protasius (now dedicated to San Vitale) was to be built from the proceeds of the sale of her jewelry.[60] Xystus (432–440) gave 5 properties, including 2 houses, which yielded 773 *solidi* and 3 *siliquae*.[61] And that is all that we hear of land grants in the recension of the *Liber Pontificalis* that extends to 715. There is not even a mention of the funding of the great second basilica of San Paolo fuori le Mura, which we know from a mosaic inscription on the chancel arch was consecrated by pope Siricius in 390, following the rebuilding of the church initiated by Valentinian II, Theodosius, and Arcadius[62] — which makes one wonder whether some of the 7 estates yielding 4,070 *solidi* supposedly donated by Constantine to the first church on the site came from these later emperors. In the light of excavation, the original "Constantinian" *memoria* has been "described as a simple hall rather than a three-aisled church."[63] This near-absence in the papal biographies of comments on land acquisition comes despite the growing evergetical activities of the popes, which have been stressed by Bronwen Neil in her examination of the fifth-century section of the papal biographies,[64] and which required considerable funds. It would appear that the donations of property ascribed to Constantine in the *Liber Pontificalis* are more concerned with portraying the Church of Rome as being a creation of the first Christian emperor than they are with providing an accurate statement of who actually transferred the estates to the Church. The *Liber Pontificalis* surely drew on genuine archival records: the Life of pope Julius states that "bonds, deeds, donations, exchanges, transfers, wills, declarations or

---

60 *Liber Pontificalis,* 42.3, 6, ed. Duchesne, vol. 1, 220–22.

61 *Liber Pontificalis,* 46.3, ed. Duchesne, vol. 1, 232–33.

62 Tyler Lansford, *The Latin Inscriptions of Rome: A Walking Guide* (Baltimore: Johns Hopkins University Press, 2009), 176–77; McKitterick, *Rome and the Invention of the Papacy,* 112.

63 Brandenburg, *Ancient Churches of Rome,* 103.

64 Bronwen Neil, "Imperial Benefactions to the Fifth-Century Roman Church," in *Basileia: Essays on Imperium and Culture in Honour of E.M. and M.J. Jeffreys,* ed. Geoffrey Nathan and Lynda Garland (Sydney: University of New South Wales, 2011), 55–66.

manumissions" should be drawn up under the supervision of the *primicerius notariorum*.[65] Moreover, the inventories of gold and silver objects can be compared with similar lists on pagan inscriptions, recording donations to temples such as that of Isis at Nemi.[66] But this is no guarantee that the gifts are associated with their true donor: some of the gifts of treasure associated with Constantine, like those of land, must belong to the post-Constantinian period, simply because the churches to which they were given had not been built before 337.

Of course, the estates listed in the *Liber Pontificalis* were not the sum total of properties acquired by the popes. For the fourth and fifth centuries, there are a handful of cases which we can compare with the foundation of Vestina's SS. Gervasius and Protasius.[67] The *Liber Pontificalis* does mention the foundation of a church of St. Stephen by Demetrias in the pontificate of Leo I (440–461), and the pope's own construction of the basilica of St. Cornelius.[68] In addition, there is the evidence of inscriptions, for example those that allude to a church of SS. John and Paul founded by Pammachius,[69] and to the endowment of the church of Sant'Andrea in Catabarbara by the Goth Valila in the days of pope Simplicius (468–483).[70] But as Julia Hillner has remarked,

---

65 *Liber Pontificalis*, 36.3, ed. Duchesne, vol. 1, 205; Raymond Davis, trans., *The Book of Pontiffs: The Ancient Biographies of the First Ninety Roman Bishops to AD 715*, revised edn. (Liverpool: Liverpool University Press, 2000), 27.

66 Liverani, "Osservazioni sul Libellus delle donazioni Costantiniane nel *Liber Pontificalis*," 182–84.

67 Curran, *Pagan City and Christian Capital*, 116–57, provides a detailed survey of the evidence for the period 337–84.

68 *Liber Pontificalis*, 47.1, 6, ed. Duchesne, vol. 1, 238–39.

69 Hillner, "Families, Patronage, and the Titular Churches," 241.

70 Mariano Armelini, *Le chiese di Roma dal secolo IV al XIX* (Rome: Tipografia Vaticana, 1891), 815–17. *Liber Pontificalis*, 49.1, ed. Duchesne, vol. 1, 249. On Valila's donation to the church of Tivoli, see Montinaro, "Les fausses donations de Constantin dans le *Liber Pontificalis*," 209. On Valila see, now, Umberto Roberto, "La corte di Antemio e i rapporti con l'Oriente," in *Procopio Antemio imperatore di Roma*, ed. Fabrizio Oppedisano (Bari: Edipuglia, 2020), 141–76, at 148, 168–70; Silvia Orlandi, "L'epigrafia sotto il regno di Antemio," in *Procopio Antemio imperatore di Roma*, ed. Fabrizio Oppedisano (Bari: Edipuglia, 2020), 177–97, at 188–91. It is worth noting

"none of these rare texts speaks of any measures of endowment of the new foundations taken by the founder or indeed of any further conditions how to use the property endowed."[71] For better evidence of the endowment of the Church of Rome we have to wait until the sixth century, and the correspondence of popes Pelagius I (556–561) and Gregory I (590–604), which has been meticulously studied by Marazzi, especially for the region of Lazio.[72] Clearly the acquisition of landed property was not something that generally interested the authors of the *Liber Pontificalis,* despite their desire to attribute as much of the endowment of the Roman Church as possible to Constantine.

Although we may be sure that some of the gifts supposedly donated to the Church of Rome were given by his successors, there is nothing to suggest that Constantine established a vogue for ecclesiastical donations. Just as there is no continuous tale of endowment to be found in the *Liber Pontificalis,* so too there is little to be found in other sources. Jones's point of departure for the history of the landed endowment of the Church is less clear-cut than might have been expected. We do, however, start to hear of sizeable property donations to non-Roman Churches in the late fourth and fifth centuries. It has been inferred from the *De obitu Satyri* that Ambrose's brother left substantial estates to the Church, although the text is not explicit about what was given.[73] But Paulinus, in the *Life of Ambrose,* does tell us that the

---

the funding of Sta. Agata dei Goti by Valila's rival, the Arian Ricimer: Ralph Mathisen, "Ricimer's Church in Rome: How an Arian Barbarian Prospered in a Nicene World," in *The Power of Religion in Late Antiquity,* ed. Noel Lenski and Andrew Cain (Farnham: Ashgate, 2009), 307–25.

71 Hillner, "Families, Patronage, and the Titular Churches," 241.

72 Marazzi, *I "Patrimonia sanctae Romanae ecclesiae" nel Lazio,* 85–107.

73 Satyrus had left his property to his siblings, who were to act as stewards, distributing the proceeds to the poor: Ambrose, *De excessu fratris Satyri,* 1.59–60, 62, ed. Otto Faller, Corpus Scriptorum Ecclesiasticorum Latinorum 73 (Vienna: Austrian Academy of Sciences Press, 1955), 209–325. See also *On the Death of Satyrus (Book I),* trans. H. de Romestin, E. de Romestin, and H.T.F. Duckworth, in *Nicene and Post-Nicene Fathers,* Second Series, vol. 10, ed. Philip Schaff and Henry Wace (Buffalo: Christian Literature Publishing Co., 1896), revised and edited for New Advent by Kevin Knight; https://www.newadvent.org/fathers/34031.htm.

bishop himself gave his property to the Church of Milan, while reserving the usufruct for his sister.[74] The importance of concern for the family we have already noted in the previous chapter.

At the end of the fourth and beginning of the fifth centuries we have a major, and well-known, block of evidence relating to the pious donations of two generations of aristocrats. We hear of Paulinus of Nola and Sulpicius Severus disposing of their wealth,[75] and also of the aristocratic women, Melania the Elder, Paula, and Melania the Younger.[76] As we have already noted, what is striking about the three women in particular is their preference for following the words of the New Testament to the letter, and for giving treasure (realized by the sale of estates) rather than landed property to the Church. This circle of ascetics provided considerable gifts for the Church, but it would not seem that they played a major part in providing it with land. Although Vestina seems to have left property that was used to endow the *titulus* of SS. Gervasius and Protasius, following instructions in her will, the church itself was built out of the funds raised from the sale of her jewelry after her death.[77] Despite the development of strategies to encourage the donation of estates,

---

74 Paulinus of Milan, *Vita Ambrosii,* 37, ed. Michele Pellegrino, *Paolino di Milano, Vita di S. Ambrogio* (Rome: Editrice Studium, 1961), 103–4; Frederick R. Hoare, trans., *The Western Fathers* (London: Sheed and Ward, 1954).

75 Paulinus of Nola, ep. 5.6, ed. Guilelmi de Hartel, Corpus Scriptorum Ecclesiasticorum Latinorum 29 (Vienna: Vindobonae, 1894), 28–29; Sulpicius Severus, *Vita Martini,* 10, ed. Jacques Fontaine, *Sulpice Sévère, Vie de saint Martin,* Sources Chrétienne, 133–134 (Paris: Éditions du Cerf, 1967), 273–75; Pomerius, *De vita contemplativa,* 2.9, Patrologia Latina 59, cols. 453–54; Sister Mary Josephine Suelzer, trans., *Julianus Pomerius, the Contemplative Life* (Westminster: Newman Press, 1947).

76 Palladius, *Historia Lausiaca,* 16, 64, ed. Adelheid Hübner, *"Historia Lausiaca": Geschichten aus dem frühen Mönchtum* (Freiburg: Herder, 2016), 136–39, 315; Jerome, ep. 108, ed. Isidore Hilberg, *Sancti Eusebii Hieronymi Epistolae,* Corpus Scriptorum Ecclesiasticorum Latinorum 55 (Leipzig: Freytag, 1912), 306–51; Gerontius, *Vita Melaniae,* 20–21, ed. Denys Gorce, *Vie de sainte Melanie (Βίος τῆς Ὁσίας Μελάνης),* Sources Chrétiennes 90 (Paris: Éditions du Cerf, 1962), 169–73; Richard Goodrich, *Contextualizing Cassian: Aristocrats, Asceticism, and Reformation in Fifth-Century Gaul* (Oxford: Oxford University Press, 2007), 162–64.

77 *Liber Pontificalis,* 41.3, ed. Duchesne, vol. 1, 218.

not least involving the cult of the saints in the fifth century,[78] the major period of Church endowment involving numerous very sizeable gifts would seem, rather, to have begun, as Cracco Ruggini and Lesne argued, in the fifth century, continuing into the sixth and seventh.[79] This is also in keeping with Hunt's cautious comparison of the wealth of the late-fourth- and early-fifth-century Church with that of the senatorial aristocracy.[80] Moreover, just as the wealth of the Church increased, so too that of the aristocracy declined, not least because of the political crises of the fifth and, in Italy especially, the sixth century.[81]

The majority of the evidence we have for the accumulation of land by the Church in the late fourth and early fifth centuries points to small-scale gifts by relatively ordinary people. Montinaro, while saying little about the size of donations, has insisted that "private charity was the essential source of ecclesiastical wealth up to the sixth century."[82] Rita Lizzi Testa has commented on Chromatius of Aquileia's appreciation of "il cumulo di modeste donazione,"[83] and Peter Brown has noted that the wealth of the Church was made up of "innumerable private benefactions."[84] Many of these, of course, were gifts of coin or treasure, such as we see recorded on the floors of the churches of northern Italy. Thus we find that Maximian and

---

78 Conrad Leyser, "Through the Eyes of a Deacon: Lesser Clergy, Major Donors, and Institutional Property in Fifth-Century Rome," *Early Medieval Europe* 29, no. 4 (2021): 487–504.

79 Cracco Ruggini, *Economia e società*, 458; Lesne, *Histoire de la propriété ecclésiastique en France*, vol. 1, 143.

80 Hunt, "The Church as a Public Institution," 261–62.

81 Samuel J.B. Barnish, "Transformation and Survival in the Western Senatorial Aristocracy, c. A.D. 400–700," *Papers of the British School at Rome* 56 (1988): 120–55; Wickham, *Framing the Early Middle Ages*, 163–64, 203–19; Latham, "From Literal to Spiritual Soldiers of Christ," 318.

82 Montinaro, "Les fausses donations de Constantin dans le *Liber Pontificalis*," 216.

83 Rita Lizzi Testa, *Vescovi e strutture ecclesiastiche nella città tardoantica: l'Italia Annonaria nel IV–V secolo d.C.* (Como: Edizioni New Press, 1989), 166.

84 Peter Brown, *Power and Persuasion in Late Antiquity: Towards a Christian Empire* (Madison: University of Wisconsin Press, 1992), 95.

Leonianus financed 100 feet of the mosaic floor of San Pietro in Brescia.[85] There are further examples from Aquileia, where Januarius financed 880 feet, and Grado, where Paulinus and Marcellina funded a colossal 1,500 feet of mosaic floor.[86] Additional examples are known from Isonzo and Fondo Tullio alla Beligna.[87] Brown has also noted the comparable evidence from the Holy Land.[88] Discussing the evidence from the patriarchates of Jerusalem and Antioch, Rudolf Haensch has pointed out that some donors are named, but that others are simply members of a pool of contributors: οἱ καρποφορήσαντες.[89] Although some of the western inscriptions do point to sizeable donations, most notably the 1,500 feet of mosaic funded by Paulinus and Marcellina, many of the donors were clearly *mediocres,* Brown's "middling sort." While Chromatius of Aquileia welcomed sizeable donations, as Lizzi Testa noted, he also appreciated more modest gifts.[90] Others have also stressed the importance of small donations.[91]

For grants of land by *mediocres* we can turn to two remarkable sermons (355 and 356) preached by Augustine on either side of the feast of Epiphany in 426, when he directly addressed the question of the property of his clergy.[92] As we have already not-

---

85 Lizzi Testa, *Vescovi e strutture ecclesiastiche nella città tardoantica,* 118.

86 Ibid., 142, n. 10, 157.

87 Ibid., 156, 159–60. On the mosaic floors see also Bryan Ward-Perkins, *From Classical Antiquity to the Middle Ages: Urban Public Building in Northern and Central Italy AD 300–850* (Oxford: Oxford University Press, 1984), 53, with n. 5.

88 Brown, *Power and Persuasion,* 95, with n. 131.

89 Rudolf Haensch, "Le financement de la construction des églises pendant l'Antiquité tardive et l'évergétisme antique," *Antiquité tardive* 14 (2006): 47–58, at 53.

90 Lizzi Testa, *Vescovi e strutture ecclesiastiche nella città tardoantica,* 166.

91 Claire Sotinel, "La recrutement des évêques en Italie aux IVe et Ve siècles. Essai denquête prosopographique," in *Vescovi e pastori in epoca teodosiana,* vol. 1 (Rome: Institutum Patristicum Augustinianum, 1997), 193–204; Thomas S. Brown, *Gentlemen and Officers: Imperial Administration and Aristocratic Power in Byzantine Italy, A.D. 554–800* (Rome: British School at Rome, 1984), 182.

92 Augustine, serm. 355 and 356, Patrologia Latina 39, cols. 1568–81.

ed, these sermons would have a significant afterlife, circulating as a freestanding work of Augustine under the titles *De vita et moribus clericorum suorum* and (less appropriately) *De gradibus ecclesiasticis.* Following the model laid out in the description of the Jerusalem community in Acts, Augustine was insistent that the clergy attached to his episcopal community at Hippo should not have any personal possessions. He had, however, discovered that one member of the community, Januarius, had held onto property which ought to have been passed on to his children (though, just to complicate matters, the children themselves had entered the Church).[93] This troubled the bishop so much that he asked all his clergy about their possessions, and set out his findings in a blow-by-blow account. It is a case that has attracted the attention of several scholars.[94]

In addition to Januarius, one other member of the Hippo community, Leporius, has attracted the attention of Peter Brown.[95] The two men fully deserve the attention that has been paid to them, but it is worth considering the other clergy described by Augustine.[96] There is Valerius, Augustine's predecessor, who had donated a plot (*hortus*) on which Augustine estab-

---

93 Augustine, serm. 355 and 356, Patrologia Latina 39, cols. 1568–81. On Januarius, Peter Brown, *Through the Eye of a Needle: Wealth, the Fall of Rome, and the Making of Christianity in the West, 350–550 AD* (Princeton: Princeton University Press, 2012), 483–84.

94 Conrad Leyser, "Augustine in the Latin West, 430–c.900," in *A Companion to Augustine,* ed. Mark Vessey (Malden: Wiley-Blackwell, 2012), 456–60; Conrad Leyser, *Authority and Asceticism from Augustine to Gregory the Great* (Oxford; Clarendon, 2000), 23–24; Conrad Leyser, "*Homo pauper, de pauperibus natum*: Augustine, Church Property, and the Cult of Stephen," *Augustinian Studies* 36, no. 1 (2005): 229–37; Neil B. McLynn, "Administrator: Augustine in His Diocese," in *A Companion to Augustine,* ed. Mark Vessey (Malden: Wiley-Blackwell, 2012), 310–22. See also Brown, *Through the Eye of a Needle,* 483–85.

95 Augustine, serm. 356.10, Patrologia Latina 39, col. 1577; Brown, *Through the Eye of a Needle,* 483–84; Peter Brown, *Poverty and Leadership in the Late Roman Empire,* The Menahem Stern Jerusalem Lectures (Lebanon: University Press of New England, 2002), 65.

96 Valerio Neri, *I marginali nell'Occidente tardoantico: "infames" e criminali nella nascente società cristiana* (Bari: Edipuglia, 1996), 120–22; Claudia Rapp, *Holy Bishops in Late Antiquity: the Nature of Christian Leadership*

lished his own monastery.[97] The deacon Valens still held some small fields (*agellos*) in common with his brother, and could not dispose of them until the two had come to an arrangement.[98] His brother, we are told, was a deacon of the Church of Milevis, and was keen to divide up the property, as well as to manumit the slaves they possessed and to provide the Church with an *alimentum*. Augustine's own nephew Patricius owned some small fields, *agelluli*, which he had not been able to dispose of while his mother was alive, since she needed the usufruct.[99] The deacon Faustinus, an ex-soldier, had a little property, *exiguum*, which he had divided with his brothers, giving his portion to the Church.[100] Another deacon, Severus, had bought a house (*unam domum*) with money given by a religious layman, to provide accommodation for his mother and sister, but the property itself he had placed under Augustine's control. He also had some small fields, *agellos*, in his native place, which he intended to give to the Church.[101] An unnamed deacon had only a few *servuli*, who he was about to emancipate.[102] The deacon Heraclius is more complicated. He had endowed a chapel of the martyr Stephen. In addition, he had bought a *possessio* that was still under his control, and he had purchased a plot (*spatia*) on which he had built a house (*domum*) that his mother might live in. He also had some slaves (*servuli*) whom he would soon emancipate.[103] But as Augustine insists, "No one says that he is rich." The priests, however, had nothing, although Barnabas had received a *villa* from Eleusinus, which he had turned into a monastery. He had also run into financial difficulties, so Augustine had entrusted him with a *fundus* belonging to the Church to

in an Age of Transition, The Transformation of the Classical Heritage 37 (Berkeley: University of California Press, 2005), 214.

97 Augustine, serm. 355.1, Patrologia Latina 39, cols. 1569–70.
98 Augustine, serm. 356.4, Patrologia Latina 39, col. 1576.
99 Augustine, serm. 356.3, Patrologia Latina 39, cols. 1575–76.
100 Augustine, serm. 356.4, Patrologia Latina 39, col. 1576.
101 Augustine, serm. 356.5, Patrologia Latina 39, col. 1576.
102 Augustine, serm. 356.6, Patrologia Latina 39, col. 1576.
103 Augustine, serm. 356.7, Patrologia Latina 39, col. 1577.

pay off the debt.[104] It is an extraordinary picture of priests and deacons, most of whom had little before entering Augustine's community, but they had still given away what they had.[105]

The donations we see in these two sermons of Augustine chime exactly with what we find in Chromatius of Aquileia. These are most certainly Brown's "middling sort,"[106] and are absolutely comparable to the deacon, lector, and *notarius* who appear together in a mosaic donation panel on the floor of San Canzian d'Isonzo.[107] They also make abundantly clear the extraordinary nature of the ecclesiastical donations of Melania,[108] which were totally out of line with what any Christian congregation might expect. The norm seems to have been a field or a house here or there — and not the vast quantities of treasure offered by a rich member of a senatorial family, although Augustine pointed out that it would be better if she offered land rather than treasure. And if the gifts of the "middling sort" scarcely compare with what Melania had to offer, it is also likely that they would have failed to measure up to the donations we find recorded on the walls of the twelfth-century temples of Andhra Pradesh, where some 390 inscriptions refer to 336 donors, in-

---

104 Augustine, serm. 356.15, Patrologia Latina 39, cols. 1580–81.

105 For another more complicated issue of property, see the discussion of the property of Antoninus of Fussala by Neil B. McLynn, "Augustine's Black Sheep: The Case of Antoninus of Fussala," in *Istituzioni, Carismi ed Esercizio del Potere (IV–VI secolo d.C.),* ed. Giorgio Bonamente and Rita Lizzi Testa (Bari: Edipulgia, 2010), 305–21, at 316–17.

106 Brown, *Through the Eye of a Needle,* 36–39, 124, 212. The "middling sort" is defined by Serena Connolly, *Lives Behind the Laws: The World of the "Codex Hermogenianus"* (Bloomington: Indiana University Press, 2010), 139, as "everyone from people just above peasant status [...] to the lower reaches of the curial class."

107 Lizzi Testa, *Vescovi e strutture ecclesiastiche nella città tardoantica,* 156.

108 Gerontius, *Vita Melaniae,* 21, ed. Gorce, *Vie de sainte Melanie* (Βίος τῆς Ὁσίας Μελάνης), 170–72; Palladius, *Historia Lausiaca,* 16, ed. Adelheid Hübner, 136–39; Andrea Giardina, "Carità eversiva. Le donazioni di Melania la Giovane et gli equilibri della società tardoromana," *Studi storici* 29 (1988): 127–42; Andrea Giardina, "Carità eversiva. Le donazioni di Melania la Giovane e gli equilibri della società tardoantica," in *Hestiasis. Studi di tarda antichità offerti a Salvatore Calderone* (Messina: Sicania, 1986), 77–102; Brown, *Through the Eye of a Needle,* 366.

cluding 26 kings, 76 feudal lords, 109 officials, 47 royal ladies, as well as 21 merchants.[109] Early fifth-century Hippo was not a temple society, even if the small community surrounding Augustine was living the life of the early Christian community in Jerusalem. For the financing of churches in the late fourth and early fifth centuries we might find a better parallel in the funding of madrasas in modern Pakistan, for which we can turn to Francis Robinson: "According to one account Pakistan had just 189 at independence, but 10,000 by 2002. This growth is a reflection of popular will; they are almost entirely dependent on public subscription. Among the reasons for this are the faith of the common people."[110]

Augustine's sermons provide us with a marvelous snapshot of the endowment of a diocese in the early fifth century. But we are still far from the landed Church of the late sixth and early seventh centuries that I sketched out in the first chapter. Augustine tells us himself that his father's property was the equivalent of about a twentieth of that of the bishopric of Hippo,[111] and he certainly did not come from a wealthy family.[112] On the other hand, there had been some accumulation of Church land already by the time of Chalcedon in 451, when, as we have already noted, we find the recommendation that a bishop appoint an *oeconomus* to deal with the financial administration of the diocese.[113] This was a point specifically cited by the Visigothic

---

109 P.S. Kanaka Durga and Y.A. Sudhakar Reddy, "Kings, Temples and Legitimation of Autochthonous Communities: A Case Study of a South Indian Temple," *Journal of the Economic and Social History of the Orient* 35 (1992): 145–66, at 155.

110 Francis Robinson, "Laboratory Nation: What Happened to Islamic Modernism?" review of Muhammad Qasim Zaman, *Islam in Pakistan, Times Literary Supplement* 6066 (July 5, 2019): 28–29.

111 Augustine, ep. 126.7, ed. Alois Goldbacher, *Augustini Epistolae* 3, Corpus Scriptorum Ecclesiasticorum Latinorum 44 (Vienna, 1904), http://www.presbytersproject.ihuw.pl/index.php?id=6&SourceID=473.

112 Peter Brown, *Augustine of Hippo: A Biography* (London: Faber & Faber, 1967), 21.

113 Council of Chalcedon, c. 26, https://www.newadvent.org/fathers/3811.htm.

bishops at the Fourth Council of Toledo (633).[114] The increasing references to the need for property managers that we find in the late fifth and sixth centuries are an indication of the accumulation of property.[115] Thus we have what Brown has called the "rise of the managerial bishop."[116]

In addition, Chalcedon also put checks on the alienation of land in the possession of the Church.[117] Already as early as 314 the Council of Ancyra had annulled the alienation of goods during an episcopal vacancy.[118] The *Apostolic Canons,* from fourth-century Syria, which were accepted by the Council in Trullo in 692, but rejected at the same time by pope Sergius, forbade a bishop from selling what he was administering.[119] In 419 the Council of Carthage deposed a bishop who had alienated *res ecclesiasticae.*[120] Chalcedon insisted that synodal approval was needed if a bishop wanted to sell property.[121] A Roman synod in 502 stated that rural and urban estates, gems, gold, silver, and cloth donated to the Church for the poor should not be transferred to anyone else,[122] and the canons of the synod concluded with a letter of pope Symmachus forbidding the alienation of Church property, the usufruct of which was only to provide for

114 Council of Toledo IV (633), c. 48, ed. Vives, *Concilios visigóticos e hispano-romanos,* 208. Also, Council of Seville II (619), c. 9, ed. Vives, *Concilios visigóticos e hispano-romanos,* 169. See Edward A. Thompson, *The Goths in Spain* (Oxford: Clarendon, 2000), 299, citing Council of Mérida (666), cc. 10, 14, ed. Vives, *Concilios visigóticos e hispano-romanos,* 332–33, 335.

115 See above.

116 Brown, *Through the Eye of a Needle,* 496–97.

117 Council of Chalcedon, cc. 3, 24, https://www.newadvent.org/fathers/3811.htm.

118 Council of Ancyra (314), c. 15, ed. Mansi, *Sacrorum Conciliorum,* vol. 2, cols. 513–39. On alienation, see Esders, "'Because Their Patron Never Dies,'" 565–68.

119 *Apostolic Canons,* c. 39. https://www.ccel.org/ccel/schaff/anf07/anf07.ix.ix.vi.html.

120 Council of Carthage (419), ed. Munier, *Concilia Africae 345–525,* 88–155.

121 Council of Chalcedon, c. 26, https://www.newadvent.org/fathers/3811.htm.

122 *Acta synhodi Romani,* a. 502, 7(3), 16, ed. Theodor Mommsen, *Cassiodorus Variae,* Monumenta Germaniae Historica, Auctores Antiquissimi 12 (Berlin: Weidmann, 1894), 446–47, 450.

priests, the poor, and *peregrini*.[123] This was, in fact, a reaffirmation of a ruling of the senate, issued by Odoacer, in 483.[124] It was reiterated by Theodoric the Ostrogoth in a law of 508.[125] On numerous occasions Gregory the Great stated that the possessions of the Church could not be alienated.[126] The point is also enshrined in the *Liber Diurnus*.[127] In addition, in several letters the pope insisted on the need for an inventory of the property of a particular church.[128] The Merovingian Church councils repeatedly stressed the inalienability of Church property.[129] In Spain, the Council of Lérida in 546 legislated to protect the possessions of a church on the death of a bishop (*sacerdos*),[130] and further legislation was added by the Councils of Valencia (549) and IX Toledo (655).[131] Among the *Antiquae* of the *Lex Visigothorum* is a requirement that inventories of land committed to priests

123 *Acta synhodi Romani*, a. 502, 13–18, ed. Mommsen, *Cassiodorus Variae*, 448–51. Calvet-Marcadé, *Assassin des pauvres*, 84–88.

124 Hillner, "Families, Patronage, and the Titular Churches," 248–52.

125 *Theoderici regis edictum Symmacho papae directum contra sacerdotes substantiae ecclesiarum alienatores A. 508*, ed. Georg Heinrich Pertz, Monumenta Germaniae Historica, Leges 5 (Hanover: Hahn, 1875–1889), 169–70.

126 Gregory I, *Register*, 4.36; 5.23; 6.1; 9.75, 142; 12.12, ed. Dag Norberg, Corpus Christianorum, Series Latina 140–140A (Turnhout: Brepols, 1982), 256–67, 290, 369–70, 630, 693–94, 985–86.

127 *Liber Diurnus, romanorum pontificum*, 71, 74, 89, 95, 97, ed. Theodor von Sickel (Vienna: Vindobonae, 1889), 67–68, 74–78, 117–19, 123–25, 127–29.

128 Gregory I, *Register*, 3.22, 41, ed. Norberg, *Registrum Epistularum*, 167–68, 186.

129 Councils of Épaon (517), cc. 7, 12; III Orléans (538), c. 13; V Orléans (549), c. 13; Clichy (626/627), cc. 15, 25, ed. Brigitte Basdevant, *Les canons des conciles mérovingiens (VIᵉ–VIIᵉ siècles)*, 2 vols., Sources Chrétiennes 353–354 (Paris: Éditions du Cerf, 1989), vol. 1, 104, 106; vol. 1, 222; vol. 1, 308; vol. 2, 538, 542.

130 Council of Lérida (546), c. 16, ed. Vives, *Concilios visigóticos e hispano-romanos*, 59–60; also (on monastic property), c. 3, p. 56. Arnold Pöschl, *Bischofsgut und mensa episcopalis. Ein Beitrag zur Geschichte des kirchlichen Vermögensrechtes, 1: Die Grundlagen* (Bonn: Hanstein, 1908), 17; Pedro Castillo Maldonado, "*In hora mortis*: deceso, duelo, rapiña y legado en la muerte del obispo visigótico," *Hispania Sacra* 64 (2012): 7–28, at 17.

131 Councils of Valencia (549), c. 3; IX Toledo (655), c. 7, ed. Vives, *Concilios visigóticos e hispano-romanos*, 62–63, 301; Castillo Maldonado, "In hora mortis," 17.

should be drawn up, to ensure that no loss was suffered.[132] The question of appropriation of Church property by bishops is also the subject of a law of Wamba from 675.[133] In the East, Justinian legislated in 537 to prevent the alienation of Church land.[134]

On the other hand, a number of leading clergy, including Ambrose and Gregory the Great, did allow for the alienation of property to support the poor, ransom captives, and construct cemeteries.[135] The alienation of wealth (usually of treasure) to fund the ransom of captives is a recurrent theme in episcopal hagiography:[136] it could be a mark of sanctity, although it could also, clearly, be contentious — as we have already noted, in the

132 *Leges Visigothorum*, 5.1.2, ed. Karl Zeumer, Monumenta Germaniae Historica, Leges Nationum Germanicarum 1 (Hanover: Hahn, 1902), 208–9, with n. 1 for the sources of the law. See also P.D. King, *Law and Society in the Visigothic Kingdom* (Cambridge: Cambridge University Press, 1972), 155; Castillo Maldonado, "*In hora mortis,*" 18–19. In addition, Councils of Toledo IV (633), c. 38; XI Toledo (675), c. 5, ed. Vives, *Concilios visigóticos e hispano-romanos,* 205–6, 358–60. David Addison, "Property and 'Publicness': Bishops and Lay-founded Churches in Post-Roman Hispania," *Early Medieval Europe* 28, no. 2 (2020): 175–96.

133 *Leges Visigothorum*, 4.5.6, ed. Zeumer, 202–5.

134 Justinian, *Novellae*, 46, ed. Rudolf Schöll and Wilhem Kroll, *Corpus Iuris Civilis, Novellae*, 6th edn. (Berlin: Weidemann, 1928), 280–82. See Wolfram Brandes, "Das Schweigen des *Liber pontificalis*. Die 'Enteignung' der päpstlichen Patrimonen Siziliens und Unteritaliens in der 50er Jahren des 8. Jahrhunderts," in *Fontes Minores* 12, ed. Wolfram Brandes, Lars Hoffmann, and Kirill Maksimovič (Frankfurt: Löwenklau-Gesellschaft, 2014), 97–203, at 136–37.

135 Ambrose, *De Officiis*, 2.136, ed. Ivor J. Davidson, 2 vols. (Oxford: Oxford University Press, 2002), vol. 2, 342–43; Gregory I, *Register,* 4.17; 7.13, 35; 9.52, ed. Norberg, *Registrum Epistularum,* 235–36, 462–63, 498–99, 610.

136 E.g., Cyprian of Toulon et al., *Vita Caesarii*, 1.32, ed. Bruno Krusch, Monumenta Germaniae Historica, Scriptores Rerum Merovingicarum 3 (Hanover: Hahn, 1896), 469; William Klingshirn, "Charity and Power: Caesarius of Arles and the Ransoming of Captives in Sub-Roman Gaul," *Journal of Roman Studies* 75 (1985): 183–203, at 189. There is a fuller list in Noel Lenski, "Captivity and Romano-Barbarian Interchange," in *Romans, Barbarians and the Transformation of the Roman World: Cultural Interaction and the Creation of Identity in Late Antiquity,* ed. Ralph Mathisen and Danuta Shanzer (Farnham: Ashgate, 2011), 185–98, at 189, n. 18, listing (among other texts) Paulinus, *Vita Ambrosii,* 38; Possidius, *Vita Augustini,* 24; Honoratus, *Vita Hilarii,* 11; and Ennodius, *Vita Epiphanii,* 115–19.

context of the discussion of whether a bishop should melt down liturgical vessels to redeem those held captive.[137] The 502 Rome synod stated explicitly that it was wrong, even sacrilegious to give away what had been offered *pro salute vel requie animarum suarum*.[138]

In the conciliar evidence Church property and its protection becomes a constant from the sixth century onwards. It is raised in the canons of the first Council of Orléans, which states that:

> concerning the gifts (*oblationibus*) and lands (*agris*) which our lord the king has deigned to give as a personal gift to churches, or those that, inspired by God, he will give to those that do not yet have them, together with a concession of immunity to those lands and priests, we declare that it is entirely right that all that God will deign to give as revenue should be used for the repair of churches, the support of bishops, and of the poor, and of the ransom of captives, and that the clergy should be committed to support the work of the Church.[139]

Here we effectively have a statement of the *Quadraticum*, but associated with royal land donation. It is certainly the earliest reference to the concession of land to the Church by a Merovingian king — and although several churches and monasteries claimed

---

137 Klingshirn, "Charity and Power"; Pauline Allen and Bronwen Neil, *Crisis Management in Late Antiquity (410–590 CE): A Survey of the Evidence from Episcopal Letters*, Vigiliae Christianae Supplement 121 (Boston and Leiden: Brill, 2013), 40–41; Michèle Renée Salzman, "The Religious Economics of Crisis: the Papal Use of Liturgical Vessels as Symbolic Capital in Late Antiquity," *Religion in the Roman Empire* 5, no. 1: *Transformations of Value: Lived Religion and the Economy* (2019): 125–41, at 132; Neri, *I marginali*, 112, with n. 115: *Codex Iustinianus*, 1.2.21 (529), https://droitromain.univ-grenoble-alpes.fr/; Justinian, *Novellae*, 65; 108; 115; 120.10 (544); 123.37; 131.11, 13, ed. Schöll and Kroll, 339, 513–16, 534–49, 589–91, 620–21, 659–660, https://droitromain.univ-grenoble-alpes.fr/; Council of Clichy (626–627), c. 25, ed. Basdevant, *Les canons des conciles mérovingiens*, vol. 2, 542.

138 *Acta synhodi Romani*, a. 502, c. 7(3), ed. Mommsen, *Cassiodorus Variae*, 446–47.

139 Council of Orléans I (511), c. 5, ed. Basdevant, *Les canons des conciles mérovingiens*, vol. 1, 76.

foundation by Clovis, none of the documentation is genuine.[140] Our authentic charters do not start until the seventh century.[141] But in this canon we have a reference to what appears to be a number of grants.

We have no genuine charters for early sixth century Francia (although we now have a charter from 522 for Spain),[142] but we do have other reasons for thinking that it was in the sixth century that large-scale donations to the Church started to become more common. Above all, we have the evidence of diocesan histories that were set down in the Carolingian period. For instance, like other Carolingian histories, the *Actus Pontificum Cenomannis* includes the texts of the testaments of bishops. Certainly, we have to be careful when using these documents: there is every reason to think that some of the *testamenta* preserved in the histories are forgeries, or contain forged elements, which the Carolingian episcopate intended to use in its claims to property.[143] At the same time, the chronology of land-giving that we find in these histories is reasonably consistent, and tallies with the impression to be gained from other types of document. The diocesan histories tend to record episcopal wills from the sixth century and later: thus, in the *History of the Bishops of Le Mans,*

---

140 Friedrich Prinz, *Frühes Mönchtum im Frankenreich: Kultur und Gesellschaft in Gallien, den Rheinlanden und Bayern am Beispiel der monastischen Entwicklung (4. bis 8. Jahrhundert)* (Kempten: Ferdinand Oechelhäuser, 1965), 152–53.

141 *Diplomata Merowingica,* 171, ed. Theo Kölzer, *Die Urkunden der Merowinger,* 2 vols., Monumenta Germaniae Historica (Hanover: Hahn 2001), vol. 1, doc. 28, 75–77 (a charter of 625); also doc. 23, 62–64 (a charter dated to the reign of Chlothar II [584–628]). There is an interpolated charter, doc. 25 (596), 68–70. For the problematic charter of Ansemundus for St-André-le-Haut, Vienne, see now Nathanaël Nimmegeers, "Saint-André-le-Haut des origines à 1031: approche historique," *Bulletin du centre d'études Auxerre,* Hors-série 10 (2016): n.p.

142 Guillermo Tomás-Faci and José Carlos Martín-Iglesias, "Cuatro documentos inéditos des monasterio visigodo de San Martín de Asán (522–586)," *Mittellateinisches Jahrbuch* 52 (2017): 261–86, at 277–78.

143 Walter Goffart, *The Le Mans Forgeries: A Chapter from the History of Church Property from the Ninth Century* (Cambridge: Harvard University Press, 1966).

although there is reference to improbable gifts of land from the time of "Decius, Nerva and Trajan,"[144] as well as extraordinary lists of gifts of wax for the pre-Constantinian period,[145] the main evidence relating to property donation dates from the episcopates of bishop Innocent (who died in 559) and his successors.[146] *The History of the Bishops of Auxerre* lists the supposed gifts of Germanus in the fifth century (surely an attempt to associate donations with the most famous saint of the diocese), but thereafter information on land grants begins with bishop Aunarius in the last quarter of the sixth century.[147] The earliest will referred to in Flodoard's *History of the Church of Rheims* is that of Bennadius (d. 459), but this first testament mentions no land, only a liturgical vessel and coin.[148] The version of the will of his successor, Remigius, who died in 533, which is preserved by Flodoard, is regarded as heavily tampered with, but a shorter version preserved by Hincmar is thought to be authentic.[149] It does include land-grants, but the scale of donation is not vast. Further wills are listed for the late sixth and seventh centuries in Flodoard's account. These *Histories,* thus, give the impression that the ma-

---

144 *Actus Pontificum Cenomannis in urbe degentium,* 1.4, ed. Margarete Weidemann, *Geschichte des Bistums Le Mans von der Spätantike bis zur Karolingerzeit,* 3 vols. (Mainz: Verlag des Römisch-Germanischen Zentralmuseums, 2002), vol. 1, 33–34.

145 *Actus Pontificum Cenomannis in urbe degentium,* 1.4, 2.4, 3.4, 4.4, ed. Weidemann, *Geschichte des Bistums Le Mans,* 33–34, 38–39, 40, 41.

146 *Actus Pontificum Cenomannis in urbe degentium,* 8, ed. Weidemann, *Geschichte des Bistums Le Mans,* vol. 1, 52–53.

147 *Gesta Pontificum Autissiodorensium,* 7, 19, ed. Michel Sot, *Les gestes des évêques d'Auxerre* (Paris: Belles lettres, 2006), vol. 1, 28–49, 63–84.

148 Flodoard, *Historia Remensis Ecclesiae,* 1.9, ed. M. Lejeune, *Histoire de l'église de Reims par Flodoard,* 2 vols. (Reims: Imprimeur de l'Académie, 1854), vol. 1, 53–54.

149 Flodoard, *Historia Remensis Ecclesiae,* 1.18, ed. Lejeune, *Histoire de l'église de Reims par Flodoard,* vol. 1, 109–30; Hincmar, *Vita Remigii,* 32, ed. Bruno Krusch, Monumenta Germaniae Historica, Scriptores Rerum Merovingicarum 3 (Hanover: Hahn, 1896), 336–40; A.H.M. Jones, Philip Grierson, and J.A. Crook, "The Authenticity of the 'Testamentum sancti Remigii,'" *Revue belge de Philologie et d'Histoire* 35, no. 2 (1957): 356–73.

jor transfer of land to the Church took place in the sixth century and later.

The Spanish testamentary evidence is a good deal slighter than that from Merovingian Gaul. The very substantial donation of property given to Mérida by the mid-sixth-century bishop Paul in his will is noted in the *Vitas Patrum Emeretensium,* but unfortunately the account provides no detail.[150] At the end of the Tenth Council of Toledo (656), there was a discussion of the testament of bishop Riccimir of Dumio, which was declared invalid on account of its conflict with the earlier will of Martin of Braga (d. 579), and was condemned as being injurious to Church property,[151] but again no detail is supplied. More informative is the will of bishop Vincent of Huesca (557–576?), much of which confirms a grant he had made to the monastery of San Martín de Asán in 551 when he was still a deacon, but the text is unfortunately incomplete, and in any case the amount of property listed is not considerable.[152] Although the Visigothic material is informative about testamentary law, it tells us little about the scale of donation to churches.

---

150 *Vitas sanctorum Patrum Emeretensium,* 4.2, ed. Antonio Maya Sánchez, Corpus Christianorum, Series Latinorum 116 (Turnhout: Brepols, 1992), 26–30; Luis García Iglesias, "Las posesiones de la iglesia emeritense en época visigoda," in *Gerión: Estudios sobre la Antigüedad en homaje al Profesor Santiago Montero Díaz,* Anejos de Gerión 2 (1989): 391–401; María J. Roca Fernández, "La distinción entre patrimonio eclesiástico y privado de obispos y clérigos en la España visigoda," *e-Legal History Review* 20 (2015): 1–16, at 10–11.

151 Council of Toledo X (656), *item aliud decretum,* ed. José Vives, *Concilios visigóticos e hispano-romanos* (Madrid: C.S.I.C., 1963), 322–24; Roca Fernández, "La distinción," 12–14.

152 Fidel Fita, "Patrología visigótica. Elpidio, Pompeyano, Vicente y Gabino, obispos de Huesca en el siglo VI," *Boletín de la Real Academia de la Historia* 49 (1906): 137–69, at 151–57; Pablo C. Díaz, "El testamento de Vicente: proprietarios y dependientes en la Hispania del s. VI," in *"Romanización" y "Reconquista" en la península Ibérica: nuevas perspectivas,* ed. María José Hidalgo de la Vega, Dionisio Pérez, and Manuel J. Rodríguez Gervás (Salamanca: Universidad de Salamanca, 1998): 257–70; Roca Fernández, "La distinción," 11–12.

Like the *Liber Pontificalis,* Agnellus's *History of the Bishops of Ravenna* does not have much to say about land, although it does note that bishop Maximian secured the woods of Vistrum in Istria for the diocese,[153] and that bishop Agnellus acquired the estate of Argentea.[154] Above all, it records Justinian's grant of the property of the Goths in cities, suburban villas, and hamlets.[155] This, in all probability, was the most important of the donations to Ravenna. The *Codex Bavarus* of the tenth century gives us an indication of the scale of landholding in the century before it was compiled. There are records of 168 transactions, most of which are leases, which show us the extent of the Church's holdings in nine *territoria* of central Italy (mainly in the region of the Marche). Only rarely do they provide evidence of the date the property was acquired, but donations are listed for the reign of Heraclius,[156] and for the episcopate of Damian (689–705),[157] while 24 of the leases are clearly dated to the seventh and eighth centuries.[158] Moreover, in the case of every lease we can assume that the property had already passed into the hands of the Church of Ravenna before the grant was made. Taken together with the evidence that we have already noted for the Sicilian landholdings of the Church of Ravenna,[159] it would seem that the major period of Church endowment involving numerous very sizeable gifts was, as Lesne argued, the sixth and seventh

---

153 Agnellus, *Liber Pontificalis ecclesiae Ravennatis,* 70, ed. Deborah Mauskopf Deliyannis, Corpus Christianorum, Continuatio Medievalis 199 (Turnhout: Brepols, 2006), 238–40.

154 Ibid., 256.

155 Ibid., 252–53. For another example of the acquisition of Arian property, see Gregory I, *Register,* 3.19, ed. Norberg, *Registrum Epistularum,* 165.

156 *Breviarium ecclesiae Ravennatis (Codice Bavaro) secoli VII–X,* 174, ed. Giuseppi Rabotti, Fonti per la Storia d'Italia 110 (Rome: Istituto storico italiano per il Medio Evo, 1985), 92.

157 *Breviarium ecclesiae Ravennatis (Codice Bavaro) secoli VII–X,* 59, ed. Rabotti, 33.

158 *Breviarium ecclesiae Ravennatis (Codice Bavaro) secoli VII–X,* 23–25, 27, 30, 32, 33–34, 36–37, 41, 63–65, 70, 80, 94, 129–30, 132, 134, 158, 170, 177, ed. Rabotti, 10–94.

159 Agnellus, *Liber Pontificalis Ecclesiae Ravennatis,* 111, ed. Mauskopf Deliyannis, 281–82.

centuries, although Cracco Ruggini is also compelling in em-
phasizing the acquisition of smaller properties in the fifth century, which were absorbed into larger ones.

This coincides neatly with the chronology of references to
the *Quadripartum.* The earliest allusion to the fourfold division comes from pope Simplicius (468–483),[160] and the first full
definition is to be found in the *Decreta* sent by pope Gelasius
(492–495) to the bishops of Lucania[161] — and we might note
that John the Deacon in his *Life of Gregory the Great* regarded
the *Quadripartum* as coming from a book of Gelasius.[162] There
is a further reference in a letter of pope Felix IV (526–530) to
Ecclesius of Ravenna, preserved by Agnellus, although it is specific only about the fourth part of the church's revenue due to
the clergy.[163] It does, however, reveal that the sum amounted to
3,000 *solidi,* which as we have seen is far less than what would
have been due later in the century. The best-known statement
comes from Gregory the Great in c. 600 in the *Responsiones* to
Augustine of Canterbury,[164] and there are additional letters in
the pope's *Register* that shed light on the working of the *Quad-*

---

160 Simplicius, ep. 1.32, ed. Andreas Thiel, *Epistolae Romanorum Pontificum
Genuinae* (Braunschweig: Brunsbergae, 1868), vol. 1, 176: "de reditibus ecclesiae et oblatione fidelium quod deceat nescienti, nihil licere permittat,
sed sola ei ex his quarta portio remittantur. Duas ecclesiasticis fabricis et
erogationi peregrinorum et pauperum profuturae."

161 Gelasius, ep. 14.27, ed. Thiel, *Epistolae Romanorum Pontificum Genuinae,*
vol. 1., 378: "Quatuor autem tam de reditu quam de oblatione fidelium,
prout cujuslibet ecclesiae facultas admittit, sicut dudum rationabiliter est
decretum, convenit fieri portiones; quarum sit una pontificis, altera clericorum, pauperum tertia, quarta fabricis applicanda."

162 John the Deacon, *Vita Gregorii,* 2.24, Patrologia Latina 75, cols. 96–97.

163 Agnellus, *Liber Pontificalis ecclesiae Ravennatis,* 60, ed. Mauskopf Deliyannis, 226–31.

164 Gregory I, *Register,* 11.56a, ed. Paul Ewald and Ludwig Hartman, Monumenta Germaniae Historica, Epistolae 2 (Berlin: Weidmann, 1899), 332–43;
Bede, *Historia Ecclesiastica Gentis Anglorum,* 1.27. http://www.thelatinli-
brary.com/bede.html; Bertram Colgrave and Roger Mynors, trans., *Bede's
Ecclesiastical History of the English Nation* (Oxford: Clarendon, 1969),
41–54. The most recent edition of the *Responsiones* is that by Valeria Mattaloni, *Rescriptum beati Gregorii papae ad Augustinum episcopum seu Libellus
responsionum* (Florence: Sismel, 2017).

ripartum.[165] In addition, a conciliar statement which alludes to the *Quadripartum* is to be found in the canons of the Council of Orléans of 511.[166] The notion of the *Quadripartum* was, therefore, being promulgated just as the scale of ecclesiastical landowning was escalating, and thus at the time when the Church had more revenue to distribute.

We need to ask what lies behind the formulation of the *Quadripartum* and its chronology. Of course, there may have been specific reasons that only applied to certain regions — and which are reflected in the differing formulations of the *Quadripartum,* and indeed in the Spanish preference for the *tertia.* For instance, one possible reason for Clovis's largesse, which provides the context for the statement on the division of ecclesiastical revenue in the Council of Orléans, may be the king's deliberate imitation of what he understood to be the actions of Constantine. In Gregory of Tours he appears as a *novus Constantinus.*[167] As we have seen, in the *Life of Silvester* contained in the *Liber Pontificalis,* which was composed a generation after Clovis's death, the first Christian emperor was remembered as being notable for his donation of property to the Church of Rome.[168] That Clovis had an interest in Rome is suggested by the *Liber Pontificalis,* which states that he sent a votive crown to St. Peter's during the pontificate of Hormisdas (514–523).[169] The date must be wrong, but there is no reason to doubt the gift. There is also a possibility that the Frankish king had an interest in the church of St. Martin in Rome.[170]

165 Gregory I, *Register,* 5.27, 39; 8.7; 9.144; 11.22; 13.45, ed. Norberg, *Registrum Epistularum,* 297, 314–18, 524, 695, 892–93, 1051–52.

166 Council of Orléans I (511), c. 5, ed. Basdevant, *Les canons des conciles mérovingiens,* vol. 1, 76.

167 Gregory of Tours, *Decem Libri Historiarum,* 2.31, ed. Bruno Krusch and Wilhelm Levison, Monumenta Germaniae Historica, Scriptores Rerum Merovingicarum 1.1 (Hanover: Hahn, 1951), 76–78.

168 *Liber Pontificalis,* 34, 35, ed. Duchesne, vol. 1, 170–204.

169 *Liber Pontificalis,* 54.10, ed. Duchesne, vol. 1, 271.

170 Monika Ozóg and Henryk Pietras, "Il battesimo di Clodoveo e sue possibili ripercussioni in Italia alla luce del *Liber Pontificalis,* ossia della chiesa romana di S. Martino ai Monti," *Gregorianum* 93 (2015): 157–74.

The formulation of the *Quadripartum* given in the Council of Orléans is also unusual in its allocation of one *quarta* to the ransoming of captives. Following close on Clovis's victories against the Visigoths, the concern presumably reflects a very specific situation, although as we have seen, the fate of captives attracted particular attention on either side of 500, and also in the pontificate of Gregory the Great.[171] Care for those in prison is, of course, advocated by Christ in Matthew 25:36: "when I was ill you came to my help, when in prison you visited me." Pauline Allen and Bronwen Neil have noted references to episcopal involvement in the ransoming of captives, and also to support for refugees, throughout the late antique period. Augustine, for instance, writes about redeeming men from Galatian people-traffickers.[172] Allen and Neil also note those displaced by the barbarians, including aristocratic refugees from Africa following Gaiseric's takeover, who appear in papal letters and in the writings of Theodoret of Cyrrhus.[173] And they point to the presence of religious refugees fleeing from pro- or anti-Chalcedonian persecution.[174]

It may seem tempting when considering the expansion of ecclesiastical landholding of the late fifth and sixth centuries to turn to Dodds's notion of an "Age of Anxiety,"[175] and to apply it to the period of the *Völkerwanderung* and the collapse of the Empire. There is even a convenient Ravenna charter of donation to the Church, where land is given in exchange for protection *adversus violentus impetos.*[176] But the charter dates to 556–561, the last stages of the Gothic Wars. It does not allow us to ascribe the increase in the donation of land to the Church to the period of the arrival of the barbarians, or of their settlement. And this negative conclusion gels suggestively with the arguments

---

171 See above.

172 Allen and Neil, *Crisis Management in Late Antiquity,* 32.

173 Ibid., 48, 61–62.

174 Ibid., 45, 66–67.

175 E.R. Dodds, *Pagan and Christian in an Age of Anxiety* (Cambridge: Cambridge University Press, 1965).

176 Tjäder, *Die nichtliterarischen Papyri Italiens auf der Zeit 445–700,* vol. 1, doc. 13, 300–308; Cracco Ruggini, *Economia e società,* 449, with n. 609.

of Pauline Allen and Bronwen Neil in their study of episcopal crisis management. Their analysis of the epistolary evidence relating to papal and episcopal charitable activity draws attention to the lack of reference to the barbarians — two papal letters, one from Innocent I and one from Pelagius I, and one letter of Augustine.[177] There are, of course, more references to barbarians in the letters of Sidonius and his successors, who lived in regions controlled by the incomers.

Although, as Allen and Neil have vividly demonstrated, crisis management was a major issue for the Church, it may only be a secondary factor in the growth in ecclesiastical landholding in the course of the fifth, sixth, and seventh centuries. Not surprisingly, it would seem that the increase in Church property went hand in hand with the growth in the number of ecclesiastics and indeed of monks and nuns. Admittedly, we have very little evidence to allow us to calculate the expansion of the clergy, but there is ecclesiastical legislation, from the councils of IV Orléans (541),[178] II Braga (571),[179] and the 597 Council of Toledo,[180] requiring that provision was made for priests when churches were founded. The *tomus* for XVI Toledo (693) actually reverses the equation: king Egica directed that every church with ten slaves or more, however poor, must have a priest, although those with fewer than ten slaves were to be attached to another parish.[181] For some dioceses we have good evidence for church founda-

177 Allen and Neil, *Crisis Management in Late Antiquity*, 30.

178 Council of Orléans IV (541), c. 33, ed. Basdevant, *Les canons des conciles mérovingiens*, vol. 1, 284. See Robert Godding, *Prêtres en Gaule mérovingienne* (Brussels: Société des Bollandistes, 2001), 257; also on the material support for clergy, 335–39.

179 Council of Braga II (571), c. 5, ed. Vives, *Concilios visigóticos e hispano-romanos*, 83. See Pöschl, *Bischofsgut und mensa episcopalis*, 15.

180 Council of Toledo (597), c. 2, ed. Vives, *Concilios visigóticos e hispano-romanos*, 156–57. Pöschl, *Bischofsgut und mensa episcopalis*, 15–16.

181 Council of Toledo XVI, *tomus*, ed. Vives, *Concilios visigóticos e hispano-romanos*, 485; also ed. Zeumer, *Leges Visigothorum*, 482; Pöschl, *Bischofsgut und mensa episcopalis*, 16; Thompson, *The Goths in Spain*, 299. For the foundation of "proprietary churches" in Spain, see Addison, "Property and 'Publicness,'" esp. 14.

tion throughout the sixth century. Above all, the information supplied by Gregory of Tours allows us to see the increase in churches in his diocese, episcopate by episcopate, until there were at least 58 in his own day.[182]

To the evidence of *vicus* churches, we can add that of monasteries. In parts of the East, the number of monastic communities would seem to have been very substantial already by the early fifth century, even if Ewa Wipszycka has seriously challenged the picture presented by Palladius, Jerome, and the *Historia Monachorum,* following her detailed investigation of the papyrus evidence.[183] The West certainly lagged behind Egypt and Palestine in the development of monasticism. But, as we have already noted, there seem to have been some 220 monasteries in Francia by 600 and 550 by the early eighth century.[184] And some of these monasteries had very considerable numbers. There may well have been between 300 and 400 monks at Corbie,[185] 300 monks and 100 *pueri* at St. Riquier,[186] and perhaps 220 at Luxeuil.[187]

Large numbers of monks needed massive donations in order to provide them with the basic necessities of life. For St. Martin de Tours we do not have a list of monks, but the so-called *documents comptables,* edited by Gasnault, supply 1,000 personal names (essentially of tenants) and 137 place-names, providing an insight into the dues owed to the abbey during the

182 Clare Stancliffe, "From Town to Country: The Christianisation of the Touraine, 370–600," in *Studies in Church History* 16: *The Church in Town and Countryside,* ed. Derek Baker (Oxford: Blackwell, 1979), 43–59, at 46–48.

183 Ewa Wipszycka, *The Second Gift of the Nile: Monks and Monasteries in Late Antique Egypt* (Warsaw: University of Warsaw, 2018), 371–99.

184 Hartmut Atsma, "Les monastères urbains du Nord de la Gaule," *Revue d'Histoire de l'Église de France* 62 (1976): 163–87, at 168.

185 Ursmer Berlière, "Les nombres des moines dans les anciens monastères," *Revue Bénédictine* 41 (1929): 231–61, at 242. See also *Revue Bénédictine* 42 (1930): 19–42.

186 Angilbert, *Libellus de ecclesia Centulae,* 9, ed. Georg Waitz, Monumenta Germaniae Historica, Scriptores 15.1 (Hanover: Hahn, 1887), 174–79, at 178; Berlière, "Les nombres des moines dans les anciens monastères," 243.

187 *Vita Walarici,* 5, ed. Bruno Krusch, Monumenta Germaniae Historica, Scriptores Rerum Merovingicarum 4 (Hanover: Hahn, 1902), 162; Paul Roth, *Geschichte des Beneficialwesens* (Erlangen, 1850), 249–51.

abbacy of Agyricus in the second half of the seventh century.[188] The community of St. Martin was close to Tours itself, but in many cases monasteries with large communities were not based in urban centers, but rather in the countryside, thus requiring a redistribution of resources to areas that had not been places of significance in the late Roman World — including, for instance, both Luxeuil and Bobbio. Historians of early medieval Ireland have been more sensitive to the impact on the landscape of the foundation of sizeable communities[189] than have specialists of the monastic church on the continent.

Support for the clergy is a constant in the allocation of the *Quadripartum*: the bishop and the clergy are each allocated a quarter by both Gelasius and Gregory the Great,[190] and it is clear from a letter of Felix IV that the clergy of Ravenna expected their fourth.[191] In the version to be found in the Council of Orléans there is the provision of alms for clerics (*sacerdotes*).[192] Clergy also feature consistently in the reference to the threefold division of ecclesiastical revenue in Spain. They are listed as recipients of a *tertia* in the First Council of Braga.[193] In Visigothic Spain, as we have seen, no allowance is made for the poor or for captives, but the clergy were supported,[194] while in the *tomus*

---

188 Shoichi Sato, "The Merovingian Accounting Documents of Tours: Form and Function," *Early Medieval Europe* 9 (2000): 143–61.

189 Wendy Davies, "Economic Change in Early Medieval Ireland: The Case for Growth," in *L'Irlanda e gli Irlandesi nell'alto Medioevo: Spoleto, 16–21 aprile 2009, Settimane di studio del Centro italiano di studi sull'alto medioevo* 57 (Spoleto: Centro italiano di studi sull'alto medioevo, 2010), 111–32.

190 Gelasius, ep. 14.27, ed. Andreas Thiel, *Epistolae Romanorum Pontificum Genuinae* (Braunschweig: Brunsbergae, 1868), vol. 1., 378; Gregory I, Register, 8.7, ed. Norberg, *Registrum Epistularum*, 524; Bede, *Historia Ecclesiastica Gentis Anglorum*, 1.27. http://www.thelatinlibrary.com/bede.html.

191 Agnellus, *Liber Pontificalis ecclesiae Ravennatis*, 60, 117–18, 121, ed. Mauskopf Deliyannis, 226–31, 288–89, 292–95.

192 Council of Orléans I (511), c. 5, ed. Basdevant, *Les canons des conciles mérovingiens*, vol. 1, 76.

193 Council of Braga I (561), c. 7, ed. Vives, *Concilios visigóticos e hispano-romanos*, 68.

194 Councils of Mérida (666), cc. 10, 14; IV Toledo (633), c. 33; IX Toledo (655), c. 6, ed. Vives, *Concilios visigóticos e hispano-romanos*, 204, 301, 332–33, 335.

for XVI Toledo (693) the upkeep of the church building was to fall to the bishop, who could draw on the *tertiae parrochialium baselicarum.*[195] The question of the state of the buildings in Spain was clearly a serious one, for it also appears in the canons of IX Toledo (655).[196]

Provision for the clergy was a constant issue, and concern for the poor attracted almost as much attention,[197] although Allen and Neil have noted that there were moments when they attracted particular concern, as for instance during the pontificate of pope Pelagius, because of the hardship caused by the Gothic Wars.[198] Care for the poor was understood to be a central feature of Christian charity from very early on, as has been shown in a number of major studies.[199] Brown in particular has stressed the importance of the phrase *amator pauperum* as an epithet for a bishop,[200] and, along with Toneatto,[201] has drawn attention to the phrase *necator pauperum* (or a variant thereof), used in the canons of the Councils of Vaison (442), Agde (506), Orléans (549), Arles (554), Paris (556–573), Tours (567), Mâcon I (581–583), Valence (583–585), and Paris (614), as well as the *Statuta Ecclesiae*

Thompson, *The Goths in Spain,* 298–99.

195 Council of Toledo XVI (693), tomus, ed. Vives, *Concilios visigóticos e hispano-romanos,* 485; ed. Zeumer, *Leges Visigothorum,* 482.

196 Council of Toledo IX (655), c. 2, ed. Vives, *Concilios visigóticos e hispano-romanos,* 298–99.

197 See Rapp, *Holy Bishops in Late Antiquity,* 225–30.

198 Pelagius I, ep. 4, 85, ed. Pius M. Gassó and Columba M. Batlle, *Scripta et documenta* 8 (Montserrat: In Abbatia Montisserati, 1956), 18, 200; Allen and Neil, *Crisis Management in Late Antiquity,* 174.

199 Évelyne Patlagean, *Pauvreté économique et pauvreté sociale à Byzance (IVᵉ–VIIᵉ siècles),* Civilisations et sociétés 48 (Paris: Mouton, 1977); Neri, *I marginali;* Lizzi Testa, *Vescovi e strutture ecclesiastiche;* Valentina Toneatto, *Les banquiers du Seigneur: Évêques et moines face à la richesse (IVᵉ–début IXᵉ siècles)* (Rennes: Presses universitaires de Rennes, 2012).

200 Peter Brown, "From *Patriae Amator* to *Amator Pauperum* and Back Again: Social Imagination and Social Change in the West between Late Antiquity and the Early Middle Ages," in *Cultures in Motion,* ed. Daniel T. Rodgers, Bhavani Raman, and Helmut Reimitz (Princeton: Princeton University Press, 2014), 87–106; Brown, *Poverty and Leadership,* 1; Brown, *Through the Eye of a Needle,* 509–17.

201 Toneatto, *Les banquiers du Seigneur,* 200–202.

Antiqua, to describe those who tried to despoil the Church of property.[202] Concern for the poor is even stated as being one of the two reasons for Guntram summoning the first Council of Mâcon, the other being *causae publicae.*[203] The second Council of Tours (567) states firmly that each *civitas* had to look after its poor and needy as best it could.[204] In Francia, in return for the Church's support, the poor, and particularly the *matricularii* registered on the poor-lists of the diocese, were a force that might turn out in support of a bishop, as indeed might those who had been ransomed by the Church.[205] It is not surprising to find that provision for the poor occurs in almost all the versions of the *Quadripartum.* Moreover, despite the fact that the Spanish tripartite division of Church wealth makes no equivalent allowance, concern for the poor, although not the phrase *necator pauperum,* appears in IV Toledo (633),[206] VI Toledo (638),[207] and X Toledo (656).[208]

The Church needed funds to carry out its charitable duties in caring for the poor, widows, and orphans, ensuring the upkeep of churches, and providing for the sustenance of the clergy.

---

202 Brown, *Through the Eye of a Needle,* 506–9; Councils of Vaison (442), c. 4 and Agde (506), c. 4, ed. Munier, *Concilia Galliae,* 97–98, 194; Councils of Orléans V (549), c. 13; Arles (554), c. 6; Tours (567), c. 25; III Paris (556–573), c. 1; I Mâcon (581–583), c. 4; and V Paris (614), c. 9, ed. Basdevant, *Les canons des conciles mérovingiens,* vol. 1, 308, 342; vol. 2, 344–48, 412–16, 430, 512; *Statuta Ecclesiae Antiqua,* c. 86, ed. Munier, *Concilia Galliae,* 180. For a full list of references in Merovingian canon law, see Michael E. Moore, "The Ancient Fathers: Christian Antiquity, Patristics and Frankish Canon Law," *Millennium* 7 (2010): 293–342, at 321–23.

203 Council of Mâcon I (581–583), praef., ed. Basdevant, *Les canons des conciles mérovingiens,* vol. 2, 428.

204 Council of Tours (567), c. 5, ed. Basdevant, *Les canons des conciles mérovingiens,* vol. 2, 354.

205 Brown, *Power and Persuasion in Late Antiquity,* 98; Brown, *Through the Eye of a Needle,* 510, 513, 516. Also Neri, *I marginali,* 97–101.

206 Council of Toledo IV (633), cc. 32, 67, ed. Vives, *Concilios visigóticos e hispano-romanos,* 204, 214.

207 Council of Toledo VI (638), c. 15, ed. Vives, *Concilios visigóticos e hispano-romanos,* 242–43.

208 Council of Toledo X (656), *item aliud decretum,* ed. Vives, *Concilios visigóticos e hispano-romanos,* 322–24.

And on occasion it was also faced with the ransoming of captives. Claudia Rapp has stressed the emergence of the bishop as "a new urban functionary."[209] For all charitable and religious actions the Church needed regular revenue, and that could not come from the donation of treasure. Moreover, the alienation of liturgical objects was distinctly questionable — although a charismatic bishop might turn the action into a virtue.[210]

Essentially, the Church needed revenue from land. The creation of a propertied Church was a straightforward matter of necessity. The growth in the number of clergy and in the number of churches and monasteries, as well as the growing expense of the liturgy (as can be seen in the need for lights), together with the burden of charity, especially in times of crisis, effectively led to the creation of a new ecclesiastical economy — of what I would call a temple society. And this largely occurred in the course of the late fifth and sixth centuries, coming to fruition only at the end of the period. This chronology is important, because it implies that the economic development of the Church comes after the great spiritual and theological achievements of the period before Chalcedon.

What we therefore have is a perfect storm of a political crisis, which had major social implications, at precisely the moment that the institution of the Church was expanding — a development that went hand in hand with a growing recognition that churches needed landed endowment. The result, by the beginning of the eighth century, was a massively wealthy Church, with enormous estates, amounting perhaps to a third of western Europe, which supported a body of clergy and other religious, which was numerically a relatively small but significant segment of the population, while caring for the marginal of society. This is as much a matter of economic as of religious history. As we will see, the economic importance of the Church also challeng-

---

209 Rapp, *Holy Bishops in Late Antiquity,* 247–89.
210 Robert Wiśniewski, "Clerical Hagiography in Late Antiquity," in *The Hagiographical Experiment: Developing Discourses of Sainthood,* ed. Christa Gray and James Corke-Webster (Boston and Leiden: Brill, 2020), 93–118, at 108.

es the notion of the centrality of the royal court in the seventh century, in Francia and perhaps in Visigothic Spain, although scarcely in the Exarchate, and probably not in the Lombard kingdom. The Church was arguably the key socio-economic institution of the period. Throughout the Latin West, the accumulation of property by the Church, and the revenue that it had at its disposal, which was distributed in line with a particular set of socio-religious ideals, means that we cannot merely see churchmen as members of an aristocratic elite. They were involved in the distribution and redistribution of wealth along totally novel lines — lines that are not dissimilar from those laid down by Appadurai and Appadurai Breckenridge in their definition of a temple society.[211] The Church of the late- and post-Roman West effected a more fundamental socio-economic revolution than most economic historians have acknowledged.

---

211 Arjun Appadurai and Carol Appadurai Breckenridge, "The South Indian Temple: Authority, Honour and Redistribution," *Contributions to Indian Sociology* 10, no. 2 (1976): 187–211, at 190.

6

The Temple Society and the State in the Early Medieval West

The Church of the post-Roman West amassed a vast amount of landed property, largely in the course of the late fifth, sixth, and early seventh centuries. The revenue from these possessions was divided between the churchmen (clergy and ascetics), church-building, the requirements of cult, and charitable activities, notably concern for the poor and, in certain specific periods, the ransom of captives. This, I have argued, constituted a redistributive process of the sort described by Arjun Appadurai and Carole Appadurai Breckenridge in their definition of a temple society. Although what has been defined as the spiritual economy of the late-antique and early medieval West has normally been discussed in socio-religious terms, I have insisted that it should also be understood as a matter of hard economics.

The model presented by Appadurai and Appadurai Breckenridge has little to say about the relationship of secular authority to the Temple, other than that protection of the temple was "one of the primary requirements for human claims to royal status."[1] Early medieval rulers unquestionably did regard themselves as

---

1   Arjun Appadurai and Carol Appadurai Breckenridge, "The South Indian Temple: Authority, Honour and Redistribution," *Contributions to Indian Sociology* 10, no. 2 (1976): 187–211, at 190.

having a duty to protect the Church and Christian religion. For instance, the bishops noted the concern for the faith ("ad religionis cultum gloriosae fidei cura") shown by Clovis in his summons to the first Council of Orléans,[2] and similar comments are made about the concerns of Childebert I at the fifth Council of Orléans (549),[3] of Charibert at the second Council of Tours (567),[4] of Clovis II at the Council of Chalon (647–653),[5] and of Childeric II at the Councils of Bordeaux and St. Jean de Losne (662–675).[6] In return, bishops and priests prayed for the king and the kingdom, as at Clermont in 535.[7] Yitzhak Hen has noted that "chants and prayers became an instrument by which heavenly protection could be sought for the benefit of the kingdom and its ruler" in the course of the Merovingian period.[8] Kings granted fiscal immunities to ecclesiastical institutions to facilitate such prayer.[9] The canons of the Catholic Council of Agde (506) in Visigothic Gaul begin with prayers for the Arian Alaric II and his kingdom,[10] while in Spain the Councils of Toledo, from the Third onwards, almost all begin with a reference to

---

2 Council of Orléans I (511), *epistola ad regem,* ed. Brigitte Basdevant, *Les canons des conciles mérovingiens (VIᵉ-VIIᵉ siècles),* 2 vols., Sources Chrétiennes 353–354 (Paris: Éditions du Cerf, 1989), vol. 1, 70.

3 Council of Orléans V (549), praef, ed. Basdevant, *Les canons des conciles mérovingiens,* vol. 1, 297–99.

4 Council of Tours II (567), praef., ed. Basdevant, *Les canons des conciles mérovingiens,* vol. 2, 348–50.

5 Council of Chalon (647–653), praef., ed. Basdevant, *Les canons des conciles mérovingiens,* vol. 2, 550.

6 Council of Bordeaux (662–675), praef; Council of St. Jean de Losne (663–675) praef., ed. Basdevant, *Les canons des conciles mérovingiens,* vol. 2, 568, 576.

7 Council of Clermont (535), praef., ed. Basdevant, *Les canons des conciles mérovingiens,* vol. 1, 210.

8 Yitzhak Hen, *The Royal Patronage of the Liturgy in Frankish Gaul* (Woodbridge: Boydell, 2001), 34.

9 Alexander C. Murray, "Merovingian Immunity Revisited," *History Compass* 8 (2010): 913–28, at 917, 920, 924.

10 Council of Agde (506), praef., ed. Charles Munier, *Concilia Africae 345–525,* Corpus Christianorum, Series Latina 144 (Turnhout: Brepols, 1974).

royal support, and some make reference to the king's presence.[11] On occasion, the conciliar decrees are followed directly by a royal statement.[12]

The significance attached to prayers for the king and the king-dom has been noted by numerous scholars.[13] This was a world in which the liturgy and the liturgical year mattered. Easter was, inevitably, a time of particular significance, and it constitutes the backdrop of a number of moments of political tension. One of the seventh-century conflicts in Francia about which we are best informed, that involving bishops Leodegar of Autun and Praeiectus of Clermont, blew up at the Easter court of Child-eric II in 675.[14] Praeiectus was accused by Hector, the *patricius* of Marseilles, of taking over the land of a woman called Clau-dia. Hector was backed by Leodegar, but Praeiectus received the backing of the *maior palatii* Wulfoald. As a result, Hector

---

11 See Councils of Toledo III (589), praef.; IV Toledo (633), praef.; V Toledo (636), praef.; VI Toledo (638), praef.; VII Toledo (646), praef.; VIII Toledo (653), praef.; IX Toledo (655), praef. and expl.; X Toledo (656), praef.; XI Toledo (675), praef. and c. 16; XII Toledo (681), praef.; XIII Toledo (683), praef, and c. 13; XIV Toledo (684), praef. and c. 12; XV Toledo (688), praef.; XVII Toledo (694), praef., ed. José Vives, *Concilios visigóticos e hispano-romanos* (Madrid: C. S. I. C., 1963), 107–24, 186–87, 226, 233, 249, 260–67, 297, 308, 344–54 and 367, 380–85, 411–14 and 431, 441, 449–54, 522–28. But see Ra-chel Stocking, *Bishops, Councils, and Consensus in the Visigothic Kingdom, 589-633* (Ann Arbor: University of Michigan Press, 2000), 87, on the clos-ing homily of III Toledo given by Leander of Seville.

12 Councils of Toledo III (589), *epistola Recharedi*; V Toledo (636), *epistola Chintilae*; VIII Toledo (653), *lex Reccesvinthi*; XV Toledo (688), *lex Egicanis*; XVI Toledo (693), *lex*; XVII Toledo (694), *lex,* ed. Vives, *Concilios visigóticos e hispano-romanos*, 144–45, 231–32, 293–96, 471, 515–18, 537.

13 Hen, *The Royal Patronage of Liturgy in Frankish Gaul,* 39–41; Gregory Hal-fond, *Bishops and the Politics of Patronage in Merovingian Gaul* (Ithaca: Cor-nell University Press, 2019), ch. 1; Marculf, *Formulary,* 1.6, ed. Karl Zeumer, Monumenta Germaniae Historica, Formulae Merowingici et Karolini Aevi (Hanover: Hahn, 1886), 46; *Bobbio Missal,* 53, ed. Elias A. Lowe, Henry Bradshaw Society 58 (London, 1920): 59–106; *Missale Francorum,* 20–21, ed. Leo Cunibert Mohlberg (Rome: Herder, 1957); *Gelasian Sacramentary,* 213–18, ed. Leo Cunibert Mohlberg, *Liber Sacramentorum Romanae aecle-siae* (Rome: Herder, 1960).

14 *Passio Praeiecti,* 23–27, ed. Bruno Krusch, Monumenta Germaniae Histori-ca, Scriptores Rerum Merovingicarum 5 (Hanover: Hahn, 1910), 239–42.

was killed, having fled from the court, and Leodegar was exiled. Subsequently, however, Praeiectus was murdered. The events give an exceptional insight into conflicts involving bishops, but it is important to note the context of the Easter court and the recurrent liturgical elements in the story. Praeiectus refused to answer a summons because it was made during the holy days of Easter. Childeric, who had withdrawn to the monastery of St. Symphorian, demonstrated his support for the bishop of Clermont by inviting him to say Mass.

Although there is little to suggest a formal Easter court in the early Merovingian period, Gregory of Tours does say that Guntram had the Treaty of Andelot read out to him and bishop Felix of Chalons-sur-Marne at Easter, before proceeding to hear Mass.[15] Gregory also notes on a number of occasions where kings held their Paschal celebrations.[16] The Easter court had already been an occasion of importance for the rulers of Gibichung Burgundy: their law-book, the *Liber Constitutionum,* was issued at Easter 517.[17] The State, in other words, functioned within the Christian calendar. But that is only a small aspect of relations between the ecclesiastical and religious authority. In this final chapter I will examine some other aspects of the relationship between Church and State in greater detail.

As we have already noted, Claudia Rapp has argued that the bishop emerged as a "new urban functionary" in the course of Late Antiquity.[18] The development is most striking in Rome,

---

15 Gregory of Tours, *Decem Libri Historiarum,* 9.20, ed. Bruno Krusch and Wilhelm Levison, Monumenta Germaniae Historica, Scriptores Rerum Merovingicarum 1.1 (Hanover: Hahn, 1951), 434–41.

16 Gregory of Tours, *Decem Libri Historiarum,* 8.4, 9, 9.29, ed. Krusch and Levison, 373–74, 376, 447–48.

17 Ian Wood, "The Legislation of *Magistri Militum*: The Laws of Gundobad and Sigismund," *La forge du droit: Naissance des identités juridiques en Europe (IVᵉ–XIIIᵉ siècles), Clio@Themis* 10 (2016): 1–16, at 4, n. 32; Liber Constitutionum, 62, ed. Ludwig R. de Salis, Leges Burgundionum, Monumenta Germaniae Historica, Leges 2.1 (Hanover: Hahn, 1882), 93.

18 Claudia Rapp, *Holy Bishops in Late Antiquity: The Nature of Christian Leadership in an Age of Transition* (Berkeley: University of California Press, 2005), 247–89. See also Claire Sotinel, "Le personnel épiscopal. Enquête

where the pope was both instructed by the emperor and had, as a matter of necessity, to oversee much of the running of the city[19] — as can be seen most obviously in the *Register* of Gregory the Great.[20] Outside Rome, it is in Francia that episcopal authority has attracted most attention, and it has been the subject of an extended discussion of what has been termed *Bischofs-herrschaft*[21] — the exercise of episcopal leadership which was at its most striking in the later Merovingian period, when bishops such as Savaric of Auxerre and Milo of Trier effectively controlled their diocesan cities.[22]

I begin with brief consideration of *Bischofsherrschaft*, which is usually discussed with relatively little reference to contemporary secular authority. I will then turn back to a more anthropological model, based on John Haldon's comparative examination of the late medieval Vijayanagaran Empire of south India, Merovingian Gaul, and early Byzantium in his formulation of the "Tributary Mode of Production,"[23] to offer some comments

---

sur la puissance de l'évêque dans la cité," in *L'évêque dans la cité du IVᵉ au Vᵉ siècle: Actes de la table ronde de Rome (1ᵉʳ et 2 décembre 1995)*, ed. Eric Rebillard (Rome: École française de Rome, 1998), 105–26.

19 Justinian, *Pragmatic Sanction, Novellae Appendix constitutionum dispersarum, 7*, ed. Rudolf Schöll and Wilhem Kroll, *Corpus Iuris Civilis, Novellae*, 6th edn. (Berlin: Weidemann, 1928), 799–803, https://droitromain.univ-grenoble-alpes.fr/; Michèle Renée Salzman, "From a Classical to a Christian City: Civic Evergetism and Charity in Late Antique Rome," *Studies in Late Antiquity* 1 (2017): 77; Robert A. Markus, *Gregory the Great and His World* (Cambridge: Cambridge University Press, 2010), 121–24. For a very different perspective, which places emphasis on the importance of the household as a model for the development of papal authority, Kristina Sessa, *The Formation of Papal Authority in Late Antique Italy: Roman Bishops and the Domestic Sphere* (Cambridge: Cambridge University Press, 2012).

20 Jeffrey Richards, *Consul of God: The Life and Times of Gregory the Great* (London: Routledge, 1980), 85–90.

21 See below.

22 *Gesta Pontificum Autissiodorensium, 26*, ed. Michel Sot, *Les gestes des évêques d'Auxerre* (Paris: Belles lettres, 2006), vol. 1, 126–27; Eugen Ewig, "Milo et eiusmodi similes," in *Spätantikes und fränkisches Gallien* (Munich: Artemis, 1979), vol. 2, 189–219.

23 John Haldon, "Mode of Production, Social Action, and Historical Change: Some Questions and Issues," in *Studies on Pre-Capitalist Modes of Produc-*

on the differences between the Frankish world and that of the Exarchate of Ravenna in the sixth and seventh centuries,[24] before looking finally at one respect in which the difference between the two regions lessened in the eighth century.

Bischofsherrschaft is a term often applied to describe the position of the bishop in Merovingian Gaul. It was promoted by Friedrich Prinz in 1973,[25] and subsequently by Reinhold Kaiser in 1981.[26] As Steffen Diefenbach has noted in the most recent general assessment of the concept, it was used primarily in an institutional sense,[27] referring to the bishop's jurisdictional and administrative activities, which stretched beyond the moral and spiritual duties associated with cult and charity to matters of legal authority in the form of the *episcopalis audientia* — although it has to be said that this is less well defined than is sometimes assumed; its limitations have been noted for some while, most recently by Caroline Humfress.[28]

To this emphasis on the bishop as administrator and judge, however, was added a notion that bishops of the Merovingian kingdom were often of senatorial extraction (whatever that

---

tion, ed. Laura da Graca and Andrea Zingarelli (Boston and Leiden: Brill, 2015), 204–36, at 223–27.

24 See Merle Eisenberg and Paolo Tedesco, "Seeing the Churches Like the State: Taxes and Wealth Redistribution in Late Antique Italy," *Early Medieval Europe* 29, no. 4 (2021): 505–34.

25 Friedrich Prinz, "Die bischöfliche Stadtherrschaft im Frankenreich vom 5. bis zum 7. Jahrhundert," *Historische Zeitschrift* 217, no. 1 (1973): 1–35.

26 Reinhold Kaiser, *Bischofsherrschaft zwischen Königtum und Fürstenmacht: Studien zur bischöflichen Stadtherrschaft im westfränkisch-französischen Reich im frühen und hohen Mittelalter*, Pariser historische Studien vol. 17 (Bonn: Röhrscheid, 1981).

27 Steffen Diefenbach, "'Bischofsherrschaft': Zur Transformation der politischen Kultur im spätantiken und frühmittelalterlichen Gallien," in *Gallien in Spätantike und Frühmittelalter: Kulturgeschichte einer Region*, ed. Steffen Diefenbach and Michael Gernot Müller (Berlin: De Gruyter, 2013), 91–149.

28 Caroline Humfress, "Bishops and Law Courts in Late Antiquity: How (Not) to Make Sense of the Legal Evidence," *Journal of Early Christian Studies* 19, no. 3 (2011): 375–400. See also the brief overview in Rapp, *Holy Bishops in Late Antiquity*, 242–44.

may mean)[29] — and that members of the aristocracy, on finding that the opportunities which had been provided by the traditional *cursus honorum* were blocked with the ending of the
Roman Empire, instead turned their attention to a career in the
Church.[30] This is in contrast with Italy, where Clare Sotinel has
noted that less than three percent of the bishops whose origins
are known were from the senatorial class.[31] In Rita Lizzi Testa's
view, the early fifth century was an age when "clergy and bishops came from lower orders, and were lacking in administrative
experience"[32] — an observation that would seem to hold true
well into the sixth. As Steffen Patzold has noted, however, there
are major problems with the traditional reading of the Gallo-
Roman and Frankish episcopate — the evidence is quite simply
not strong enough to support the notion that the Merovingian
Church was dominated by the senatorial aristocracy.[33] To il-
lustrate the aristocratic nature of the Gallo-Roman Church a

---

29 For a compelling argument that what we are really looking not at the de-
    scendants of the old imperial senatorial class, but rather a continuing curial
    class, see the forthcoming study by Andrew Wallace-Hadrill, *The Idea of the
    City after Antiquity: Studies in Resilience.*
30 Rapp, *Holy Bishops in Late Antiquity,* 193.
31 Claire Sotinel, "La recrutement des évêques en Italie aux IVᵉ et Vᵉ siècles.
    Essai d'enquête prosopographique," in *Vescovi e pastori in epoca teodosiana,*
    vol. 1 (Rome: Institutum Patristicum Augustinianum, 1997), 193–204, at 196;
    Rapp, *Holy Bishops in Late Antiquity,* 191.
32 Rita Lizzi Testa, *Vescovi e strutture ecclesiastiche nella città tardoantica:
    l'Italia Annonaria nel IV–V secolo d.C.* (Como: Edizioni New Press, 1989),
    169: "clero e vescovi provennero da strati più bassi, privi di esperienza am-
    ministrativa."
33 Steffen Patzold, "Zur Socialstruktur des Episkopats und zur Ausbildung
    bischöflicher Herrschaft in Gallien zwischen Spätantike und Frühmittelal-
    ter," in *Völker, Reiche und Namen im frühen Mittelalter,* ed. Matthias Becher
    and Stefanie Dick, Mittelalterliche Studien 22 (Munich: Wilhelm Fink,
    2010), 121–40; Steffen Patzold, "Bischöfe, soziale Herkunft und die Organ-
    isation lokaker Herrschaft um 500," in *Chlodwigs Welt: Organisation von
    Herrschaft um 500,* ed. Mischa Meier and Steffen Patzold (Stuttgart: Steiner,
    2014), 523–43. The traditional interpretation was accepted by Rapp, *Holy
    Bishops in Late Antiquity,* 193–94, who presents the Gallo-Roman Church in
    being unusual in its senatorial make-up: the percentage of known senatorial
    bishops in Gaul may be higher than elsewhere, but the figures are still low.

handful of examples are regularly produced. Above all, there are bishops from the intermarried families of the Apollinares and the Aviti in Clermont and Vienne, as well as the Nicetii in Lyon, the Ruricii in Limoges, the Gregorii in Langres and Tours, and the Leontii in Bordeaux. But despite these examples, as Patzold points out, there are plenty of cities whose bishops are known not to have been of senatorial origin, and even more dioceses where we have no evidence for the social origins of the bishop.

In Bernhard Jussen's reading of *Bischofsherrschaft*, more important than the social origins of the bishops was the religious aspect of episcopal authority, especially in those cases where the bishop was an ascetic.[34] And even those bishops who were not ascetic had oversight of the performance of cult in their cities. In fact, the idealized image of *Bischofsherrschaft* had already received its fullest analysis in Martin Heinzelmann's study of the epitaphs of the bishops of Lyon, published in 1976.[35] Heinzelmann demonstrated that there was a set of virtues, above all ascetic, but also charitable and associated with episcopal authority and action, that were invoked regularly in describing the holy bishop and his exercise of office.

Although the ideal is certainly promoted in Merovingian sources — in epitaphs and in narratives (both hagiographical texts and the *Histories* of Gregory of Tours) — it is important to recognize that it is an ideal. As Simon Loseby has stated, the bishop of Tours's "model of *Bischofsherrschaft* [...] corresponded only imperfectly to reality, as he knew well. Gregory was striving as far as possible to present bishops as the leaders of an undifferentiated urban *populus*."[36] Despite the fact that bishops

---

34 Bernhard Jussen, "Über 'Bischofsherrschaften' und die Prozeduren politisch-sozialer Umordnung in Gallien zwischen 'Antike' und 'Mittelalter'," *Historische Zeitschrift* 260 (1995): 673–718.

35 Martin Heinzelmann, *Bischofsherrschaft in Gallien* (Munich: Artemis, 1976).

36 Simon Loseby, "Decline and Change in the Cities of Late Antique Gaul," in *Die Stadt in der Spätantike — Niedergang oder Wandel? Akten des internationalen Kolloquiums in München am 30. und 31. Mai 2003*, ed. Jens-Uwe Krause and Christian Witschel (Stuttgart: Steiner, 2006), 67–104, at 91.

did indeed have powers conferred on them in law, both secular and ecclesiastical, there are well-known occasions where they found their position challenged by the local count, as is well-known from the evidence for Clermont,[37] and Tours,[38] but also by unnamed but equally dangerous opponents, as in Cahors,[39] and on occasion by their own clergy (for instance in the cases of Sidonius Apollinaris[40] and later of Leodegar of Autun[41]), and, as Greg Halfond has noted, by other bishops.[42] The most extreme cases of challenge offered to bishops are to be found in the episcopal martyrdoms of the seventh century, studied by Paul Fouracre[43] — which are a witness both to the power of the bishop and to the perilous nature of his position: in Fouracre's words "it was, after all, the power which bishops exercised, and the struggles for power, at local, regional, and supra-regional level, which were behind the killings."[44] Halfond has placed the

---

37 Gregory of Tours, *Decem Libri Historiarum,* 4.35, ed. Krusch and Levison, 138–39; Ian Wood, "The Ecclesiastical Politics of Merovingian Clermont," in *Ideal and Reality in Frankish and Anglo-Saxon Society: Studies Presented to John Michael Wallace-Hadrill,* ed. Patrick Wormald (Oxford: Blackwell, 1983), 34–57, at 44–45.

38 Gregory of Tours, *Decem Libri Historiarum,* 5.48, ed. Krusch and Levison, 257–58.

39 *Vita Desiderii Cadurcae urbis,* 4, 8, ed. Bruno Krusch, Monumenta Germaniae Historica, Scriptores Rerum Merovingicarum 4 (Hanover: Hahn, 1902), 565–66, 568–69; Jean Durliat, "Les attributions civiles des évêques mérovingiens: l'exemple de Didier, évêque de Cahors (630–655)," *Annales du Midi* 91, no. 143 (1979): 237–54.

40 Gregory of Tours, *Decem Libri Historiarum,* 2.23, ed. Krusch and Levison, 68–69.

41 *Passio Leudegarii I,* 10, ed. Bruno Krusch, Monumenta Germaniae Historica, Scriptores Rerum Merovingicarum 5 (Hanover: Hahn, 1910), 292–93. See Paul Fouracre and Richard Gerberding, *Late Merovingian France: History and Hagiography 640-720* (Manchester: Manchester University Press, 1996), 198, 200.

42 Halfond, *Bishops and the Politics of Patronage,* 97–106.

43 Paul Fouracre, "Why Were So Many Bishops Killed in Merovingian Francia?" in *Bischofsmord im Mittelalter,* ed. Natalie Fryde and Dirk Reitz (Göttingen: Vandenhoeck und Ruprecht, 2003), 13–35; Paul Fouracre, "Merovingian History and Merovingian Hagiography," *Past and Present* 127 (1990): 3–38.

44 Fouracre, "Why Were So Many Bishops Killed in Merovingian Francia?" 34.

relations between bishops and the royal court at the start of his recent discussion of the Merovingian episcopate.[45] In Francia, episcopal authority was potentially considerable, but although there were some cities that were effectively episcopal republics in the final third of the Merovingian period — notably Auxerre under Savaric[46] and Trier under Milo[47] — they were the exception rather than the rule.

To judge by the evidence of the Councils of Toledo, the episcopate played an even greater role in Visigothic government and certainly of the formulation of royal rule in Spain than it did in Francia.[48] The letter known as the *De fisco Barcinonense,* which was probably composed in the context of the Second Council of Zaragoza (592), reveals that they also had a role in the oversight of the collection of taxation.[49] Despite this, in the seventh century, Visigothic kings (especially Chindaswinth and Recceswinth) were fairly ruthless in their exploitation of the Church.[50] There is nothing comparable in the relations between Merovingian kings and their bishops in the seventh century (despite episcopal martyrdoms), although one can see tensions between Guntram and the Burgundian episcopate in the sixth.[51]

45 Halfond, *Bishops and the Politics of Patronage,* ch. 1.

46 Paul Fouracre, *The Age of Charles Martel* (Harlow: Longman, 2000), 90.

47 Ewig, "Milo et eiusmodi similes."

48 Stocking, *Bishops, Councils, and Consensus*; Sam Koon and Jamie Wood, "Unity from Disunity: Law, Rhetoric, and Power in the Visigothic Kingdom," *European Review of History* 16 (2009): 793–808.

49 *De fisco Barcinonensi,* ed. Vives, *Concilios visigóticos e hispano-romanos,* 54. See Damián Fernández, "What Is the *de fisco Barcinonensi* About?" *Antiquité Tardive* 14 (2006): 217–24.

50 Michael J. Kelly, "Recceswinth's *Liber Iudiciorum*: History, Narrative and Meaning," *Visigothic Symposium* 1 (2017): 110–30; Ruth Miguel Franco, "Braulio de Zaragoza, el Rey Chindasvinto, y Eugenio de Toledo: imagen y opinión en el Epistularium de Braulio de Zaragoza," *Emerita, Revista de Lingüística y Filología Clásica* 79, no. 1 (2011): 155–76.

51 Helmut Reimitz, "True Differences: Gregory of Tours' Account of the Council of Mâcon (585)," in *The Merovingian Kingdoms and the Mediterranean World: Revisiting the Sources,* ed. Stefan Esders, Yitzhak Hen, Pia Lucas, and Tamar Rotman (London: Bloomsbury, 2019), 19–28.

Bischofsherrschaft is a concept, then, that should be invoked with precision and care. Bishops were frequently powerful, but their authority was curtailed by local and supra-regional circumstances. In any case, my present concerns are not simply with the episcopate, but rather with the position of the Church as a whole within the wider society. Christianity did not just impinge on politics — it also had an influence on the fiscal and economic structures of kingdoms. One reason that bishops were potentially powerful that has not been much emphasized in discussions of *Bischofsherrschaft* is their wealth and the ways in which they might deploy it — not least their charitable actions, although scholars have noted the support that a Church might receive from the *matricularii,* those on its poor list.[52] But, as we have seen, the landed wealth controlled by a bishop could be colossal. It is significant that when Charles Martel broke the power of the bishops of Auxerre, he did so by alienating their estates.[53]

According to Haldon, "Christian rulers in the East and the West legitimated the extraction and distribution of surplus [...] through political/theological systems of thought which highlighted the duty of the state and its rulers to defend the faith and to promote the variety of associated activities which this entailed [...]. This institutional Christianisation of society [...] directly affected how labour was exploited and how surpluses were appropriated and consumed."[54] In Haldon's reading of the early Frankish World, the process begins with the "conquests

---

52 Peter Brown, *Power and Persuasion in Late Antiquity* (Madison: University of Wisconsin Press, 1992), 98; Peter Brown, *Through the Eye of a Needle: Wealth, the Fall of Rome, and the Making of Christianity in the West, 350–550 AD* (Princeton: Princeton University Press, 2012), 483–84, 510, 513, 516. Also Valerio Neri, *I marginali nell'Occidente tardoantico: "infames" e criminali nella nascente società cristiana* (Bari: Edipuglia, 1996), 97–101.

53 *Gesta Pontificum Autissiodorensium,* 32, ed. Sot, *Les gestes des évêques d'Auxerre,* 135–37. There is a chronological problem with the entry, which relates to bisop Aidulf (supposedly 751–766), but talks of the actions of Charles Martel (d. 741). That Auxerre lost its estates, however, is reasonably clear, despite the chronological confusion. See also Fouracre, *The Age of Charles Martel,* 90–93, 123.

54 Haldon, "Mode of Production, Social Action, and Historical Change," 226.

and extension of Merovingian royal power, together with the institutional and administrative means of extracting wealth which the first Merovingian kings adopted," which in turn created a class of warriors who invested some of their wealth in "secular property and warfare," but also "in the Church: bishoprics and the ecclesiastical lands to which they thereby had access, and monastic foundations."[55]

Military activity was unquestionably a major issue in the sixth century, as the Merovingians established themselves throughout Gaul, clashed with the Visigoths, and intervened in Italy. Thereafter, however, it is not clear that warfare (as opposed to minor conflict — some of it, admittedly, destructive) was a particularly significant feature of Merovingian society. Certainly, any able-bodied man might find himself called upon to fight,[56] but few did with any regularity or for any length of time, and almost all the conflicts that we hear of in the seventh century would seem to have been between the military followings of rival aristocrats. It is surely significant that Charles Martel was actually defeated by the Frisian *dux* or *rex* Radbod in 715/716, and that he withdrew from the northern Rhineland until after the Frisian ruler's death three years later.[57] Yet Radbod himself was scarcely in a position to raise a substantial trained army — Frisia was no centralized state, and, in any case, its waterlogged geography militated against it producing large armies.[58] When faced with a major military threat, that of the Muslims, it is interesting that Charles had to turn to the Lombard king Liutprand for

---

55   Ibid., 226.

56   *Lex Ribvaria,* 68, ed. Franz Beyerle and Rudolf Buchner, Monumenta Germaniae Historica, Leges 3.2 (Hanover: Hahn, 1954), 119.

57   *Liber Historiae Francorum,* 52, ed. Bruno Krusch, Monumenta Germaniae Historica, Scriptores Rerum Merovingicarum 2 (Hanover: Hahn, 1885), 240; *Chronicon Moissacense,* s.a. 716, ed. Georg H. Pertz, Monumenta Germaniae Historica, Scriptores 1 (Hanover: Hahn, 1826), 291.

58   For the regional nature of Frisia, Johan Nicolay, *The Splendour of Power: Early Medieval Kingship and the Use of Gold and Silver in the Southern North Sea Area (5th to 7th century AD)* (Groningen: Barkhuis, 2014).

help — a point that is registered by Paul the Deacon,[59] but not in the Frankish chronicles and annals (and therefore overlooked by historians). Unlike the Franks, of course, the Lombards had remained a militarized society throughout the seventh century, because of the threat posed by the Byzantine Exarchate. The much-cited Frankish Marchfield is not mentioned in contemporary sources between the sixth century and 761, which was the start of a sequence of such gatherings.[60] The meetings would seem to have been the revival, perhaps even the creation of a political institution. It is by no means clear that the reference to the *campus Martius* to be found in Gregory's account of the Vase of Soissons story, when Clovis was inspecting his army, is to an annual institutionalized meeting.[61] Although attendance at the *bannum* when necessary was required by seventh-century law,[62] Charles Martel may have initiated much of what we regard as "Merovingian military organization."

Despite the fact that the Merovingian kingdom was founded on a series of successful wars, in the seventh century it was dominated not by the military, but by the Church. We have noted the significance of the religion for the political life of the *regnum,* as well as the growth in churches, monasteries, and above all in their possession of property in the post-Roman period. To this we can add the extension of immunities from taxation and from various obligations on ecclesiastical land.

As the Church acquired property, so too it acquired privileges. In a law preserved by Eusebius, Constantine exempted clergy from public services.[63] In the course of the fourth and fifth cen-

---

59 Paul the Deacon, *Historia Langobardorum,* 6.54, 58, ed. Georg Waitz, Monumenta Germaniae Historica, Scriptores Rerum Germanicarum 48 (Hanover: Hahn, 1878), 237–38.

60 Fredegar, *continuationes,* s.a. 761, 763, 766, 767, ed. Bruno Krusch, Monumenta Germaniae Historica, Scriptores Rerum Merovingicarum 2 (Hanover: Hahn, 1888), 186–91.

61 Gregory of Tours, *Decem Libri Historiarum,* 2.27, ed. Krusch and Levison, 71–73; Fredegar, 3.16, ed. Krusch, 94.

62 *Lex Ribvaria,* 68, ed. Beyerle and Buchner, 119.

63 Eusebius, *Historia Ecclesiastica,* 10.7, ed. T.E. Page et al., trans. J.E.L. Oulton, Loeb Classics, 2 vols. (Cambridge: Harvard University Press, 1942), 463–65.

turies churches were exempted from some taxes[64] and public services.[65] In 359/360 the Council of Rimini exempted Church property from the compulsory provision of public service, and, although the Council was condemned as Arian, its rulings in this respect passed into law.[66] Further exemptions from *munera sordida,* including the menial services of road building and the repair of roads and bridges, were issued from the 380s onwards[67] — we are almost in the world of the *trinoda necessitas* of eighth-century Anglosaxon England (which surely derived from Roman precedent). They could, however, be reimposed: exemptions from public service were removed by Valentinian in the crisis of 441, when the emperor insisted that neither the imperial household nor the Church should be exempt from any compulsory public service because of the burdens faced by other taxpayers.[68] It is perhaps not surprising that there is a lack of clarity in the Merovingian period as to whether or not a church was exempt from certain taxes and obligations.

Whether or not there was any significant break in the exemptions enjoyed by the Church, in Francia we find them again already in the canons of I Orléans.[69] The property donated by Clovis which yielded the revenue to be divided between the restoration of churches, the bishop, the poor, and the ransom of captives was explicitly granted immunity, both with regard to the land and to the clergy.[70] The *Praeceptio* of Chlothar II provides further detail on the grant of immunity (both fiscal, from public charges, and judicial, from the *introitus* of a judge).

For exemption from public services, see Eisenberg and Tedesco, "Seeing the Churches Like the State," 511–12.

64 *Codex Theodosianus,* 11.1.1, https://droitromain.univ-grenoble-alpes.fr/.

65 *Codex Theodosianus,* 16.2.9.

66 *Codex Theodosianus,* 16.12.15.

67 *Codex Theodosianus,* 11.16, 15, 18, 21–22; 15.3, 6; 16.2, 2, 3, 6, 7, 9, 11, 14, 15, 16, 24, 36, 38, 40, 46, 47; *Sirmondian Constitution,* 11, https://droitromain.univ-grenoble-alpes.fr/; also *Codex Theodosianus,* 11.1, 33; 16, 21.

68 Valentinian III, *Novellae,* 10, https://droitromain.univ-grenoble-alpes.fr/.

69 Council of Orléans I (511), c. 5, ed. Basdevant, *Les canons des conciles mérovingiens,* vol. 1, 76.

70 See Murray, "Merovingian Immunity Revisited," 915.

Clause 11 states: "We grant to the Church out of the devotion of our faith dues from cleared land, from pasturage and the tithe of pigs, so no royal agent or tax collector may have access onto Church property. Public agents should demand no obligation from the Church or from clergy, who deserved immunity from our grandfather or father."[71] Chlothar II, in other words, traced these immunities back to Chlothar I and Chilperic I — that is, to the period after Clovis's death in 511.

Some immunities were granted to specific religious institutions and were not general concessions to the Church. Gregory tells us that he managed to convince Guntram's tax collectors that the city of Tours had been exempt from tax since the days of Chlothar I, but those same collectors had just successfully revised the tax lists for Poitiers, which they had updated, and where they had made allowance for the poor and the infirm.[72] But although the bishop was involved in the arguments about tax in these instances, it is unclear whether the taxation of ecclesiastical property and of the clergy was actually at issue. There was a disagreement over whether the *pauperes* and *iuniores* of the *ecclesia* and basilica of Tours were exempt from military service — Chilperic eventually agreed that they were,[73] but *iudices* subsequently tried to claim that the *homines sancti Martini* were liable to serve.[74] Certainly the exemption was not general: the *Lex Ribvaria* lists fines for non-attendance at the *bannum,* along with a failure to offer hospitality to a royal agent, although a *Romanus,* a *homo regius,* and a *homo ecclesiasticus* was fined at

---

71 Chlothar II, *Praeceptio,* c. 11, ed. Alfred Boretius, Monumenta Germaniae Historica, Leges, Capitularia Regum Francorum 1 (Hanover: Hahn, 1883), 19: "Agraria, pascuaria vel decimus porcarum aecclesiae pro fidei nostrae devotione concedimus, ita ut actor aut decimatur in rebus ecclesiae nullus accedat. Ecclesiae vel clericis nullam requirant agentes publici functionem, qui avi vel genitoris nostri immunitatem meruerunt."

72 Gregory of Tours, *Decem Libri Historiarum,* 9.30, ed. Krusch and Levison, 448–49.

73 Gregory of Tours, *Decem Libri Historiarum,* 5.26, ed. Krusch and Levison, 232–33.

74 Gregory of Tours, *Decem Libri Historiarum,* 7.42, ed. Krusch and Levison, 364.

half the rate of the rest of the population[75] — but the clear implication is that some churchmen were required to serve in the army. A further illustration of a concession to a particular diocese comes in Gregory's statement that Childebert II remitted for the diocese of Clermont all taxes "due from churches, monasteries, clergy who were attached to a given parish, and indeed anyone who was employed by the Church."[76]

Our most precise evidence for exemptions comes in the charter material of the seventh century. This provides plenty of evidence for the concession of immunities, occasionally to lay persons, but above all to the Church — both episcopal and monastic.[77] The great charters of fiscal and judicial immunity have become the backbone of the study of the seventh-century Frankish Church, not least since the studies of Eugen Ewig.[78] A number of monasteries are known to have received exemptions from taxes and the performance of public services, and also to have been freed from any interference by secular judges. A further set of episcopal immunities removed certain monasteries from the oversight of the bishop. Many of these grants would have been financially considerably advantageous, but there are also some marvelously specific concessions. The second part of the grant of Chilperic II to Corbie issued in 716 that confirmed the concession of toll income (*telloneum*) at the southern port of Fos, which we have already noted, also deals with the exemption from toll for 10 of the monastery's couriers (*viredus sive paraveridus*), and with them 10 loaves of good bread and of coarse bread, a *modius* of wine, 2 *modii* of beer, 10 pounds of bacon, 20

---

75 *Lex Ribvaria*, 68, ed. Beyerle and Buchner, 119.

76 Gregory of Tours, *Decem Libri Historiarum*, 10.7, ed. Krusch and Levison, 488.

77 See most recently Murray, "Merovingian Immunity Revisited." But see also Paul Fouracre, "Eternal Light and Earthly Needs: Practical Aspects of the Development of Frankish Immunities," in *Property and Power in the Early Middle Ages*, ed. Wendy Davies and Paul Fouracre (Cambridge: Cambridge University Press, 1995), 53–81, and Barbara Rosenwein, *Negotiating Space: Power, Restraint, and Privileges of Immunity in Early Middle Europe* (Ithaca: Cornell University Press, 1999).

78 Ewig, *Spätantikes und fränkisches Gallien*, vol. 2, 411–583.

pounds of other meat, 12 pounds of cheese, a goat, 5 chickens, 10 eggs, 2 pounds of oil, 1 pound of garum, an ounce of pepper, 2 ounces of cumin, as well as sufficient salt, greens, and wood.[79] In other words, the couriers could take subsistence for their journeys with them.

The concessions made to the Church certainly annoyed some kings. Famously, according to Gregory of Tours, Chilperic I complained that "my treasury is always empty. All our wealth has fallen into the hands of the Church. There is no one with any power left except the bishops. Nobody respects me as king: all respect has passed to bishops in their cities."[80] Gregory presents the king as being unreasonable (and irreligious), but there is good reason for thinking that he had a valid point. In the previous generation, Chramn had been advised by Leo that the churches of saints Martial and Martin had denuded the royal treasury.[81] There is some evidence that Dagobert I secularized some Church property.[82] But this assault on ecclesiastical landholding cannot have amounted to much. And in any case, kings continued to endow the Church with property, and the late seventh century would seem to mark a highpoint in the granting of immunities. But essentially, because the Franks were not involved in large-scale foreign wars between the early seventh century and the arrival of the Arabs, the Merovingians had no need for the revenues that the Church had acquired. What they

---

79 *Diplomata Merowingica,* 171, ed. Theo Kölzer, *Die Urkunden der Merowinger,* 2 vols., Monumenta Germaniae Historica (Hanover, 2001), vol. 1, 424–26.

80 Gregory, *Decem Libri Historiarum,* 6.46, ed. Krusch and Levison, 319–21; Lewis Thorpe, trans., Gregory of Tours, *The History of the Franks* (London: Penguin, 1974), 380.

81 Gregory, *Decem Libri Historiarum,* 4.16, ed. Krusch and Levison, 147–50.

82 Michel Rouche, "*Religio calcata et dissipata* ou les premières sécularisations de terre d'Église par Dagobert," in *The Seventh Century: Change and Continuity: Proceedings of a Joint French and British Colloquium held at the Warburg Institute 8–9 July 1988,* ed. Jacques Fontaine and Jocelyn N. Hillgarth (London: The Warburg Institute, 1992), 236–46; Ian Wood, "Entrusting Western Europe to the Church, 400–750," *Transactions of the Royal Historical Society* 23 (2013): 37–73, at 60.

needed to do was to serve God, and this they did pretty well. In doing so, they facilitated the emergence of an ecclesiastical economy. In the words of Alexander C. Murray, the immunities reveal that the Merovingian State "employed fiscal means to encourage religious works, and in the seventh century, to judge by surviving charters, to finance the liturgical activities of clerics praying solemnly for the health of the kingdom and its king."[83] This comes remarkably close to the criteria of a temple society laid down by Appadurai and Appadurai Breckenridge.

A further comparison with southern India, as described by Isabelle Clark-Decès, is striking:

> medieval royal gifts indicate a peculiar cultural conception of statecraft that involves neither (or involves minimally) the use of large standing armies nor of elaborate bureaucracies [...] the Pallava and Cola kings [...] were less interested in conquering and administering the lives of their subjects, than in dramatizing their generosity, and hence political superiority, through the construction of enormous temple complexes, and the patronage of temple worship.[84]

Although the scale of the Indian temple complexes dwarfs anything in the Merovingian world, the description is otherwise applicable to the states of the early medieval West. On the other hand, it contrasts with another model of a temple society discussed by Haldon, that of the Vijayanagar Empire, as interpreted by Burton Stein (though one might note that Stein has not been universally accepted),[85] which, unlike the interpretation of the Pallava and Cola kingdoms, does place some emphasis on the military: "Political authority, and the potential to extract resources in the Vijayanagar Empire, depended on a combination of military/political coercion and connections of a ritual

---

83 Murray, "Merovingian Immunity Revisited," 917.

84 Isabelle Clark-Decès, "Towards an Anthropology of Exchange in Tamil Nadu," *International Journal of Hindu Studies* 22 (2018): 197–215, at 199–200.

85 Sanjay Subrahmanyam, "Agreeing to Disagree: Burton Stein on Vijayanagara," *South Asian Research* 17 (1997): 127–39.

nature."[86] Other studies, like that of the early medieval Kalukyan State based on the temple of Draksarama by P.S. Kanaka Durga and Y.A. Sudhakar Reddy, have placed the mobilization of warriors at the heart of a temple society: "the temple provided human resources to the caste society, which, in turn gradually made use of the services of [...] militant tribes and drew them into statecraft."[87] Although the "military/political coercion" to be seen in the seventh-century Merovingian world was relatively slight, this was not the case elsewhere.

The Frankish Church would seem to have been unusual in the exemptions and immunities it received from the State, although there are parallels to be drawn with Anglosaxon England, where churches in the early eighth century were exempt from certain services, most notably that to provide fighting men.[88] This was not the case in Visigothic Spain, at least by the end of the seventh century. According to the *Life of Fructuosus of Braga,* so many men joined his foundation at Nono that the local *dux* was worried about military recruitment.[89] Shortly thereafter, however, in a law of Wamba from 675, clergy were explicitly required to serve in the army when necessity demanded.[90] This, however, was rescinded by Erwig six years later, which only put the obligation to fight on the *dux, comes,* and *gardingus,* omitting the *episcopus sive etiam in quocumque ecclesiastico ordine constitutus.*[91] Equally, churches were obliged to pay some taxes, despite

86 Haldon, "Mode of Production, Social Action, and Historical Change," 225.

87 P.S. Kanaka Durga and Y.A. Sudhakar Reddy, "Kings, Temples and Legitimation of Autochthonous Communities: A Case Study of a South Indian Temple," *Journal of the Economic and Social History of the Orient* 35 (1992): 145–66, at 166.

88 Ian Wood, "Land Tenure and Military Obligations in the Anglo-Saxon and Merovingian Kingdoms: The Evidence of Bede and Boniface in Context," *Bulletin of International Medieval Research* 9–10 (2005): 3–22.

89 *Vita Fructuosi,* 14, ed. Manuel Díaz y Díaz, *La vida de San Fructuoso de Braga* (Braga: Diário do Minho, 1974), 104–6.

90 *Leges Visigothorum,* 9.2.8, ed. Karl Zeumer, Monumenta Germaniae Historica, Leges Nationum Germanicarum 1 (Hanover: Hahn, 1902), 370–73.

91 *Leges Visigothorum,* 9.2.9, ed. Zeumer, 374–79; E.A. Thompson, *The Goths in Spain* (Oxford: Clarendon, 2000), 262–64. On the distinction between the two laws, Michael J. Kelly, "The *Liber Iudiciorum*: A Visigothic Literary

the fact that in 633, on Sisenand's instructions, the bishops at IV Toledo announced tax-exemptions for all free-born clerics.[92] In XVI Toledo from 693 bishops were forbidden from drawing on parish revenues to pay *exactiones* or *angaria* (transport dues).[93] As E.A. Thompson noted, this is the one direct piece of evidence from the seventh century to suggest that the Visigothic Church was subject to tax.[94] There is, moreover, no indication that clergy could avoid paying the *census,* which was demanded from all landowners, with no exception specified.[95] In his survey of Visigothic taxation, Santiago Castellanos invokes Haldon's model of the "Tributary Mode," and its value for understanding "political relations in the distribution of surplus production."[96] Unlike Francia, however, Visigothic Spain does not bear much comparison with the model of a temple society as defined by Appadurai and Appadurai Breckenridge, although there are other models which perhaps come closer.

In his discussion of temple societies, Haldon contrasts the Byzantine World with that of the South Indian temples. He notes the importance in the Empire of liturgy and ritual for the expression of the symbolic order, which clearly does stand some comparison with the Indian situation.[97] Here the Merovingian world could scarcely compete, despite the regular expression of prayers for the king and for the state, and also despite Simon Loseby's observation that "[e]very [Frankish] city had its own liturgical round, orchestrated by the bishop [...]. It was on feast days, in particular, that the city-community came together to

---

Guide to Institutional Authority and Self-Interest," in *The Visigothic Kingdom: The Negotiation of Power in Post-Roman Iberia,* ed. Paulo Pachá and Sabine Panzram (Amsterdam: Amsterdam University Press, 2020), 257–72.

92 Council of Toledo IV (633), c. 47, ed. Vives, *Concilios visigóticos e hispanoromanos,* 210–211; Thompson, *The Goths in Spain,* 177–78.

93 Council of Toledo XVI (693), c. 5, ed. Vives, *Concilios visigóticos e hispanoromanos,* 501–2.

94 Thompson, *The Goths in Spain,* 299–300.

95 *Leges Visigothorum,* 10.1.15, ed. Zeumer, 388.

96 Santiago Castellanos, "The Political Nature of Taxation in Visigothic Spain," *Early Medieval Europe* 12, no. 3 (2003): 201–28.

97 Haldon, "Mode of Production, Social Action, and Historical Change," 226.

join the great and the good in procession, to exchange their surplus at market, and in hopeful expectation of miraculous happenings in and around the churches of the saints."[98] Haldon notes the importance in Byzantium of the closeness of Church and State, but he goes on to argue that "in this particular historical formation, and in contrast to the South Indian examples, it did not express itself also, or serve as, a key institution of surplus distribution necessary to the economic survival of the state institution."[99] I would argue, however, that compared with the Merovingian State, the Byzantine Exarchate in Italy did depend on the redistribution of surplus from estates that had been donated to the Church.[100]

The difference between Francia and the Exarchate is apparent from a strikingly under-exploited passage to be found in a letter sent by Gregory the Great to kings Theudebert II and Theuderic II, to which Murray has drawn attention: "We have heard that the properties of churches do not pay taxes, and we marvel greatly at this circumstance if there is a desire to receive illicit gains [that is simony] from those [that is bishops] to whom licit gains [that is taxes] are transferred."[101] Gregory clearly expected the Church to pay tax, and he was surprised that the churches of Francia did not do so.[102]

There are a number of references to taxation in Gregory the Great's Register, which give an indication of the range of taxes to which the Church of the Exarchate and its tenants might be subject. In one letter the pope refers to the *sextariaticum* (a mar-

98 Simon Loseby, "Decline and Change in the Cities of Late Antique Gaul," in *Die Stadt in der Spätantike — Niedergang oder Wandel? Akten des internationalen Kolloquiums in München am 30. und 31. Mai 2003,* ed. Jens-Uwe Krause and Christian Witschel (Stuttgart: Steiner, 2006), 87.

99 Haldon, "Mode of Production, Social Action, and Historical Change," 226.

100 See Eisenberg and Tedesco, "Seeing the Churches Like the State," 528–33.

101 Gregory I, *Register,* 9.216, ed. Dag Norberg, *Registrum Epistularum,* Corpus Christianorum, Series Latina, 140–140A (Turnhout: Brepols, 1982), 776–79: "Audivimus autem quia ecclesiarum praedia tributa non praebeant, et magna super hoc admiratione suspendimur, si ab eis illicita quaerantur accipi, quibus etiam licita relaxantur."

102 Murray, "Merovingian Immunity Revisited," 920–21.

itime tax covering risk), an *exactio* which could amount to 73 and a half *solidi,* a grain levy, *pondera excepta* and *vilicilia* (steward's taxes), *burdatio* (public tax on cultivated land), and a tax levied on farmers when they married.[103] Some of these were levies raised by the Church or its agents, but some were State taxes, and these could be very high. In a letter to the empress Constantina, Gregory commented that some Corsicans were finding the tax burden so heavy that they were moving to Lombard territory.[104] Despite the details, however, nothing in the *Register* allows a sense of the overall scale of tax-paying, although Tom Brown argued that "at a time when civilian tax-payers were impoverished by war and the state was fighting for its life against the Lombards, ecclesiastical property was called upon to make a major contribution to the government's revenues."[105] But Gregory does mention a loan of 600 pounds of gold to the Exarch.[106]

We get some sense of the burden from the *Liber Pontificalis,* where we hear that Justinian II remitted the *annonocapita/annonacapita* (poll-tax) for Sicily and Calabria during the pontificate of John V (685–686), and 200 *annonocapita* for Bruttium and Lucania during that of Conon (686–687).[107] In the ac-

---

103 Gregory I, *Register,* 1.42, ed. Norberg, *Registrum Epistularum,* 49–56.

104 Gregory I, *Register,* 5.38, ed. Norberg, *Registrum Epistularum,* 312–14.

105 Thomas S. Brown, "The Church of Ravenna and the Imperial Administration in the Seventh Century," *The English Historical Review* 94, no. 370 (1979): 1–28, at 3, with n. 1, listing F. Homes Dudden, *Gregory the Great: His Place in History and Thought* (Oxford: Longmans, Green, and Company, 1905), vol. 2, 238–48.

106 Gregory I, *Register,* 9.240, ed. Norberg, *Registrum Epistularum,* 823–24.

107 *Liber Pontificalis,* 84.1, 85.3, ed. Louis Duchesne, *"Liber Pontificalis": Texte, Introduction et Commentaire,* 2 vols. (Paris: E. Thorin, 1886–1892), vol. 2, 336, 308–9. On *annonocapita,* see John Haldon, "Synônê: Reconsidering a Problematic Term of Middle Byzantine Fiscal Administration," *Byzantine and Modern Greek Studies* 18 (1994): 116–53, at 134–35; John Haldon, *Byzantium in the Seventh Century: The Transformation of a Culture* (Cambridge: Cambridge University Press, 1990), 229; Vivien Prigent, "Le rôle des provinces d'Occident dans l'approvisionnement de Constantinople (618–717): témoignages numismatique et sigillographique," *Mélanges de l'École française de Rome, Moyen Âge* 118, no. 2 (2006): 269–99, at 293; Wolfram Brandes, "Das Schweigen des *Liber pontificalis.* Die 'Enteignung' der päpstlichen Patrimonen Siziliens und Unteritaliens in der 50er Jahren des 8. Jahrhunderts,"

count of this last pontificate we also hear of the return of the dependents of the Roman patrimony taken as a pledge for the payment of tax arrears. A further indication of the significance of the tax paid by the papacy to the empire is to be found in Gregory II's threat of a tax boycott in c. 724–726, recorded by the *Liber Pontificalis*,[108] and by Theophanes, who notes: "When Gregory, the Pope of Rome, had been informed of this ['the removal of the holy and venerable icons'], he withheld the taxes of Italy and Rome and wrote to Leo a doctrinal letter."[109] The pope subsequently distributed particularly large amounts of money to the poor, to prevent the Exarch Eutychius getting hold of it.[110] Even more striking is the evidence provided by Theophanes on the supposed confiscation of papal estates in Sicily by the emperor Leo III, and his demand that the tenants pay three and a half talents of gold to the treasury:[111] "Now the emperor, who was furious with the pope for the secession of Rome and Italy [...] imposed a capitation tax on one third of the people of Sicily and Calabria.[112] As for the so-called Patrimonies of the holy chief apostles who are honored in the Elder Rome (these, amounting to three and a half talents of gold, had been from olden times

in *Fontes Minores* 12, ed. Wolfram Brandes, Lars Hoffmann, and Kirill Maksimovič (Frankfurt: Löwenklau-Gesellschaft, 2014), 97–203, at 146–47.

108 *Liber Pontificalis*, 91.16, ed. Duchesne, vol. 1, 403–4.

109 Theophanes, *Chronographia, AM 6217 (724/725)*, ed. Carl de Boor (Bonn: Teubner, 1883), 404; Cyril A. Mango and Roger Scott, *The Chronicle of Theophanes the Confessor* (Oxford: Oxford University Press, 1997), 558. See also Wolfram Brandes, "Byzantinischer Bilderstreit, das Papsttum und die Pippinische Schenkung. Neue Forschungen zum Ost-West Verhältnis im 8. Jahrhundert," in *Menschen, Bilder, Spracher, Dinge. Wege der Kommunikation zwischen Byzanz und dem Westen, 2: Menschen und Worte,* ed. Falko Daim, Christian Gastgeber, Dominik Heher, and Claudia Rapp (Mainz: Verlag des Römisch-Germanischen Zentralmuseums, 2018), 63–79, at 65–67; Brandes, "Das Schweigen des Liber pontificalis," esp. 118–20.

110 *Liber Pontificalis*, 91, 19–20, ed. Duchesne, vol. 1, 405–7.

111 Theophanes, *Chronographia, AM 6224 (731/732)*, ed. Carl de Boor, 410; Brandes, "Byzantinischer Bilderstreit, das Papsttum und die Pippinische Schenkung," 65–67; Brandes, "Das Schweigen des *Liber pontificalis*," 111–16.

112 Mango and Scott, *The Chronicle of Theophanes the Confessor,* 568, n. 3, state that this means "a general increase of tax 'by one third.'"

paid to the churches), he ordered them to be paid to the Public Treasury."[113] The *Chronicle* of Theophanes dates this expropriation to 731/732, but as Wolfram Brandes has argued (not least because of the silence of the *Liber Pontificalis*), the date is probably incorrect — and the loss of the papal estates should be placed much later in the century.[114]

More specific is the evidence for Ravenna.[115] From a fragmentary papyrus we learn that at some point between 565 and 570 the Church of Ravenna received 2,171.5 *solidi* from some property (probably part of the former Gothic territory granted by Justinian), of which 932.5 *solidi* went to the *comes patrimonii* and a further 1,153.5 to the prefect, leaving 85.5 *solidi*.[116] Agnellus reveals that the Ravenna Church paid 15,000 *solidi* to the Empire out of the revenue of its Sicilian estates[117] — that is very nearly half of the total yield of 31,000.[118] This, we are told, was an annual payment. In other words, the Empire received large amounts of revenue from the Church.

Tom Brown has argued that the Empire granted out lands to the Church in exchange for tax and rents: "This policy was followed precisely because the alternative of entrusting state property to secular officials involved a serious risk of alienation, especially since the whole centralised machinery of domanial administrators and palatine inspectors was breaking down."[119] Although this is highly likely, it is largely an argument from si-

---

113 These were in Sicily and Calabria, as in Nicolas I, ep. 82, to Michael III (860), ed. Ernst Perels, Monumenta Germaniae Historica, Epistolae 6, Epistolae Karolini Aevi 4 (Berlin: Weidmann, 1925), 439.

114 Brandes, "Das Schweigen des *Liber pontificalis*."

115 Eisenberg and Tedesco, "Seeing the Churches Like the State," 525–28.

116 Jan-Olof Tjäder, *Die nichtliterarischen lateinischen Papyri italiens aus der Zeit 445–700,* 2 vols. (Lund: Gleerup, 1955–1982), vol. 1, doc. 2.

117 Agnellus, *Liber Pontificalis ecclesiae Ravennatis,* 111, ed. Deborah Mauskopf Deliyannis, Corpus Christianorum, Continuatio Medievalis 199 (Turnhout: Brepols, 2006), 281–82.

118 Thomas S. Brown, *Gentlemen and Officers: Imperial Administration and Aristocratic Power in Byzantine Italy, A.D. 554–800* (Rome: British School at Rome, 1984), 7.

119 Brown, *Gentlemen and Officers,* 123; Brown, "The Church of Ravenna and the Imperial Administration," 4.

lence: there are numerous references in Gregory the Great's letters to agents of the imperial patrimony, but very few thereafter.
We do, however, have extraordinary evidence for leases agreed
by the Church of Ravenna. The tenth-century *Codex Bavarus*
or *Breviarium ecclesiae Ravennatis* details the land transactions of the Church in 8 *territoria* of central Italy — largely in
the Marche. This deals with 168 transactions (mainly leases, but
also a handful of donations), most of which are unfortunately
undated. In the period of the Exarchate we know of 10 transactions from the episcopate of Damian (692–709)[120] and 14 from
that of Sergius (744–769).[121] We also hear of grants to the exarch
Theodore Calliopa, who was in post 643–645, and again from
653–666, from both the *Codex Bavarus*,[122] and from the Ravenna
papyri, where he was granted the lease of a property that his father had originally donated to the Church.[123] Theodore is known
from Agnellus to have built a monastery dedicated to his namesake, in the region of the city known as the Chalchi, and he was
a patron of the church of Sta. Maria ad Blachernas.[124]

Tom Brown describes the papyrus contract between Theodore and the Church of Ravenna as an emphyteutic lease.[125]

---

120 *Breviarium Ecclesiae Ravennatis (Codice Bavaro) secoli VII–X*, 23–25, 30,
32, 37, 59, 64, 94, 130, ed. Giuseppi Rabotti, Fonti per la Storia d'Italia 110
(Rome: Istituto storico italiano per il Medio Evo, 1985), 10–74.

121 *Breviarium ecclesiae Ravennatis (Codice Bavaro) secoli VII–X*, 27, 33, 34, 41,
63, 65, 70, 71, 80, 129, 132, 134, 158, 177, ed. Rabotti, 12–94.

122 *Breviarium ecclesiae Ravennatis (Codice Bavaro) secoli VII–X*, 140, ed. Rabotti, 77: "Pet(icio) qua(m) petiv(it) Theodorus magister militu(m) a Ioh(ann)
e archiep(iscop)o de sorte et porcione in fund(o) Venilia et por(cione) de
fund(o) Fatini, ter(ritorio) Ausimano, sub pen(sione) sol(idum) 1."

123 Tjäder, *Die nichtliterarischen lateinischen Papyri italiens*, vol. 2, doc. 44,
176–79; François Burdeau, "L'administration des fonds patrimoniaux et
emphytéotiques au bas-empire romain," *Revue internationale des droits
d'antiquité* 20 (1973): 285–310.

124 Agnellus, *Liber Pontificalis ecclesiae pontificum*, 119, ed. Mauskopf Deliyannis, 290–91; Deborah Mauskopf Deliyannis, trans., *The Book of the Pontiffs
of the Church of Ravenna* (Washington, DC: Catholic University of America,
2004), 10–11, n. 17.

125 Brown, "The Church of Ravenna and the Imperial Administration," 5, 10,
18–19; Brown, *Gentlemen and Officers*, 187, 199, 208; Justinian, *Novellae*, 7.3
(535), ed. Schöll and Kroll, 54–56.

These were long-term leases, originally of estates of the imperial patrimony. We find, for instance, in a law of Theodosius from 393: "The emphyteutic right, by which landed estates belonging to our patrimonial domain or the privy purse are assigned to possessors in perpetuity, is maintained, not only by our orders but also by those of our predecessors, as so indefeasible that once an estate has been delivered, it can never be occupied by Us or by anyone else while the others are in possession."[126] The books of the *Corpus Iuris Civilis* have numerous clauses on emphyteusis, including a full title on "emphyteutical contracts and leases."[127] The basic significance of emphyteutic leases is contained in a law of Gordian: "It is perfectly evident that the possessor of land under emphyteusis cannot be deprived of the same without his consent, if the rent is paid regularly at the time it is due."[128] In other words, an emphyteutic lease had the advantage for the lessee that the lease was permanent, and for the lessor that the revenue could be guaranteed. From the government's point of view, this also meant that they could be relied upon to provide their required services. A law of Constantine from 323 states that emphyteutic farms "shall be considered exempt from all extraordinary burdens, so that they shall pay only the regular and customary dues."[129] But in the straightened circumstances of 416, a law of Honorius and Theodosius II states that: "no house [...] subject to emphyteutic right [...] shall be exempt from such a compulsory public service"[130] — that is, from regular taxation.

Although it would seem that in origin emphyteutic leases were associated with the imperial patrimony, a law of Valentinian, Theodosius, and Arcadius also envisages that they could be

126 *Codex Theodosianus,* 5.14.33; trans. Clyde Pharr, *The Theodosian Code* (Princeton: Princeton University Press, 1952), 113.

127 Justinian, *Codex,* 4.66.0; *Digest,* 6.3.0, https://droitromain.univ-grenoble-alpes.fr/.

128 Justinian, *Codex,* 11.30.1.

129 *Codex Theodosianus,* 11.16.2; trans. Pharr, *The Theodosian Code,* 306.

130 *Codex Theodosianus,* 11.5.2; trans. Pharr, *The Theodosian Code,* 298.

issued by churches.[131] Even more significantly for territory under the control of the Byzantine emperor, in a Novel of 544 Justinian enshrined in law the right of churches to make emphyteutic grants.[132] Not surprisingly, the wording of the ecclesiastical contracts seems to have been modelled on that of the imperial chancery.[133] Tom Brown has suggested that ecclesiastical leases in Italy were made with the encouragement of the government, which would clearly benefit from the regular oversight of the payment of services[134] — the empire was effectively using the Church as an agent,[135] much as it was using the Church to continue State evergetism — as in Justinian's order that pope Vigilius supervise the distribution of the *annona civica*. Brown has also argued that bishops used grants of land to gain influence over generals, citing the very favorable lease offered to Theodore Calliopa.[136] The result was the economic interdependence of the Church and the military.[137]

Brown offers a reading of the material which is one that is essentially seen through the eyes of the State. It is significant that his main statement of the case is to be found in a monograph entitled *Gentlemen and Officers*. The same case might equally be made with greater ecclesiastical emphasis — the key players would then be Churchmen and Officers. This fits with F. Homes Dudden's insistence that Gregory the Great saw no distinction between Church and State.[138] And here a model of a temple so-

131 Justinian, *Codex*, 7.38.2.

132 Justinian, *Novellae*, 120.5–6 (544), ed. Schöll and Kroll, 581–85. For the significance of this law, see David J.D. Miller and Peter Sarris, trans., *The Novels of Justinian: A Complete Annotated English Translation* (Cambridge: Cambridge University Press, 2018), 781, n. 1. See also Federico Montinaro, "Les fausses donations de Constantin dans le *Liber Pontificalis*," *Millennium* 12 (2015): 203–30.

133 Brown, *Gentlemen and Officers*, 187.

134 Ibid.

135 Brown, "The Church of Ravenna and the Imperial Administration," 10.

136 Tjäder, *Die nichtliterarischen lateinischen Papyri italiens*, vol. 2, doc. 44, 172–73.

137 Brown, "The Church of Ravenna and the Imperial Administration," 11.

138 Dudden, *Gregory the Great: His Place in History and Thought*, vol. 2, 238–39.

ciety — albeit not necessarily that of Appadurai and Appadurai Breckenridge — is worth bearing in mind.

There is good reason for putting considerable emphasis on the Church. If we take the *Codex Bavarus,* which is one of the main sources to show the support given by the Church to the military, we should note how small a percentage of the leases is granted to military officers. In its 168 entries I have noted 8 references to *magistri militum,*[139] 8 (or 9) to *duces,*[140] 14 to *tribuni,*[141] 2 to gastalds,[142] and 1 each to a *vicarius numeri,* a *miles numeri,* an *auctenta numeri,* an *exercitalis,* and to a *scabinus*[143] — in other words, military men appear in approximately 20 percent of the leases and donations listed in the Codex. Moreover, 2 of the leases in question were granted to *ex-tribuni,*[144] and 4 were to the widows of military men.[145] And on a number of occasions the soldier is only one petitioner among several for property — the others sometimes being named as relatives, some of whom were also clerics. Interestingly, women are listed in almost all of the contracts, either as wives (even of clergy), widows, or as daughters — the significance of the wives and widows is clear from the fact that *conjugalis* is among the most common descriptors to be found in the text. Hardly any of the leases can be dated to the period before the end of the Exarchate, and some of them are unquestionably later, but 10 are from the episcopate of Damian

---

139 *Breviarium ecclesiae Ravennatis (Codice Bavaro) secoli VII–X,* 32, 33, 63, 71, 77, 80, 140, 164, ed. Rabotti, 25–87.

140 *Breviarium ecclesiae Ravennatis (Codice Bavaro) secoli VII–X,* 17, 18, 20, 39, 76, 125, 167, 183, ed. Rabotti, 15–98.

141 *Breviarium ecclesiae Ravennatis (Codice Bavaro) secoli VII–X,* 21, 22, 26, 27, 28, 29, 34, 43, 45, 48, 70, 76, 95, 177, ed. Rabotti, 17–94.

142 *Breviarium ecclesiae Ravennatis (Codice Bavaro) secoli VII–X,* 146, 153, ed. Rabotti, 79–80, 81–82.

143 *Breviarium ecclesiae Ravennatis (Codice Bavaro) secoli VII–X,* 64, 76, 132, 169, 186, ed. Rabotti, 33, 39, 74, 90, 100.

144 *Breviarium Ecclesiae Ravennatis, (Codice Bavaro) secoli VII–X,* 43–45, ed. Rabotti, 21–22.

145 *Breviarium ecclesiae Ravennatis (Codice Bavaro) secoli VII–X,* 20, 32, 80, 164, ed. Rabotti, 10, 17, 44, 87.

(692–709)[146] and 14 from that of Sergius (744–769),[147] and there is no reason to think that all the undated leases listed (which constitute the majority) relate to a later period. In other words, support for soldiers and veterans is present, but the *Codex Bavarus* is a document of Church economics, not of military finance. Moreover, alongside all the leases listed in the *Codex Bavarus,* there are also donations to the Church of Ravenna, including one by a *tribunus* and another by a gastald.[148] And if we turn to the Ravenna papyri, we find the grants of a *spatarius* from c. 600,[149] another from the son of a general from 625,[150] and a third from a soldier from 629.[151]

The army surely dominated the Exarchate to an extent that it did not dominate late-seventh-century Francia, not least because of the ever-present threat of the Lombards — Tom Brown has estimated that most of land of the peninsula was in the hands of the Church or of military commanders.[152] But if we are thinking, as anthropologists do, of redistributive processes, it is the Church which has the greater role to play.

But while one needs to treat the significance of emphyteutic leases for the support of the military in Italy with a slight amount of caution, it is worth noting that the model of ecclesiastical support for the military would take on much greater significance in Francia in the course of the eighth century. The leases of the *Codex Bavarus* have the title *petitio*: at least in theory the lease was a response to a petition. In origin, the same is true of the *precaria*.[153] Legal historians have insisted emphyteutic

---

146 *Breviarium ecclesiae Ravennatis (Codice Bavaro) secoli VII–X,* 23–25, 30, 32, 37, 59, 64, 94, 130, ed. Rabotti, 12–74.

147 *Breviarium ecclesiae Ravennatis (Codice Bavaro) secoli VII–X,* 27, 33, 34, 41, 63, 65, 70, 71, 80, 129, 132, 134, 158, 177, ed. Rabotti, 15–94.

148 *Breviarium ecclesiae Ravennatis (Codice Bavaro) secoli VII–X,* 48, 153, ed. Rabotti, 24, 81–82.

149 Tjäder, *Die nichtliterarischen lateinischen Papyri italiens,* vol. 1, 16.

150 Ibid., vol. 1, 21.

151 Ibid., vol. 1, 22.

152 Brown, *Gentlemen and Officers,* 195.

153 Paul Fouracre, "The Use of the Term *beneficium* in the Frankish Sources: A Society Based on Favours," in *Languages of Gift in the Early Middle Ages,* ed.

leases and *precaria* are indistinguishable.[154] I am not sure that a Merovingian abbot would have agreed — he would have hoped that any grant of land he was obliged to make to a layman was not permanent, or at least was limited to a small number of generations. And in this he would have had the support of Justinian and Isidore, both of whom saw *precaria* as temporary concessions of usufruct.[155]

I would, nevertheless, suggest that it is worth considering the *precaria* that Merovingian abbeys and dioceses were forced to make by Charles Martel alongside Tom Brown's interpretation of the emphyteutic leases in the Exarchate. According to the *Gesta abbatum Fontanellensium,* an inventory of the holdings of the monastery of St. Wandrille was drawn up in 787, according to which 2,120 out of 4,264 *mansi* were let out as *precaria* at the time[156] — in fact, if one adds up the figures provided in the text, the upper number is incorrect and should read 3,964.[157] We are given greater detail on the properties granted out to *comes* Ratharius during the abbacy of Teutsind.[158] These included 3 large

---

Wendy Davies and Paul Fouracre (Cambridge: Cambridge University Press, 2010), 62–88; Ian Wood, "Teutsind, Witlaic, and the History of Merovingian *precaria,*" in *Property and Power in the Early Middle Ages,* ed. Wendy Davies and Paul Fouracre (Cambridge: Cambridge University Press, 1995), 31–52.

154 Henry Hallam, *Supplemental Notes to the View of the State of Europe During the Middle Ages* (London: J. Murray, 1848), 117: "Does it appear from the ancient use of the words 'precaria' and 'beneficium' that they were convertible, as the former is said by Muratori and Lehouerou, to have been with emphyteusis? […] The word *precaria* is for the most part applied to ecclesiastical property, which, by some usurpation, had fallen into the hands of laymen. These afterwards, by way of compromise, were permitted to continue as tenants of the Church, for a limited term, generally for life, on payment of a fixed rate."

155 Justinian, *Digest,* 43.26.1, https://droitromain.univ-grenoble-alpes.fr/; Isidore of Seville, *Etymologiae,* 5.25, ed. William M. Lindsay, 2 vols. (Oxford: Clarendon, 1911), 190–93; Wood, "Teutsind, Witlaic and the History of Merovingian *precaria,*" 45–46.

156 *Gesta Abbatum Fontanellensium,* 11.3, ed. Pascal Pradié, *Chronique des abbés de Fontenelle* (Paris: Les Belles Lettres, 1999).

157 Wood, "Teutsind, Witlaic and the History of Merovingian *precaria,*" 38.

158 *Gesta Abbatum Fontanellensium,* 6.2, ed. Pradié, *Chronique des abbés de Fontenelle.*

estates and vineyards that had been given by king Childeric II, together with other properties, totaling 29 *domaines*. Among other churches that suffered in the course of the secularization of property under Charles Martel was that of Auxerre, where, according to the *Gesta Pontificum Autissiodorensium,* the bishop was left with 100 *mansi,* the rest being divided up between 6 *principes baioarios*.[159] It would seem that the beneficiaries of the *precaria* were often men who might be called upon to fulfil military obligations.

The secularizations of the eighth century, in both Francia and England, seem to have been sizeable.[160] But they were probably necessary, at least in Francia, where the Muslim threat presented a totally new challenge to the Franks, who for almost a century had enjoyed comparative peace, even if factions, religious and secular, had been in competition, which sometimes spilled over into violence. The actions of Charles Martel certainly struck a blow at the economic power of bishops and abbots. But in the course of the later eighth and ninth centuries there would be some redress: Herlihy's estimate of the extent of Church land in the ninth century is not unlike the estimate I have given for the seventh.[161] In fact, Charles Martel did not intend to undermine the centrality of the Church within the Christian society of the Franks — he was concerned primarily with ensuring that it supported his followers: it was still to play a crucial role in the process of the redistribution of landed resources. He himself donated the royal estate of Clichy to St. Denis in 741,[162] and over the following decade Pippin III started to uphold the same monastery's claims to property.[163] A charter issued in 751 was, in

159 *Gesta Pontificum Autissiodorensium,* 32, ed. Sot, *Les gestes des évêques d'Auxerre,* 135–37.

160 Wood, "Land Tenure and Military Obligations in the Anglo-Saxon and Merovingian Kingdoms."

161 David Herlihy, "Church Property on the Continent, 700–1200," *Speculum* 36, no. 1 (1961): 81–105, at 89.

162 Ingrid Heidrich, ed., *Die Urkunden der Arnulfinger* (Bad Münsterfeld: H-C-I, 2001), doc. 14, pp. 90–92.

163 Ibid., doc. 18, 21, 22, 23, pp. 102–3, 107–17.

Michael Wallace-Hadrill's words, "like wholesale restitution."[164] Pippin also issued legislation protecting monastic property at the Council of Soissons in 744.[165] And it is worth remembering that the second most substantial will from the Merovingian period is that of Abbo, a close supporter of Charles, who left the majority of his vast landed wealth to his foundation of Novalesa in 739.[166] The Council of Estinnes, authorized by Pippin's brother Carloman in 743, recognized the need for support for the army in a time of crisis, but put strict limits on the use of *precaria*.[167]

Scholars have, of course, long been aware that the Merovingian and Carolingian Churches were very rich, as indeed was the Church of Rome and that of Ravenna. But, on the whole, they have not seen the accumulation of wealth as leading to a distinctive pattern of economic distribution. I have tried to suggest, however, that to reduce the wealth of the Church to being no more than a segment of the elite is to fail to register the extent to which it was an integral part of a socio-economic structure that was dominated by the priorities of Christianity. These priorities, the performance of cult and the provision of charity, were funded with the income from perhaps a third of the property of the post-Roman West — although in the Exarchate a good proportion of that revenue was also transferred to the State. Many churchmen may have been decidedly unchristian in their personal actions, but the injunctions of the Gospel, which I have cited on numerous occasions, were nevertheless

164 J.M. Wallace-Hadrill, *The Long-haired Kings, and Other Studies in Frankish History* (London: Methuen, 1962), 241.

165 Council of Soissons (744), c. 3, ed. Albert Werminghoff, *Concilia Aevi Karolini* 1.1, Monumenta Germaniae Historica, Leges 3, Concilia 2.1 (Hanover: Hahn, 1906), 33–36. Gaëlle Calvet-Marcadé, *Assassin des pauvres: l'église et l'inaliénabilité des terres à l'époque carolingienne* (Turnhout: Brepols, 2019), 55–56.

166 Patrick J. Geary, *Aristocracy in Provence: The Rhône Basin at the Dawn of the Carolingian Age* (Stuttgart: Hiersemann, 1985).

167 Council of Estinnes (743), c. 2, ed. Werminghoff, *Concilia Aevi Karolini* 1.1, 5–7; Calvet-Marcadé, *Assassin des pauvres*, 52–55, and (for the unsatisfactory nature of the term "secularization"), 105–6.

hugely influential. In order to appreciate the nature of the early medieval economy it is more useful, I have argued, to turn to the models of temple societies that have been constructed by anthropologists, than it is to invoke modern western economic theory. And, one might note, that the temple societies of southern India provide examples of the integration of the military into the equation.

The temple societies of western Europe did not emerge overnight, with the conversion of Constantine: indeed, I have tried to suggest that the fundamental notion of supporting religion with landed endowment was relatively slow in taking hold, not least because the Gospels provided no guidance on the possession of land (indeed they challenged it). The emergence of a landed Church instead went hand in hand with the establishment of churches and the recruitment of clergy: the endowment of the Church which effectively ended in the establishment of temple societies in some areas of the early medieval West took place over a period of centuries. But the process of redistribution, which anthropologists have seen as essential to their models, did not follow the same line in all parts of the post-Roman West. The economic process was different in Francia from what it was in the Exarchate. Anglosaxon England would seem to have had much in common with Francia, to judge by the secularizations of the early eighth century,[168] but, although its Christianity may have been influenced from the continent, it was largely a new import of the early seventh century. Spain looks curiously different — but how much the difference is a matter of social reality, how much it reflects the source material, and how much it is the result of historiographical traditions is an interesting question. Despite the variety all these areas had one thing in common — churches that came, in the course of the sixth and seventh centuries, to be hugely well endowed with land, and which used the revenues from that land to support kingdoms that made some attempt to abide by a set of religious

---

168 Wood, "Land Tenure and Military Obligations in the Anglo-Saxon and Merovingian Kingdoms."

and ethical concerns that had only entered the mainstream in the early fourth century. The grand narrative of Western Civilization tends to lead us to see the emergence of Christian society as perfectly straightforward. Looking at the post-Roman period through the prism of models created to understand the temple societies of India helps us to break away from a rather teleological vision, and to have a sharper appreciation of some of the more distinctive aspects of the socio-economic structures of the early medieval West.

Bibliography

Primary

Acta synodi Romani. Edited by Theodor Mommsen. *Cassiodorus Variae.* Monumenta Germaniae Historica. Auctores Antiquissimi 12. Berlin: Weidmann, 1894.

Actus Pontificum Cenomannis in urbe degentium. Edited by Margarete Weidemann. *Geschichte des Bistums Le Mans von der Spätantike bis zur Karolingerzeit,* 3 vols. Mainz: Verlag des Römisch-Germanischen Zentralmuseums, 2002.

Adso of Montierender. *Vita Walberti.* Edited by Monique Goullet, *Adso Dervensis Opera Hagiographica.* Corpus Christianorum, Continuation Medievalis 198. Turnhout: Brepols, 2003.

Agnellus. *Liber Pontificalis ecclesiae Ravennatis.* Edited by Deborah Mauskopf Deliyannis. Corpus Christianorum, Continuatio Medievalis 199. Turnhout: Brepols, 2006. Translated by Deborah Mauskopf Deliyannis, *The Book of the Pontiffs of the Church of Ravenna.* Washington, DC: Catholic University of America, 2004.

Angilbert. *Libellus de ecclesia Centulae.* Edited by Georg Waitz. Monumenta Germaniae Historica, Scriptores 15.1. Hanover: Hahn, 1887.

Ahistulfi leges. Edited by Claudio Assara and Stefano Gasparri. *Le leggi dei Longobardi. Storia, memoria e diritto di un populo germanico.* Rome: Viella, 2005.

Ambrose. *De excessu fratris Satyri.* Edited by Otto Faller. Corpus Scriptorum Ecclesiasticorum Latinorum 73. Vienna: Austrian Academy of Sciences Press, 1955.

———. *De Officiis.* Edited by Ivor J. Davidson, 2 volumes. Oxford: Oxford University Press, 2002.

———. *Epistulae.* Translated by J.H.W.G. Liebeschuetz. *Ambrose of Milan: Political Letters and Speeches.* Liverpool: Liverpool University Press, 2005.

———. *On the Death of Satyris (Book I).* Translated by H. de Romestin, E. de Romestin, and H.T.F. Duckworth. *Nicene and Post-Nicene Fathers.* Second Series. Volume 10. Edited by Philip Schaff and Henry Wace. Buffalo: Christian Literature Publishing Co., 1896. Revised and edited for *New Advent* by Kevin Knight. http://www.newadvent.org/fathers/34031. htm.

Ammianus Marcellinus. *Res gestae.* http://thelatinlibrary.com/ ammianus.html.

Angilbert. *Libellus de ecclesia Centulae.* Edited by Georg Waitz, 174–81. Monumenta Germaniae Historica, Scriptores 15.1. Hanover: Hahn, 1887.

Apostolic Canons. Translated by Alexander Roberts and James Donaldson. *The Ante-Nicene Fathers: Translations of the Writings of the Fathers Down to A.D. 325.* Edinburgh: T&T Clark and Grand Rapids: Wm. B. Eerdmans Publishing Company, 1886. https://www.ccel.org/ccel/schaff/anf07/ anf07.ix.ix.vi.html.

Athanasius. *Historia Arianorum.* Edited by Hans-George Opitz. *Athanasius Werke* 2.1. Berlin: De Gruyter, 1935. Translated by Richard Flower. *Imperial Invectives against Constantius II, Athanasius of Alexandria, Hilary of Poitiers and Lucifer of Cagliari.* Liverpool: Liverpool University Press, 2016.

Augustine. *Epistulae.* Edited by Alois Goldbacher. *Augustini Epistolae* 3. Corpus Scriptorum Ecclesiasticorum Latinorum 44. Vienna, 1904.

―――. *Praeceptum.* Edited by Luc Verheijen. *La règle de saint Augustin.* Paris: Études augustiniennes, 1967.

―――. *Sermons.* Patrologia Latina 39.

Avitus. *Epistulae.* Edited by Rudolf Peiper. Monumenta Germaniae Historica, Auctores Antiquissimi 6.2. Berlin: Weidmann, 1883. Translated by Danuta Shanzer and Ian Wood. *Avitus of Vienne: Letters and Selected Prose.* Liverpool: Liverpool University Press, 2002.

Bede. *De templo.* Edited by David Hurst. *Opera exegetica* 2A. Corpus Christianorum, Series Latina 119A. Turnhout: Brepols, 1969.

―――. *Historia Ecclesiastica Gentis Anglorum.* http://www.thelatinlibrary.com/bede.html. Translated by Bertram Colgrave and Roger Mynors. *Bede's Ecclesiastical History of the English Nation.* Oxford: Clarendon, 1969.

―――. *Responsiones.* Edited by Valeria Mattaloni. *Rescriptum beati Gregorii papae ad Augustinum episcopum seu Libellus responsionum.* Florence: Sismel, 2017.

Benedict. *Regula.* Edited by Adalbert de Vogüé and Jean Neufville. *La règle de saint Benoît.* Sources Chrétiennes, 182. Paris: Éditions du Cerf, 1972.

Bobbio Missal. Edited by Elias A. Lowe. Henry Bradshaw Society 58. London, 1920.

Breviary Alaricianum. Edited by Gustav Haenel. *Lex Romana Visigothorum.* Leipzig: Teubner, 1848.

Breviarium ecclesiae Ravennatis (Codice Bavaro) secoli VII–X. Edited by Giuseppi Rabotti. Fonti per la Storia d'Italia 110. Rome: Istituto storico italiano per il Medio Evo, 1985.

Caesarius of Arles. *Sermons.* Edited by Germain Morin. Corpus Christianorum, Series Latina 103–104. Turnhout: Brepols, 1953.

―――. *Statuta sanctarum virginum.* Edited by Adalbert de Vogüé and Joël Courreau. *Césaire d'Arles, Œuves monas-*

tiques, Volume 1: *Œuvres pour les moniales.* Sources Chrétiennes 345. Paris: Éditions du Cerf, 1988.

Cassian. *Institutiones.* Edited by Jean Claude Guy. *Jean Cassien, Institutions cénobitiques.* Sources Chrétiennes 109. Paris: Éditions du Cerf, 1965.

Cassiodorus. *Expositio in Psalterium.* Patrologia Latina 70.

Chronicon Moissacense. Edited by Georg H. Pertz. Monumenta Germaniae Historica, Scriptores 1. Hanover: Hahn, 1826.

Chlothar II. *Praeceptio.* Edited by Alfred Boretius. Monumenta Germaniae Historica, Leges. Capitularia regum Francorum 1. Hanover: Hahn, 1883.

Codex Carolinus. Edited by Wilhelm Gundlach, Monumenta Germaniae Historica, Epistolae III, Merowingici et Karolini Aevi I. Berlin: Weidmann, 1892. Translated by Rosamond McKitterick, Dorine van Espelo, Richard Pollard, and Richard Price. *Codex Epistolaris Carolinus: Letters from the Popes to the Frankish Rulers, 739–791.* Liverpool: Liverpool University Press, 2021.

Codex Euricianus. Edited by Karl Zeumer. *Leges Visigothorum,* Monumenta Germaniae Historica. Leges Nationum Germanicarum 1. Hanover: Hahn, 1902.

Codex Iustinianus. https://droitromain.univ-grenoble-alpes.fr.

Codex Theodosianus. https://droitromain.univ-grenoble-alpes. fr. Translated by Clyde Pharr. *The Theodosian Code.* Princeton: Princeton University Press, 1952.

Codice diplomatico del monastero di S. Colombano di Bobbio. Edited by Carlo Cipolla. Fonti per la Storia d'Italia 52–54, 3 volumes. Rome: Tipografria del Buzzi, 1918.

Codice Diplomatico Longobardo. Edited by Luigi Schiaparelli. Fonti per la Storia d'Italia 62. Volume 1. Rome: Istituto storico italiano, 1929.

Collectio Avellana. Edited by Otto Günther. Corpus Scriptorum Ecclesiasticorum Latinorum 35.1. Vienna: F. Tempsky, 1895.

Collectio Flaviniacensis. Edited by Karl Zeumer. *Formulae Merowingici et Karolini Aevi.* Monumenta Germaniae Historica, Legum 5. Hanover: Hahn, 1886.

Concilia Africana sec. trad. coll. Hispanae. Edited by Charles Munier. *Concilia Africae 345–525*. Corpus Christianorum, Series Latina 149. Turnhout: Brepols, 1974.

Council of Ancyra (314). Edited by Giovanni Domenico Mansi. *Sacrorum Conciliorum nova et amplissima collectio*. Florence, 1759.

Council of Antioch (330/341). Edited by Giovanni Domenico Mansi. *Sacrorum Conciliorum nova et amplissima collectio*. Florence, 1759.

Council of Chalcedon (451). Edited by Eduard Schwartz, *Acta Concilium Œcumenicorum, Concilium universale Chalcedonense (AD 451)*, 6 volumes. Bonn, 1932–1938. Translated by Richard M. Price, *The Acts of the Council of Chalcedon*, 3 volumes. Liverpool: University Press, 2007.

Council of Estinnes (743). Edited by Albert Werminghoff. *Concilia Aevi Karolini* 1.1. Monumenta Germaniae Historica, Leges 3, Concilia 2.1. Hanover: Hahn, 1906.

Council of Soissons (744). Edited by Albert Werminghoff. *Concilia Aevi Karolini* 1.1. Monumenta Germaniae Historica, Leges 3, Concilia 2.1. Hanover: Hahn, 1906.

Councils of the African Church. Edited by Charles Munier. *Concilia Africae 345–525*. Corpus Christianorum, Series Latina 144. Turnhout: Brepols, 1974.

Councils of the Gallic Church. Edited by Charles Munier. *Concilia Galliae, c. 314 –c. 506*. Corpus Christianorum, Series Latina 148. Turnhout: Brepols, 1963.

Councils of the Merovingian Church. Edited by Brigitte Basdevant. *Les Canons des Conciles Mérovingiens (VIᵉ–VIIᵉ siècles)*, 2 volumes. Sources Chrétiennes 353–354. Paris: Éditions du Cerf, 1989.

Councils of the Visigothic Church. Edited by Gonzalo Martínez Díez and (from 1982 forward as co-editor) Félix Rodríguez. *La Colección Canónica Hispana*, 6 volumes. Madrid, 1966–2002; Edited and translated by José Vives. *Concilios Visigóticos e Hispano-Romanos*. Barcelona and Madrid: Consejo Superior de Investigaciones Científicas, 1963.

Cyprian of Toulon, et al. *Vita Caesarii*. Edited by Bruno Krusch. Monumenta Germaniae Historica, Scriptores Rerum Merovingicarum 3. Hanover: Hahn, 1896. Translated by William Klingshirn. *Caesarius of Arles, Life, Testament, Letters*. Liverpool: Liverpool University Press, 1994.

Diplomata Merowingica. Edited by Theo Kölzer. *Die Urkunden der Merowinger*, 2 volumes. Monumenta Germaniae Historica. Hanover, 2001.

Domitii Ulpiani Fragmenta. Edited by Edward Böcking. Bonn: Marcus, 1831.

Edictum Theodorici. Edited by Ingemar König. *Edictum Theodorici regis. Das "Gesetzbuch" des Ostgotenkönigs Theoderich des Großen*. Darmstadt: Wissenschaftliche Buchgesellschaft, 2018.

Ennodius. *Vita Epifani*. Edited by Frideric Vogel. Monumenta Germaniae Historica. Auctores Antiquissimi 7. Berlin: Weidmann, 1885.

Eucherius of Lyon. *Letter to Philo*. Edited by Alain Dubreucq. "Les sources textuelles relatives aux monastère de l'Île-Barbe au Haut Moyen Âge," forthcoming.

Eugippius. *Vita Severini*. Edited by Philippe Régerat. *Eugippe, Vie de saint Séverin*. Sources Chrétiennes 374. Paris: Éditions du Cerf, 1991.

Eusebius. *Life of Constantine*. Translated by Averil Cameron and Stuart Hall. Oxford: Clarendon, 1999.

———. *Historia Ecclesiastica*. Edited by T.E. Page et al. Translated by J.E.L. Oulton. Loeb Classics, 2 volumes. Cambridge: Harvard University Press, 1942.

Ex concilio bracarense. Edited by Gonzalo Martínez Díez. *El Epítome Hispánico: una colección canónica española del siglo VII: estudio y texto crítico*. Santander: Universidad Pontificia de Comillas, 1961.

Flodoard. *Historia Remensis Ecclesiae*. Edited by M. Lejeune. Histoire de l'Église de Reims par Flodoard, 2 volumes. Reims: Imprimeur de l'Académie, 1854.

Fredegar. *Chronicle and continuationes.* Edited by Bruno Krusch. Monumenta Germaniae Historica, Scriptores Rerum Merovingicarum 2. Hanover: Hahn, 1888.

Gelasian Sacramentary. Edited by Leo Cunibert Mohlberg. *Liber Sacramentorum Romanae aeclesiae.* Rome: Herder, 1960.

Gelasius I. *Epistolae.* Edited by Andreas Thiel. *Epistolae Romanorum Pontificum Genuinae.* Braunschweig: Brunsbergae, 1868.

Gerontius. *Vita Melaniae.* Edited by Denys Gorce. *Vie de sainte Melanie (Βίος τῆς Ὁσίας Μελάνης).* Sources Chrétiennes 90. Paris: Éditions du Cerf, 1962.

Gesta Abbatum Fontanellensium. Edited by Pascal Pradié. *Chronique des abbés de Fontenelle.* Paris: Les Belles Lettres, 1999.

Gesta Pontificum Autissiodorensium. Edited by Michel Sot. *Les gestes des évêques d'Auxerre,* 3 volumes. Paris: Belles lettres, 2006.

Gregory of Tours. *Decem Libri Historiarum.* Edited by Bruno Krusch and Wilhelm Levison. Monumenta Germaniae Historica, Scriptores Rerum Merovingicarum 1.1. Hanover: Hahn, 1951.

———. *Liber Vitae Patrum.* Edited by Bruno Krusch. Monumenta Germaniae Historica, Scriptores Rerum Merovingicarum 1.2. Hanover: Hahn, 1969 (1885).

Gregory the Great. *Epistulae.* Edited by Dag Norberg. *Registrum Epistularum.* Corpus Christianorum, Series Latina 140–140A. Turnhout: Brepols, 1982. Translated by John R.C. Martyn. *The Letters of Gregory the Great,* 3 volumes. Toronto: Pontifical Institute of Mediaeval Studies, 2004.

Guérard, M., ed. *Cartulaire de l'abbaye de Saint-Victor de Marseille.* Volume 2. Paris, 1857.

Hadrian I. *Epistolae.* Edited by Wilhelm Gundlach. Monumenta Germaniae Historica, Epistolae 3, Merowingici et Karolini Aevi, 469–657. Berlin: Weidmann, 1892. Translated by Rosamond McKitterick, Dorine van Espelo, Richard Pollard, and Richard Price. *Codex Epistolaris Carolinus: Letters from the Popes to the Frankish Rulers, 739–891.* Liverpool: Liverpool University Press, 2021.

Heidrich, Ingrid, ed. *Die Urkunden der Arnulfinger*. Bad Münsterfeld: H-C-I, 2001.

Heraclius. *Novellae*. Edited by Iohannes Konidaris. "Die Novellen des Kaiser Heracleios." In *Fontes Minores* 5, edited by Dieter Simon, 33–106. Forschungen zum byzantinischen Rechtsgeschichte 8. Frankfurt am Main: Löwenklau Gesellschaft, 1982.

Hincmar. *Vita Remigii*. Edited by Bruno Krusch. Monumenta Germaniae Historica, Scriptores Rerum Merovingicarum 3. Hanover: Hahn, 1896.

Ildefonsus. *De viris illustribus*. Edited by Carmen Codoñer Merino. *Ildefonsi Toletani episcopi Opera*. Corpus Christianorum, Series Latinorum 114A. Turnhout: Brepols, 2007.

Isidore of Seville. *De officiis ecclesiasticis*. Edited by Christopher M. Lawson. Corpus Christianorum, Series Latinorum 113. Turnhout: Brepols, 1989.

———. *Etymologiae*. Edited by William M. Lindsay, 2 volumes. Oxford: Clarendon, 1911.

———. *Historia Gothorum*. Edited and translated (Sp.) by Cristobal Rodríguez Alonso. *Las Historias de los Godos, los Vandalos y los suevos de Isidoro de Sevilla*. León: Centro de Estudios e Investigación "San Isidoro," 1975. Translated (Eng.) by Kenneth Baxter Wolf. *Conquerors and Chroniclers of Early Medieval Spain*. Liverpool: Liverpool University Press, 1999.

———. *Sententiae*. Edited by Pierre Cazier. Corpus Christianorum, Series Latina 111. Turnhout: Brepols, 1998.

Jaffe, Philipp. *Register Pontificum Romanorum*. 2nd edition. Leipzig: Graz, 1885.

Jerome. *De viris illustribus*. Patrologia Latina 23.

———. *Epistulae*. Edited by Isidore Hilberg. *Sancti Eusebii Hieronymi Epistolae*. Corpus Scriptorum Ecclesiasticorum Latinorum 55. Leipzig: Freytag, 1912.

John the Deacon. *Vita Gregorii*. Patrologia Latina 75.

John Lydus. *On Powers*. Edited by Anastasius C. Bandy. Philadelphia: American Philosophical Society, 1983.

Jonas of Bobbio. *Vita Columbani*. Edited by Bruno Krusch. Monumenta Germaniae Historica, Scriptores Rerum Germanicarum. Hanover: Hahn, 1905. Translated by Alexander O'Hara and Ian Wood. *Jonas of Bobbio, Life of Columbanus, Life of John of Réomé, and Life of Vedast.* Liverpool: Liverpool University Press, 2017.

Julian the Apostate. *Epistulae.* Translated by Wilmer Cave Wright. *The Works of the Emperor Julian,* 3 volumes. New York: Putnam, 1923.

Justinian. *Digest.* http://thelatinlibrary.com/justinian.html. Translated by Alan Watson. *The Digest of Justinian,* 4 volumes. Philadelphia: University of Pennsylvania, 1998.

Justinian. *Novellae.* Edited by Rudolf Schöll and Wilhem Kroll. *Corpus Iuris Civilis, Novellae,* 6th edn. Berlin: Weidemann, 1928. Translated by David J.D. Miller and Peter Sarris. *The Novels of Justinian: A Complete Annotated English Translation.* Cambridge: Cambridge University Press, 2018.

Leo I. *Sermons.* Edited by Antonius Chavasse. *Leo Magnus Tractatus.* Corpus Christianorum, Series Latinorum 138. Turnhout: Brepols, 1978.

Lex Ribvaria. Edited by Franz Beyerle and Rudolf Buchner. Monumenta Germaniae Historica, Leges 3.2. Hanover: Hahn, 1954.

Liber Constitutionum. Edited by Ludwig R. de Salis. *Leges Burgundionum.* Monumenta Germaniae Historica, Leges 2.1. Hanover: Hahn, 1882.

Liber de virtutibus sancti Juliani. Edited by Bruno Krusch. Monumenta Germaniae Historica, Scriptores Rerum Merovingicarum 1.2. Hanover: Hahn, 1885.

Liber de virtutibus sancti Martini. Edited by Bruno Krusch. Monumenta Germaniae Historica, Scriptores Rerum Merovingicarum 1.2. Hanover: Hahn, 1885.

Liber Diurnus, romanorum pontificum. Edited by Theodor von Sickel. Vienna: Vindobonae, 1889.

Liber Historiae Francorum. Edited by Bruno Krusch. Monumenta Germaniae Historica, Scriptores Rerum Merovingicarum 2. Hannover, 1885.

Liber Iudiciorum. Edited by Karl Zeumer. *Leges Visigothorum.* Monumenta Germaniae Historica, Leges Nationum Germanicarum 1. Hanover: Hahn, 1902. See also the forthcoming translation in the Liverpool series by Damián Fernández and Noel Lenski.

Liber Pontificalis. Edited by Louis Duchesne. *"Liber Pontificalis": Texte, Introduction et Commentaire,* 2 volumes. Paris, 1886–1892. Translated by Raymond Davis. *The Book of Pontiffs: The Ancient Biographies of the First Ninety Roman Bishops to* AD *715.* Revised edition. Liverpool: Liverpool University Press, 2000.

Marculf. *Formulary.* Edited by Karl Zeumer. Monumenta Germaniae Historica, Formulae Merowingici et Karolini Aevi. Hanover: Hahn, 1886.

Missale Francorum. Edited by Leo Cunibert Mohlberg. Rome: Herder, 1957.

Nicolas I. *Epistulae.* Edited by Ernst Perels. Monumenta Germaniae Historica, Epistolae 6, Epistolae Karolini Aevi 4. Berlin: Weidmann, 1925.

Olympiodorus. *Fragments.* Edited by Roger C. Blockley. *The Fragmentary Classicising Historians of the Later Roman Empire.* Volume 2. Liverpool: Cairns, 1983.

Palladius. *Historia Lausiaca.* Edited by Adelheid Hübner. *"Historia Lausiaca": Geschichten aus dem frühen Mönchtum.* Freiburg: Herder, 2016.

Parochiale Suevum. Edited by Frater Glorie. *Itineraria et alia Geographica.* Corpus Christianorum, Series Latina 175. Turnhout: Brepols, 1965.

Passio Leudegarii I. Edited by Bruno Krusch. Monumenta Germaniae Historica, Scriptores Rerum Merovingicarum 5. Hanover: Hahn, 1910.

Passio Praeiecti. Edited by Bruno Krusch. Monumenta Germaniae Historica, Scriptores Rerum Merovingicarum 5. Hanover: Hahn, 1910.

Paulinus of Milan. *Vita Ambrosii.* Edited by Michele Pellegrino. Paolino di Milano, *Vita di S. Ambrogio.* Rome: Editrice Studium, 1961. Translated by Frederick R. Hoare. *The Western Fathers.* London: Sheed and Ward, 1954.

Paulinus of Nola. *Epistulae.* Edited by Guilelmi de Hartel. Corpus Scriptorum Ecclesiasticorum Latinorum 29. Vienna: Vindobonae, 1894.

Paul the Deacon. *Historia Langobardorum.* Edited by Georg Waitz. Monumenta Germaniae Historica, Scriptores Rerum Germanicarum 48. Hanover: Hahn, 1878.

Pelagius I. *Epistulae.* Edited by Pius M. Gassó and Columba M. Batlle. *Pelagii Papae epistolae quae supersunt (556–61).* Montserrat: In Abbatia Montisserati, 1956.

Philostorgius. *Historia Ecclesiastica.* Patrologia Graeca 65.

Plutarch. *Life of Numa.* Edited by Bernadotte Perrin. Plutarch, *Parallel Lives.* Volume 1. Cambridge: Harvard University Press, 1914.

Pomerius. *De vita contemplativa.* Patrologia Latina 59. Translated by Sister Mary Josephine Suelzer. *Julianus Pomerius, the Contemplative Life.* Westminster: Newman Press, 1947.

Possidius. *Vita Augustini.* Edited by Wilhelm Geerlings. Paderborn: Schöningh, 2005.

Rowland Rea, John, ed. *The Oxyrhynchus Papyri,* XL. London: The Egypt Exploration Society, 1972.

Rufinus. *Historia Ecclesiastica.* Patrologia Latina 21.

Salvian. *Œuvres.* Edited by Georges Lagarrigue. *Salvien de Marseille, Œuvres.* Volume 1. Sources Chrétiennes 176. Paris: Éditions du Cerf, 1971.

Sidonius Apollinaris. *Epistulae.* Edited by André Loyen. *Sidoine Apollinaire,* 3 volumes. Paris: Les Belles Lettres, 1960–1970.

Simplicius. *Epistolae.* Edited by Andreas Thiel. *Epistolae Romanorum Pontificum Genuinae.* Braunschweig: Brunsbergae, 1868.

Socrates Scholasticus. *Historia Ecclesiastica.* Edited by Günther C. Hansen. *Die griechischen christlichen Schriftsteller.* Berlin: Akademie, 1995.

Sozomen. *Historia Ecclesiastica.* Patrologia Graeca 67.

Statuta Ecclesiae Antiqua. Edited by Charles Munier. *Concilia Galliae, c. 314–c. 506.* Corpus Christianorum, Series Latinorum 148. Turnhout: Brepols, 1968.

Sulpicius Severus. *Vita Martini*. Edited by Jacques Fontaine.*Sulpice Sévère, Vie de saint Martin*. Sources Chrétienne 133–134. Paris: Éditions du Cerf, 1967.

Theodoret. *Historia Ecclesiastica*. Patrologia Graeca 82.

Theoderici regis edictum Symmacho papae directum contra sacerdotes substantiae ecclesiarum alienatores A. 508. Edited by Georg Heinrich Pertz. Monumenta Germaniae Historica, Leges 5. Hanover: Hahn, 1875–1889.

Theodorus Lector. *Excerpta ex Historia Ecclesiastica*. Patrologia Graeca 86.

Theodosius. *Sirmondian Constitution*. Edited by Theodor Mommsen and Paul M. Meyer. *Theodosiani libri XVI cum constitutionibus Sirmondianis et Leges novellae ad Theodosianum pertinentes*. Berlin: Weidmann, 1905. Edited by Y. Lassard and A. Koptev. *Constitutiones Sirmondianae, The Sirmondian Constitutions (AD 333–425)*. The Roman Law Library. https://droitromain.univ-grenoble-alpes.fr.

Theophanes. *Chronographia*. Edited by Carl de Boor. Bonn: Teubner, 1883. Translated by Cyril A. Mango and Roger Scott. *The Chronicle of Theophanes the Confessor: Byzantine and Near Eastern History, AD 284–813*. Oxford: Oxford University Press, 1997.

Valentinian III. *Novelae*. Edited by Theodor Mommsen and Paul M. Meyer. *Theodosiani libri XVI cum constitutionibus Sirmondianis et Leges novellae ad Theodosianum pertinentes*. Berlin: Weidmann, 1905. Edited by Y. Lassard and A. Koptev. *Leges Novellae Ad Theodosianum Pertinentes*. The Roman Law Library. https://droitromain.univ-grenoble-alpes.fr.

Varro. *De re rustica*. Edited by William D. Hooper and Harrison B. Ash. Cambridge: Harvard University Press, 1934.

Vita Clari. Acta Sanctorum der Bollandisten, Ökumenisches Heiligenlexikon. https://www.heiligenlexikon.de/ASJanuar/Clarus_von_Vienne.html

Vita Desiderii Cadurcae urbis. Edited by Bruno Krusch, Monumenta Germaniae Historica, Scriptores Rerum Merovingicarum 4. Hanover: Hahn, 1902. *Vita vel Actus beati Desiderii*. Edited by Keith Bate, Élizabeth Carpentier, and Georges Pon.

La Vie de saint Didier évêque de Cahors (630–655). Hagiologia, vol. 16. Turnhout: Brepols, 2021.

Vita Fructuosi. Edited by Manuel Díaz y Díaz. *La vida de San Fructuoso de Braga*. Braga: Diário do Minho, 1974.

Vitas sanctorum Patrum Emeretensium. Edited by Antonio Maya Sánchez. Corpus Christianorum, Series Latinorum 116. Turnhout: Brepols, 1992. Translated by Andrew T. Fear. *Lives of the Visigothic Fathers*. Liverpool: Liverpool University Press, 1997.

Vita Vasii. Acta Sanctorum der Bollandisten, Ökumenisches Heiligenlexikon. https://www.heiligenlexikon.de/ActaSanctorum/ 16.April.html.

Vita Walarici. Edited by Bruno Krusch. Monumenta Germaniae Historica, Scriptores Rerum Merovingicarum 4. Hanover: Hahn, 1902.

Secondary

Addison, David. "Property and 'Publicness': Bishops and Lay-founded Churches in Post-Roman Hispania." *Early Medieval Europe* 28, no. 2 (2020): 175–96. DOI: 10.1111/emed.12392.

Allen, Pauline, and Bronwen Neil. *Crisis Management in Late Antiquity (410–590 CE): A Survey of the Evidence from Episcopal Letters*. Vigiliae Christianae Supplement 121. Boston and Leiden: Brill, 2013. DOI: 10.1163/9789004254824.

Anderson, Mark Alan. "Hospitals, Hospices and Shelters for the Poor in Late Antiquity." PhD diss., Yale University, 2012.

Appadurai, Arjun, and Carol Appadurai Breckenridge. "The South Indian Temple: Authority, Honour and Redistribution." *Contributions to Indian Sociology* 10, no. 2 (1976): 187–211. DOI: 10.1177/006996677601000201.

Armelini, Mariano. *Le chiese di Roma dal secolo IV al XIX*. Rome: Tipografia Vaticana, 1891.

Atsma, Hartmut. "Les monastères urbains du Nord de la Gaule." *Revue d'Histoire de l'Église de France* 62 (1976): 163–87. DOI: 10.3406/rhef.1976.1572.

Banaji, Jairus. *Agrarian Change in Late Antiquity: Gold, Labour, and Aristocratic Dominance*. Oxford: Oxford University Press, 2001.

———. *Exploring the Economy of Late Antiquity, Selected Essays*. Cambridge: Cambridge University Press, 2016.

Barnes, Timothy. *Athanasius and Constantius: Theology and Politics in the Constantinian Empire*. Cambridge: Harvard University Press, 1993.

Barnish, Samuel J. B. "Transformation and Survival in the Western Senatorial Aristocracy, c. A.D. 400–700." *Papers of the British School at Rome* 56 (1988): 120–55. DOI: 10.1017/S0068246200009582.

Berlière, Ursmer. "Les nombres des moines dans les anciens monastères." *Revue Bénédictine* 41 (1929): 231–61. DOI: 10.1484/J.RB.4.01919; 42 (1930): 19–42. DOI: 10.1484/J.RB.4.04783.

Bowman, Alan K. *Egypt after the Pharaohs 332 BC–AD 642*. London: British Museum, 1986.

Brandenburg, Hugo. *Ancient Churches of Rome from the Fourth to the Seventh Century*. Turnhout: Brepols, 2004.

Brandes, Wolfram. "Byzantinischer Bilderstreit, das Papsttum und die Pippinische Schenkung. Neue Forschungen zum Ost-West Verhältnis im 8. Jahrhundert." In *Menschen, Bilder, Spracher, Dinge. Wege der Kommunikation zwischen Byzanz und dem Westen*, Vol. 2: *Menschen und Worte*, edited by Falko Daim, Christian Gastgeber, Dominik Heher, and Claudia Rapp, 63–79. Mainz: Verlag des Römisch-Germanischen Zentralmuseums, 2018.

———. "Das Schweigen des *Liber pontificalis*. Die 'Enteignung' der päpstlichen Patrimonen Siziliens und Unteritaliens in der 50er Jahren des 8. Jahrhunderts." In *Fontes Minores* 12, edited by Wolfram Brandes, Lars Hoffmann, and Kirill Maksimovič, 97–203. Frankfurt: Löwenklau-Gesellschaft, 2014.

Brassous, Laurent. "Late Roman Spain." In *The Visigothic Kingdom: the Negotiations of Power in Post-Roman Iberia*, edited by Sabine Panzram and Paulo Pachá, 39–55. Amsterdam:

Amsterdam University Press, 2020. DOI: 10.2307/j.ctv1c5c-s6z.6.

Brown, Peter. *Augustine of Hippo: A Biography*. London: Faber & Faber, 1967.

———. "From *Patriae Amator* to *Amator Pauperum* and Back Again: Social Imagination and Social Change in the West between Late Antiquity and the Early Middle Ages." In *Cultures in Motion*, edited by Daniel T. Rodgers, Bhavani Raman, and Helmut Reimitz, 87–106. Princeton: Princeton University Press, 2014. DOI: 10.1515/9781400849895-005.

———. *Poverty and Leadership in the Late Roman Empire*. Lebanon: University Press of New England, 2002.

———. *Power and Persuasion in Late Antiquity: Towards a Christian Empire*. Madison: University of Wisconsin Press, 1992.

———. *Society and the Holy in Late Antiquity*. London: Faber and Faber, 1982.

———. *The Ransom of the Soul: Afterlife and Wealth in Early Western Christianity*. Cambridge: Harvard University Press, 2015.

———. *The Rise of Western Christendom: Triumph and Diversity, A.D. 200–1000*. Anniversary edition. Oxford: Oxford University Press, 2013.

———. *Through the Eye of a Needle: Wealth, the Fall of Rome, and the Making of Christianity in the West, 350–550 AD*. Princeton: Princeton University Press, 2012.

———. *Treasure in Heaven: The Holy Poor in Early Christianity*. Charlottesville: University of Virginia, 2016.

Brown, Thomas S. *Gentlemen and Officers: Imperial Administration and Aristocratic Power in Byzantine Italy, A.D. 554–800*. Rome: British School at Rome, 1984.

———. "The Church of Ravenna and the Imperial Administration in the Seventh Century." *English Historical Review* 94, no. 370 (1979): 1–28. DOI: 10.1093/ehr/XCIV.CCCLXX.1.

Bruce-Mitford, Rupert. "The Art of the *Codex Amiatinus*." *Journal of the British Archaeological Association,* 3rd ser., 32 (1969): 1–25. DOI: 10.1080/00681288.1969.11894883.

Bullough, Donald. "Early Medieval Social Groupings: The Terminology of Kinship." *Past and Present* 45 (1969): 3–18. DOI: 10.1093/past/45.1.3.

Burdeau, François. "L'administration des fonds patrimoniaux et emphytéotiques au bas-empire romain." *Revue internationale des droits d'antiquité* 20 (1975): 285–310.

Cabrol, Fernand, and Henri Leclercq. *Dictionnaire d'archéologie chrétienne et de liturgie.* Volume 10. Paris: Letouzey et Ané, 1931.

Calvet-Marcadé, Gaëlle. *Assassin des pauvres: l'église et l'inaliénabilité des terres à l'époque carolingienne.* Turnhout: Brepols, 2019. DOI: 10.1484/M.HAMA-EB.5.114497.

Caner, Daniel. "Towards a Miraculous Economy: Christian Gifts and Material 'Blessings' in Late Antiquity." *Journal of Early Christian Studies* 14, no. 3 (2006): 329–77. DOI: https://doi:10.1353/earl.2006.0048.

Carrié, Jean-Michel. "Les distributions alimentaires dans les cités de l'empire romain tardif." *Mélanges de l'École française de Rome* 87, no. 2 (1975): 995–1101. DOI: 10.3406/mefr.1975.5461.

———. "Pratique et idéologie chrétiennes de l'économique (IVᵉ–VIᵉ siècles)." *Antiquité Tardive* 14 (2006): 17–26. DOI: 10.1484/J.AT.2.302417.

Castellanos, Santiago. "The Political Nature of Taxation in Visigothic Spain." *Early Medieval Europe* 12, no. 3 (2003): 201–28. DOI: 10.1111/j.0963-9462.2004.00127.x.

Castillo Maldonado, Pedro. "*In hora mortis*: deceso, duelo, rapiña y legado en la muerte del obispo visigótico." *Hispania Sacra* 64 (2012): 7–28. DOI: 10.3989/hs.2012.001.

Castro, Dolores, and Michael J. Kelly. "Isidore's *Sententiae,* the *Liber Iudiciorum,* and Paris BnF Lat. 4667." *Visigothic Symposium* 4 (2020–2021): 144–68.

Chandler, Tertius, and Gerald Fox. *Three Thousand Years of Urban Growth.* New York: Academic Press, 1974.

Charles-Edwards, Thomas. "The Distinction Between Land and Moveable Wealth in Anglo-Saxon England." In *Medieval Settlement: Continuity and Change,* edited by Peter Sawyer, 180–87. London: Edward Arnold, 1976.

Chavarría Arnau, Alexandra. "Churches as Assembly Places in Early Medieval Italy." In *Power and Place in Europe in the Early Middle Ages,* edited by Jayne Carroll, Andrew Reynolds and Barbara Yorke, 203–15. Oxford: Oxford University Press, 2019. DOI: 10.5871/bacad/9780197266588.003.0009.

———. "¿Quanto costaba construir una iglesia tardoantigua?" In *Academica Libertas. Essais en l'honneur du Professeur Javier Arce,* edited by Dominic Moreau and Raúl González Salinero, 345–52. Turnhout: Brepols, 2020.

Christie, Neil. *The Lombards: The Ancient Langobards.* Oxford: Blackwell, 1995.

Clark-Decès, Isabelle. "Towards an Anthropology of Exchange in Tamil Nadu." *International Journal of Hindu Studies* 22 (2018): 197–215. DOI: 10.1007/s11407-018-9231-7.

Claussen, Martin A. T*he Reform of the Frankish Church. Chrodegang of Metz and the "Regula Canonicorum" in the Eighth Century.* Cambridge: Cambridge University Press, 2004.

Connolly, Serena. *Lives Behind the Laws: the World of the "Codex Hermogenianus."* Bloomington: Indiana University Press, 2010.

Cooper, Kate. "Property, Power and Conflict: Rethinking the Constantinian Revolution." In *Making Early Medieval Societies: Conflict and Belonging in the Latin West, 300–1200,* edited by Kate Cooper and Conrad Leyser, 16–32. Cambridge: Cambridge University Press, 2016. DOI: 10.1017/CBO9781316481714.003.

Courtois, Christian. *Les vandales et l'Afrique.* Paris: Arts et Métiers Graphiques, 1954.

Cracco Ruggini, Lellia. *Economia e società nell' "Italia annonaria": Rapporti fra agricoltura e commercio dal IV al VI secolo d.C.* Milan: A. Giuffre, 1961.

Curran, John. *Pagan City and Christian Capital: Rome in the Fourth Century.* Oxford: Clarendon, 2000.

Davies, Wendy. *An Early Welsh Microcosm: Studies in the Llandaff Charters.* London: Royal Historical Society, 1978.

———. "Economic Change in Early Medieval Ireland: the Case for Growth." In *L'Irlanda e gli Irlandesi nell'alto Medioevo:*

Spoleto, 16–21 aprile 2009, Settimane di studio del Centro italiano di studi sull'alto medioevo 57, 111–32. Spoleto: Centro italiano di studi sull'alto medioevo, 2010.

Davies, Wendy, and Paul Fouracre, eds. *Languages of Gift in the Early Middle Ages.* Cambridge: Cambridge University Press, 2010.

———, eds. *The Settlement of Disputes in Early Medieval Europe.* Cambridge: Cambridge University Press, 1986.

Davis, Raymond. *The Book of the Pontiffs (to A.D. 715).* Liverpool: Liverpool University Press, 1989.

Devroey, Jean Pierre. *Économie rurale et société dans l'Europe franque (VIᵉ–IXᵉ siècles), 1: Fondements matériels, échanges et lien social.* Paris: Belin, 2003.

———. "Elaboration et usage des polyptyques. Quelques éléments de réflexion à partir de l'exemple des descriptions de l'Église de Marseille (VIIIᵉ–IXᵉ siècles)." In *Akkulturation: Probleme einer germanisch-romanischen Kultursynthese in Spätantike und frühem Mittelalter,* edited by Dieter Hägermann, Wolfgang Haubrichs, and Jörg Jarnut, 436–72. Berlin: De Gruyter, 2004.

Díaz, Pablo C. "El testamento de Vicente: proprietarios y dependientes en la Hispania del s. VI." In *"Romanización" y "Reconquista" en la península Ibérica: nuevas perspectivas,* edited by María José Hidalgo de la Vega, Dionisio Pérez, and Manuel J. Rodríguez Gervás, 257–70. Salamanca: Universidad de Salamanca, 1998.

———. "Visigothic Political Institutions." In *The Visigoths from the Migration Period to the Seventh Century: An Ethnographic Perspective,* edited by Peter Heather, 321–73. Woodbridge: The Boydell Press, 1999.

Diefenbach, Steffen. "'Bischofsherrschaft': Zur Transformation der politischen Kultur im spätantiken und frühmittelalterlichen Gallien." In *Gallien in Spätantike und Frühmittelalter: Kulturgeschichte einer Region,* edited by Steffen Diefenbach and Michael Gernot Müller, 91–149. Berlin: De Gruyter, 2013. DOI: 10.1515/9783110260779.91.

Dodds, E.R. *Pagan and Christian in an Age of Anxiety: Some Aspects of Religious Experience from Marcus Aurelius to Constantinus.* Cambridge: Cambridge University Press, 1965. DOI: 10.1017/CBO9780511583582.

Duchesne, Louis. *Fastes épiscopaux de l'ancienne Gaule,* 3 volumes. Paris: Fontemoing, 1894–1915.

———. "Les évêchés d'Italie et l'invasion lombarde." *Mélanges d'Archéologie et d'Histoire de l'École française de Rome* 23 (1903): 83–116; 25 (1905): 365–99. DOI: 10.3406/mefr.1903.6292.

Dudden, F. Homes. *Gregory the Great: His Place in History and Thought.* Oxford: Longmans, Green, and Company, 1905.

Durliat, Jean. *De l'Antiquité au Moyen Âge. L'Occident de 313–800.* Lyon: Ellipses, 2002.

———. "Les attributions civiles des évêques mérovingiens: l'exemple de Didier, évêque de Cahors (630–655)." *Annales du Midi* 91, no. 143 (1979): 237–54. DOI: 10.3406/anami.1979.1762.

Eisenberg, Merle, and Paolo Tedesco. "Seeing the Churches Like the State: Taxes and Wealth Redistribution in Late Antique Italy." *Early Medieval Europe* 29, no. 4 (2021): 505–34. DOI: 10.1111/emed.12500.

Esders, Stefan. "'Because Their Patron Never Dies': Ecclesiastical Freedmen, Socio-Religious Interaction, and Group Formation under the Aegis of 'Church Property' in the Early Medieval West (Sixth to Eleventh Centuries)." *Early Medieval Europe* 29, no. 4 (2021): 555–85. DOI: 10.1111/emed.12497.

———. *Die Formierung der Zensualität.* Ostfildern: Thorbecke, 2010.

Ewig, Eugen. "Milo et eiusmodi similes." In *Spätantikes und fränkisches Gallien,* vol. 2, 189–219. Munich: Artemis, 1979.

Fernández, Damián. "Property, Social Status and Church Building in Visigothic Iberia." *Journal of Late Antiquity* 9, no. 2 (2016): 512–41. DOI: 10.1353/jla.2016.0022.

———. "What Is the *de fisco Barcinonensi* About?" *Antiquité Tardive* 14 (2006): 217–24. DOI: 10.1484/J.AT.2.302430.

Ferngren, Gary B. *Medicine and Health Care in Early Christianity.* Baltimore: Johns Hopkins University Press, 2009.

Filson, Floyd V. "Ancient Greek Synagogue Inscriptions." *The Biblical Archaeologist* 32, no. 2 (1969): 41–46. DOI: 10.2307/3210988.

Fita, Fidel. "Patrología visigótica. Elpidio, Pompeyano, Vicente y Gabino, obispos de Huesca en el siglo VI." *Boletín de la Real Academia de la Historia* 49 (1906): 137–69.

Fogel, Joshua A. "The Debates over the Asiatic Mode of Production in Soviet Russia, China and Japan." *The American Historical Review* 93, no. 1 (1988): 56–79. DOI: 10.2307/1865689.

Foster, Benjamin. "A New Look at the Sumerian Temple State." *Journal of the Economic and Social History of the Orient* 24, no. 3 (1981): 225–41. DOI: 10.2307/3631906.

Fouracre, Paul. *Eternal Light and Earthly Concerns: Belief and the Shaping of Medieval Society.* Manchester: Manchester University Press, 2021. DOI: 10.7765/9781526113993.

———. "Eternal Light and Earthly Needs: Practical Aspects of the Development of Frankish Immunities." In *Property and Power in the Early Middle Ages,* edited by Wendy Davies and Paul Fouracre, 53–81. Cambridge: Cambridge University Press, 1995. DOI: 10.1017/CBO9780511628665.005.

———. "Framing and Lighting: Another Angle on Transition." In *Italy and Early Medieval Europe,* edited by Ross Balzaretti, Julia Barrow, and Patricia Skinner, 305–14. Oxford: Oxford University Press, 2018.

———. "Lights, Power and the Moral Economy of Early Medieval Europe." *Early Medieval Europe* 28, no. 3 (2020): 367–87. DOI: 10.1111/emed.12409.

———. "Merovingian History and Merovingian Hagiography." *Past and Present* 127 (1990): 3–38. DOI: 10.1093/past/127.1.3.

———. *The Age of Charles Martel.* Harlow: Longman, 2000.

———. "The Use of the Term *beneficium* in the Frankish Sources: A Society Based on Favours." In *The Languages of Gift in the Early Middle Ages,* edited by Wendy Davies and Paul Fouracre, 62–88. Cambridge: Cambridge University Press, 2010.

———. "Why Were So Many Bishops Killed in Merovingian Francia?" In *Bischofsmord im Mittelalter,* edited by Natalie

Fryde and Dirk Reitz, 13–35. Göttingen: Vandenhoeck und Ruprecht, 2003.

Fouracre, Paul, and Richard Gerberding. *Late Merovingian France: History and Hagiography 640–720.* Manchester: Manchester University Press, 1996.

Fox, Yaniv. *Power and Religion in Merovingian Gaul: Columbanian Monasticism and the Frankish Elites.* Cambridge: Cambridge University Press, 2014. DOI: 10.1017/CBO9781107587649.

Ganz, David. "The Ideology of Sharing: Apostolic Community and Ecclesiastical Property in the Early Middle Ages." In *Property and Power in the Early Middle Ages,* edited Wendy Davies and Paul Fouracre, 17–30. Cambridge: Cambridge University Press, 1995. DOI: 10.1017/CBO9780511628665.003.

García Iglesias, Luis. "Las posesiones de la iglesia emeritense en época visigoda." In *Gerión. Estudios sobre la Antigüedad en homenaje al Profesor Santiago Montero Díaz, Anejos de Gerión* 2 (1989): 391–401.

García Moreno, Luis. "Los monjes y monasterios en las ciudades de las Españas tardorromanas y visigodas." *Habis* 24 (1993): 179–92.

García Sanjuán, Alejandro. *Till God Inherits the Earth: Islamic Pious Endowments in Al-Andalus (9–15th centuries).* Boston and Leiden: Brill, 2007. DOI: 10.1163/ej.9789004153585.i-549.

Gasnault, Pierre. "Deux nouveaux documents comptables de l'époque mérovingienne." *Bulletin de la Société Nationale des Antiquaires de France* (1989): 164–65. DOI: 10.3406/bsnaf.1991.9480.

———. "Deux nouveaux feuillets de la comptabilité domaniale de l'abbaye Saint-Martin de Tours à l'époque mérovingienne." *Journal des Savants* 2 (1995): 307–9. DOI: 10.3406/jds.1995.1591.

———. *Documents comptables de Saint-Martin de Tours à l'époque mérovingienne.* Paris: Bibliotheque Nationale, 1975.

———. "Nouveaux fragments de la comptabilité mérovingienne de Saint-Martin de Tours." *Comptes rendues des séances l'Académie des Inscriptions et Belles Lettres* 133, no. 2 (1989): 371–72. DOI: 10.3406/crai.1989.14734.

Gasparri, Stefano. "Il regno longobardo in Italia. Struttura e funzionamento di uno stato altomedievale." In *Il regno dei Longobardi in Italia. Archeologia, società e istituzioni*, edited by Stefano Gasparri, 1–88. Spoleto: Centro italiano di studi sull'Alto Medioevo, 2004.

Gaudemet, Jean. *L'Église dans l'empire romain (IVe–Ve siècles).* Paris: Sirey, 1958.

Geary, Patrick J. *Aristocracy in Provence: The Rhône Basin at the Dawn of the Carolingian Age.* Stuttgart: Hiersemann, 1985.

Giardina, Andrea. "Carità eversiva. Le donazioni di Melania la Giovane e gli equilibri della società tardoantica." In *Hestiasis. Studi di tarda antichità offerti a Salvatore Calderone*, 77–102. Messina: Sicania, 1986.

———. "Carità eversiva. Le donazioni di Melania la Giovane e gli equilibri della società tardoromana." *Studi storici: Rivista trimestrale* 29, no. 1 (1988): 127–42.

Godding, Robert. *Prêtres en Gaule mérovingienne.* Brussels: Sociétè des Bollandistes, 2001.

Goffart, Walter. *The Le Mans Forgeries: A Chapter from the History of Church Property from the Ninth Century.* Harvard Historical Studies 76. Cambridge: Harvard University Press, 1966.

Goodrich, Richard. *Contextualizing Cassian: Aristocrats, Asceticism, and Reformation in Fifth-Century Gaul.* Oxford: Oxford University Press, 2007. DOI: 10.1093/acprof:oso/9780199213139.001.0001.

Guérout, Jean. "Le testament de sainte Fare: Matériaux pour l'étude et l'édition critique de ce document." *Revue d'histoire ecclésiastique* 60, no. 3 (1965): 761–821.

Guidobaldi, Federico. "'Topografia ecclesiastica' di Roma (IV–VII) secolo." In *Roma dall'antichita al medioevo: Archeologia e storia*, edited by Maria Stella Arena, Paolo Delogu, Lidia Paroli, Marco Ricci, Lucia Sagui, and Laura Vendittelli, 40–51. Volume 1. Milan: Electa, 2001.

Hachlili, Rachel. *Ancient Synagogues — Archaeology and Art: New Discoveries and Current Research*. Boston and Leiden: Brill, 2013. DOI: 10.1163/9789004257726.

Haensch, Rudolf. "Le financement de la construction des églises pendant l'Antiquité tardive et l'évergétisme antique." *Antiquité Tardive* 14 (2006): 47–58. DOI: 10.1484/J.AT.2.302420.

Haldon, John. *Byzantium in the Seventh Century: The Transformation of a Culture*. Cambridge: Cambridge University Press, 1990. DOI: 10.1017/CBO9780511582318.

———. "Mode of Production, Social Action, and Historical Change: Some Questions and Issues." In *Studies on Pre-Capitalist Modes of Production*, edited by Laura da Graca and Andrea Zingarelli, 204–36. Boston and Leiden: Brill, 2015. DOI: 10.1163/9789004263703_008.

———. "*Synônê*: Reconsidering a Problematic Term of Middle Byzantine Fiscal Administration." *Byzantine and Modern Greek Studies* 18 (1994): 116–53. DOI: 10.1179/byz.1994.18.1.116.

———. *The State and the Tributary Mode of Production*. London: Verso, 1993.

Halfond, Gregory. *Bishops and the Politics of Patronage in Merovingian Gaul*. Ithaca: Cornell University Press, 2019. DOI: 10.7591/9781501739323.

Hallam, Henry. *Supplemental Notes to the View of the State of Europe during the Middle Ages*. London: J. Murray, 1848.

Harries, Jill. *Sidonius Apollinaris and the Fall of Rome, AD 407–485*. Oxford: Oxford University Press, 1994.

Head, Peter M. "Some Recently Published NT Papyri from Oxyrhynchus: An Overview and Preliminary Assessment." *Tyndale Bulletin* 51, no. 1 (2000): 1–16.

Heinzelmann, Martin. *Bischofsherrschaft in Gallien*. Munich: Artemis, 1976.

Hen, Yitzhak. *The Royal Patronage of the Liturgy in Frankish Gaul: To the Death of Charles the Bald (877)*. Woodbridge: Boydell, 2001.

Herlihy, David. "Church Property on the Continent, 700–1200." *Speculum* 36, no. 1 (1961): 81–105. DOI: 10.2307/2849846.

Herzog, Roman. *Staaten der Frühzeit: Ursprünge und Heer-schaftsformen.* Munich: Beck, 1998.

Hillner, Julia. "Families, Patronage, and the Titular Churches of Rome, c. 300-c. 600." In *Religion, Dynasty and Patronage in Early Christian Rome, 300-900,* edited by Kate Cooper and Julia Hillner, 225-61. Cambridge: Cambridge University Press, 2007. DOI: 10.1017/CBO9780511482731.009.

Horden, Peregrine. "Public Health, Hospitals and Charity," forthcoming.

Humfress, Caroline. "Bishops and Law Courts in Late Antiq-uity: How (Not) to Make Sense of the Legal Evidence." *Jour-nal of Early Christian Studies* 19, no. 3 (2011): 375-400. DOI: 10.1353/earl.2011.0033.

Humphries, Mark. "Emperors, Usurpers and the City of Rome: Performing Power from Diocletian to Theodosius." In *Con-tested Monarchy: Integrating the Roman Empire in the Fourth Century AD,* edited by Johannes Wienand, 151-68. Oxford: Oxford University Press, 2015.

———. "*In nomine Patris*: Constantine the Great and Constan-tius II in Christological Polemic." *Historia: Zeitschrift für Alte Geschichte* 46, no. 4 (1997): 448-64.

———. "Narrative and Subversion: Exemplary Rome and Im-perial Misrule in Ammianus Marcellinus." In *Some Organic Readings in Narrative: Ancient and Modern,* edited by Ian Redpath and Fritz-Gregor Hermann, 233-54. Groningen: Eelde & Barkhuis, 2019.

Hunt, David. "The Church as a Public Institution." In *The Late Empire A.D. 337-425,* edited by Averil Cameron and Peter Garnsey, 238-76. The Cambridge Ancient History 13. Cam-bridge: Cambridge University Press, 1998.

Inowlocki, Sabrina. "Eusebius of Caesarea's *Interpretatio Chris-tiana* of Philo's *De vita contemplativa*." *Harvard Theo-logical Review* 97, no. 3 (2004): 305-28. DOI: 10.1017/S0017816004000720.

Janes, Dominic. *God and Gold in Late Antiquity.* Cambridge: Cambridge University Press, 1998. DOI: 10.2307/3170872.

Jenal, Georg. *Italia ascetica atque monastica: das Asketen- und Mönchtum in Italien von den Anfängen bis zur Zeit der Langobarden (ca. 150/250–604),* 2 volumes. Stuttgart: Hiersemann, 1995.

Jones, A.H.M. "Church Finance in the Fifth and Sixth Centuries." *Journal of Theological Studies* 11, no. 3 (1960): 84–94. DOI: 10.1093/jts/XI.1.84.

———. *The Later Roman Empire 284–602.* Oxford: Blackwell, 1964.

Jones, A.H.M., Philip Grierson, and J.A. Crook. "The Authenticity of the 'Testamentum sancti Remigii.'" *Revue belge de Philologie et d'Histoire* 35, no. 2 (1957): 356–73. DOI: 10.3406/rbph.1957.2035.

Jussen, Bernhard. "Über 'Bischofsherrschaften' und die Prozeduren politisch-sozialer Umordnung in Gallien zwischen 'Antike' und 'Mittelalter.'" *Historische Zeitschrift* 260 (1995): 673–718. DOI: 10.1524/hzhz.1995.260.jg.673.

Kaiser, Reinhold. *Bischofsherrschaft zwischen Königtum und Fürstenmacht. Studien zur bischöflichen Stadtherrschaft im westfränkisch-französischen Reich im frühen und hohen Mittelalter.* Pariser historische Studien, vol. 17. Bonn: Röhrscheid 1981.

Kanaka Durga, P.S., and Y.A. Sudhakar Reddy. "Kings, Temples and Legitimation of Autochthonous Communities: A Case Study of a South Indian Temple." *Journal of the Economic and Social History of the Orient* 35, no. 2 (1992): 145–66. DOI: 10.1163/156852092X00084.

Kelly, Michael J. "Recceswinth's *Liber Iudiciorum*: History, Narrative and Meaning." *Visigothic Symposium* 1 (2017): 110–30.

———. "The *Liber Iudiciorum*: A Visigothic Literary Guide to Institutional Authority and Self-Interest." In *The Visigothic Kingdom: The Negotiation of Power in Post-Roman Iberia,* edited by Paulo Pachá and Sabine Panzram, 257–72. Amsterdam: Amsterdam University Press, 2020. DOI: 10.2307/j.ctv1c5cs6z.17.

King, P.D. *Law and Society in the Visigothic Kingdom.* Cambridge: Cambridge University Press, 1972.

Klauser, Theodor. "Eine Stationsliste der Metzer Kirche aus dem 8. Jahrhunderts, wahrscheinlich ein Werk Chrodegangs." *Ephemerides Liturgicae* 44 (1930): 162–93.

Klingshirn, William. *Caesarius of Arles: The Making of a Christian Community in Late Antique Gaul.* Cambridge Studies in Medieval Life and Thought, 4th series, 22. Cambridge: Cambridge University Press, 1994. DOI: 10.3828/978-0-85323-368-8.

———. "Charity and Power: Caesarius of Arles and the Ransoming of Captives in Sub-Roman Gaul." *Journal of Roman Studies* 75 (1983): 183–203. DOI: 10.2307/300659.

Koon, Sam, and Jamie Wood. "Unity from Disunity: Law, Rhetoric, and Power in the Visigothic Kingdom." *European Review of History* 16, no. 6 (2009): 793–808. DOI: 10.1080/13507480903368061.

Lansford, Tyler. *The Latin Inscriptions of Rome: A Walking Guide.* Baltimore: Johns Hopkins University Press, 2009.

Latham, Jacob A. "From Literal to Spiritual Soldiers of Christ: Disputed Episcopal Elections and the Advent of Christian Processions in Late Antique Rome." *Church History* 81, no. 2 (2012): 298–327. DOI: 10.1017/S0009640712000613.

Leader-Newby, Ruth. *Silver and Society in Late Antiquity: Functions and Meanings of Silver Plate in the Fourth to Seventh Centuries.* Aldershot: Ashgate, 2004.

Lenski, Noel. "Captivity and Romano-Barbarian Interchange." In *Romans, Barbarians and the Transformation of the Roman World,* edited by Ralph Mathisen and Danuta Shanzer, 185–98. Farnham: Ashgate, 2011.

Leone, Anna. *Changing Townscapes in North Africa from Late Antiquity to the Arab Conquest.* Bari: Edipuglia, 2007.

Lesne, Émile. *Histoire de la propriété ecclésiastique en France,* vol. 1: *Époques romaine et mérovingienne.* Lille: R. Giard, 1910.

Levison, Wilhelm. "Das Testament Diakons Adalgisel-Grimo vom Jahre 634." *Trierer Zeitschrift* 7 (1932): 69–80.

Leyser, Conrad. "Augustine in the Latin West, 430–c.900." In *A Companion to Augustine,* edited by Mark Vessey, 456–60.

Malden: Wiley-Blackwell, 2012. DOI: 10.1002/9781118255483. ch34.

———. *Authority and Asceticism from Augustine to Gregory the Great.* Oxford: Clarendon, 2000.

———. "*Homo pauper, de pauperibus natum*: Augustine, Church Property, and the Cult of Stephen." *Augustinian Studies* 36, no. 1 (2005): 229–37. DOI: 10.5840/augstudies200536116.

———. "Through the Eyes of a Deacon: Lesser Clergy, Major Donors, and Institutional Property in Fifth-Century Rome." *Early Medieval Europe* 29, no. 4 (2021): 487–504. DOI: 10.1111/emed.12502.

Leyser, Karl. "Maternal Kin in Early-Medieval Germany: A Reply." *Past and Present* 49 (1970): 126–34. DOI: 10.1093/past/49.1.126.

Liebeschuetz, J.H.W.G. "Transformation and Decline: Are the Two Really Incompatible?" In *Die Stadt in der Spätantike: Niedergang oder Wandel,* edited by Jens-Uwe Krause and Christian Witschel, 463–83. Stuttgart: Steiner, 2006.

Lifshitz, Baruch. *Donateurs et fondateurs dans les synagogues juives: répertoire des dédicaces grecques relatives à la construction et à la réfection des synagogues.* Paris: Gabalda, 1967.

Liverani, Paolo. "Osservazioni sul Libellus delle donazioni Costantiniane nel *Liber Pontificalis.*" *Athenaeum* 107 (2019): 169–217.

Lizzi Testa, Rita. *Vescovi e strutture ecclesiastiche nella città tardoantica: l'Italia Annonaria nel IV–V secolo d.C.* Como: Edizioni New Press, 1989.

Llewellyn, Peter. *Rome in the Dark Ages.* London: Constable, 1971.

López Quiroga, Jorge. "El I y II Concilios de Braga y el 'Parroquial Suevo'. Élites eclesiásticas y control del territorio en la Gallaecia del siglo VI." In *In tempore Sueborum: el tiempo de los suevos en la Gallaecia (411–585), el primo reino medieval de occidente. Volumen de estudios,* edited by Jorge López Quiroga, 139–44. Ourense: Deputación Provincial de Ourense, 2018.

———. "Monasterios altomedievales hispanos: lugares de emplazamiento y ordenación de sus espacios." In *Los monasterios medievales en sus emplazamientos: lugares de memoria de lo sagrado,* edited by José Ángel García de Cortázar and Ramón Teja, 66–99. Aguilar de Campoo: Fundación Santa María la Real, Centro de Estudios del Románico, 2016.

Loseby, Simon. "Decline and Change in the Cities of Late Antique Gaul." In *Die Stadt in der Spätantike — Niedergang oder Wandel?,* edited by Jens-Uwe Krause and Christian Witschel, 67–104. Stuttgart: Steiner, 2006.

———. "Marseille and the Pirenne Thesis II: Ville morte." In *The Long Eighth Century: Production, Distribution and Demand,* edited by Inge Lise Hansen and Chris Wickham, 167–93. Boston and Leiden: Brill, 2000. DOI: 10.1163/9789004473454_010.

Loth, Julien, ed. *Histoire de l'abbaye royale de St-Pierre de Jumièges.* Rouen: Société de l'Histoire Normandie, 1882.

Magnou-Nortier, Elisabeth. *Aux origines de la fiscalité moderne: le système fiscal et sa gestion dans le royaume des Francs à l'épreuve des sources (V^e–XIe siècles).* Geneve: Droz, 2012.

Marazzi, Federico. *I "patrimonia sanctae Romanae ecclesiae" nel Lazio (secoli IV–X).* Rome: Nella Sede Dell'Istituto Palazzo Borromini, 1998.

Markus, Robert A. *Gregory the Great and His World.* Cambridge: Cambridge University Press, 2010.

Martínez Tejera, Artemio. "Monasticism in Late Antique Iberia: Its Origins and Influences." *Visigothic Symposium* 2 (2017–2018): 176–94.

Mathisen, Ralph. "Ricimer's church in Rome: How an Arian Barbarian Prospered in a Nicene World." In *The Power of Religion in Late Antiquity,* edited by Noel Lenski and Andrew Cain, 307–25. Farnham: Ashgate, 2009.

Maiuro, Marco. "Archivi, amministrazione del patrimonio e proprietà imperiali nel *Liber Pontificalis.* La redazione del Libellus imperiale copiato nell *Vita Silvestri.*" In *La proprietà imperiali nell'Italia romana. Economia, produzione, amministrazione,* edited by Daniela Pupillo, 235–58. Florence: Le lettere, 2007.

McCormick, Michael. *Charlemagne's Survey of the Holy Land: Wealth, Personnel, and Buildings of a Mediterranean Church between Antiquity and the Middle Ages.* Washington, DC: Dumbarton Oaks Research Library and Collection, 2011.

———. *Origins of the European Economy: Communications and Commerce AD 300–900.* Cambridge: Cambridge University Press, 2001.

McKitterick, Rosamond. *Rome and the Invention of the Papacy: The "Liber Pontificalis."* Cambridge: Cambridge University Press, 2020. DOI: 10.1017/9781108872584.

McLynn, Neil B. "Administrator: Augustine in His Diocese." In *A Companion to Augustine,* edited by Mark Vessey, 310–22. Malden: Wiley-Blackwell, 2012. DOI: 10.1002/9781118255483.ch24.

———. "Augustine's Black Sheep: The Case of Antoninus of Fussala." In *Istituzioni, Carismi ed Esercizio del Potere (IV–VI secolo d.C.),* edited by Giorgio Bonamente and Rita Lizzi Testa, 305–21. Bari: Edipulgia, 2010.

Miguel Franco, Ruth. "Braulio de Zaragoza, el Rey Chindasvinto, y Eugenio de Toledo: imagen y opinión en el Epistularium de Braulio de Zaragoza." *Emerita, Revista de Lingüística y Filología Clásica* 79, no. 1 (2011): 155–76. DOI: 10.3989/emerita.2011.07.1009.

Mochi Onory, Sergio. *Vescovi e città (sec. IV–VI).* Bologna: Nicola Zanichelli, 1933.

Montinaro, Federico. "Les fausses donations de Constantin dans le *Liber Pontificalis.*" *Millennium* 12, no. 1 (2015): 203–30. DOI: 10.1515/mill-2015-0109.

Moore, Michael E. "The Ancient Fathers: Christian Antiquity, Patristics and Frankish Canon Law." *Millennium* 7, no. 1 (2010): 293–342. DOI: 10.1515/9783110223057.293.

Moreno Martín, Francisco José. *La arquitectura monástica hispana entre la Tardoantigüedad y la Alta Edad Media.* BAR, International Series 2287. Oxford: Archaeopress, 2011. DOI: 10.30861/9781407308647.

Mulryan, Michael. "A Few Thoughts on the *tituli* of Equitius and Sylvester in the Late Antique and Early Medieval

Subura in Rome." In *Religious Practices and the Christianisation of the Late Antique City (4th–7th century)*, edited by Aude Busine, 166–78. Boston and Leiden: Brill, 2015. DOI: 10.1163/9789004299047_008.

Murray, Alexander C. *Germanic Kinship Structures in Law and Society in Antiquity and the Early Middle Ages*. Turnhout: Brepols, 1983. DOI: 10.1111/j.1478-0542.2010.00720.x.

———. "Merovingian Immunity Revisited." *History Compass* 8 (2010): 913–28.

Nehring, Przemysław. "Disposal of Private Property: Theory and Practice in the Earliest Augustinian Monastic Communities." In *La vie quotidienne des moines en Orient et en Occident (IVe–Xe siècle)*, vol. 2: *Questions transversales*, edited by Olivier Delouis and Maria Mossakowska-Gaubert, 393–411. Paris: Institut français d'archéologie orientale, 2019.

———. "Literary Sources for Everyday Life of the Early Monastic Communities in North Africa." In *La vie quotidienne des moines en Orient et en Occident (IVe–Xe siècle)*, vol. 1: *L'état des sources* edited by Olivier Delouis and Maria Mossakowska-Gaubert, 325–35. Paris: Institut français d'archéologie orientale, 2015.

Neil, Bronwen. "Crisis and Wealth in Byzantine Italy: The *Libri Pontificales* of Rome and Ravenna." *Byzantion* 82 (2012): 279–303. https://www.jstor.org/stable/44173261.

———. "Imperial Benefactions to the Fifth-Century Roman Church." In *Basileia: Essays on Imperium and Culture in Honour of E.M. and M.J. Jeffreys,* edited by Geoffrey Nathan and Lynda Garland, 55–66. Sydney: University of New South Wales Press, 2011.

Neri, Valerio. *I marginali nell'Occidente tardoantico: "infames" e criminali nella nascente società cristiana*. Bari: Edipuglia, 1996.

Nicolay, Johan. *The Splendour of Power: Early Medieval Kingship and the Use of Gold and Silver in the Southern North Sea Area (5th to 7th century AD)*. Groningen: Barkhuis, 2014.

Nimmegeers, Nathanaël. "Saint-André-le-Haut des origines à 1031: approche historique." *Bulletin du centre d'études Auxerre,* Hors-série 10 (2016): n.p.

Nonn, Ulrich. "Merowingische Testamenta: Studien zum Fortleben einer römischen Urkundenform im Frankenreich." *Archiv für Diplomatik* 18 (1972): 1–129. DOI: 10.7788/afd.1972.18.jg.1.

Ó Cróinín, Dáibhí. "Hiberno-Latin literature to 1169." In *A New History of Ireland,* vol. 1: *Prehistoric and Early Ireland,* edited by Dáibhí Ó Cróinín, 371–404. Oxford: Oxford University Press, 2005.

Orlandi, Silvia. "L'epigrafia sotto il regno di Antemio." In *Procopio Antemio imperatore di Roma,* edited by Fabrizio Oppedisano, 177–97. Bari: Edipuglia, 2020.

Ozóg, Monika, and Henryk Pietras. "Il battesimo di Clodoveo e sue possibili ripercussioni in Italia alla luce del Liber Pontificalis, ossia della chiesa romana di S. Martino ai Monti." *Gregorianum* 93 (2015): 157–74.

Patlagean, Évelyne. *Pauvreté économique et pauvreté sociale à Byzance (IVᵉ–VIIᵉ siècles).* Paris: Mouton, 1977. DOI: 10.1515/9783110805192.

Patzold, Steffen. "Bischöfe, soziale Herkunft und die Organisation lokaker Herrschaft um 500." In *Chlodwigs Welt: Organisation von Herrschaft um 500,* edited by Mischa Meier and Steffen Patzold, 523–43. Stuttgart: Steiner, 2014.

———. "Zur Socialstruktur des Episkopats und zur Ausbildung bischöflicher Herrschaft in Gallien zwischen Spätantike und Frühmittelalter." In *Völker, Reiche und Namen im frühen Mittelalter,* edited by Matthias Becher and Stefanie Dick, 121–40. Mittelalterliche Studien 22. Munich: Wilhelm Fink, 2010. DOI: 10.30965/9783846748916_010.

Patzold, Steffen, and Carine van Rhijn. "The Carolingian Local Ecclesia as a 'Temple Society'?" *Early Medieval Europe* 29, no. 4 (2021): 535–54. DOI: 10.1111/emed.12496.

Pierce, Richard Holton. "Land Use, Social Organisation and Temple Economy." *RAIN* 15 (1976): 15–17. DOI: 10.2307/3032612.

Pietri, Charles. "Évergétisme et richesses ecclésiastiques dans l'Italie du IVe à la fin du Ve siècles: l'exemple romain." *Ktema: Civilisations de l'Orient, de la Grèce et de Rome Antiques* 3 (1978): 317–37. Reprinted in Charles Pietri. *Christiana respublica. Éléments d'une enquête sur le christianisme antique*, 813–33. Paris and Rome: École française de Rome, 1997. DOI: 10.3406/ktema.1978.1807.

———. *Roma Christiana: recherches sur l'Église de Rome, son organisation, sa politique, son idéologie de Miltiade à Sixte III (311–440)*, 2 volumes. Paris and Rome: École française de Rome, 1976.

Pontal, Odette. *Die Synoden im Merowingerreich*. Paderborn: Schöningh, 1986.

Pöschl, Arnold. *Bischofsgut und mensa episcopalis. Ein Beitrag zur Geschichte des kirchlichen Vermögensrechtes*, 1: *Die Grundlagen*. Bonn: P. Hanstein, 1908.

Prigent, Vivien. "Le rôle des provinces d'Occident dans l'approvisionnement de Constantinople (618–717): témoinages numismatique et sigillographique." *Mélanges de l'École française de Rome, Moyen Âge* 118, no. 2 (2006): 269–99.

———. "Les empereurs isauriens et la confiscation des patrimoines pontificaux d'Italie du Sud." *Mélanges de l'École française de Rome, Moyen Âge* 116, no. 2 (2004): 557–94.

Prinz, Friedrich. "Die bischöfliche Stadtherrschaft im Frankenreich vom 5. bis zum 7. Jahrhundert." *Historische Zeitschrift* 217, no. 1 (1973): 1–35. DOI: 10.1524/hzhz.1973.217.jg.1.

———. *Frühes Mönchtum im Frankenreich: Kultur und Gesellschaft in Gallien, den Rheinlanden und Bayern am Beispiel der monastischen Entwicklung (4.-8. Jh.)*. Kempten: Ferdinand Oechelhäuser, 1965.

Rapp, Claudia. *Holy Bishops in Late Antiquity: The Nature of Christian Leadership in an Age of Transition*. Berkeley: University of California Press, 2005. DOI: 10.1525/california/9780520242968.001.0001.

Reimitz, Helmut. "True Differences: Gregory of Tours' Account of the Council of Mâcon (585)." In *The Merowingian*

Kingdoms and the Mediterranean World: Revisiting the Sources, edited by Stefan Esders, Yitzhak Hen, Pia Lucas, and Tamar Rotman, 19–28. London: Bloomsbury, 2019. DOI: 10.5040/9781350048416.ch-002.

Richards, Jeffrey. *Consul of God: The Life and Times of Gregory the Great.* London: Routledge, 1980.

———. *The Popes and the Papacy in the Early Middle Ages, 476–752.* London: Routledge, 1979.

Richter, Michael. *Bobbio in the Early Middle Ages: The Abiding Legacy of Columbanus.* Dublin: Four Courts Press, 2008.

Ricl, Marijana. "Society and Economy of Sanctuaries in Roman Lydia and Phrygia." *Epigraphica Anatolica* 35 (2003): 77–101.

Roberto, Umberto. "La corte di Antemio e i rapporti con l'Oriente." In *Procopio Antemio imperatore di Roma,* edited by Fabrizio Oppedisano, 141–76. Bari: Edipuglia, 2020.

Robinson, Francis. "Laboratory Nation: What Happened to Islamic Modernism?" Review of Muhammad Qasim Zaman, *Islam in Pakistan, Times Literary Supplement* 6066, July 5, 2019, 28–29.

Roca Fernández, María J. "La distinción entre patrimonio eclesiástico y privado de obispos y clérigos en la España visigoda." *e-Legal History Review* 20 (2015): 1–16.

Rosenwein, Barbara. *Negotiating Space: Power, Restraint, and Privileges of Immunity in Early Middle Europe.* Ithaca: Cornell University Press, 1999. DOI: 10.7591/9781501718687.

Roth, Paul. *Geschichte des Beneficialwesens von den ältesten Zeiten bis ins 10. Jahrhundert.* Erlangen, 1850.

Rouche, Michel. "*Religio calcata et dissipata* ou les premières sécularisations de terre d'Église par Dagobert." In *The Seventh Century: Change and Continuity,* edited by Jacques Fontaine and Jocelyn N. Hillgarth, 236–46. London: The Warburg Institute, 1992.

Salmito, Jean-Marie. "Les dendrophores dans l'Empire chrétien. À propos de Code Théodosien, XIV, 8, 1, et XVI, 10, 20, 2." *Mélanges de l'école française de Rome* 99, no. 2 (1987): 991–1018. DOI: 10.3406/mefr.1987.1576.

Salzman, Michèle Renée. "From a Classical to a Christian City: Civic Evergetism and Charity in Late Antique Rome." *Studies in Late Antiquity* 1 (2017): 65–85. DOI: 10.1525/sla.2017.1.1.65.

———. "The Religious Economics of Crisis: The Papal Use of Liturgical Vessels as Symbolic Capital in Late Antiquity." *Religion in the Roman Empire* 5, no. 1: *Transformations of Value: Lived Religion and the Economy* (2019): 125–41. DOI: 10.1628/rre-2019-0008.

Sánchez Pardo, José Carlos. "Organización eclesiástica y social en la Galicia tardoantigua. Una perspectiva geográfico-arqueológica del Parroquial suevo." *Hispania Sacra* 66 (2014): 439–80. DOI: 10.3989/hs.2014.058.

Sato, Shoichi. "The Merovingian Accounting Documents of Tours: Form and Function." *Early Medieval Europe* 9, no. 2 (2000): 143–61. DOI: 10.1111/1468-0254.00063.

Schopen, Gregory. "Monastic Law Meets the Real World: A Monk's Continuing Right to Inherit Family Property in Classical India." *History of Religions* 35, no. 2 (1995): 101–23. DOI: 10.1086/463416.

Sessa, Kristina. *The Formation of Papal Authority in Late Antique Italy: Roman Bishops and the Domestic Sphere.* Cambridge: Cambridge University Press, 2012. DOI: 10.1017/CBO9781139017336.

Sharpe, Richard. *Medieval Irish Saint's Lives: An Introduction to the "Vitae sanctorum Hiberniae."* Oxford: Clarendon Press, 1991. DOI: 10.1093/acprof:oso/9780198215820.001.0001.

Shiozawa, Kimio. "Marx's View of Asian Society and His 'Asiatic Mode of Production.'" *The Developing Economies* 4, no. 3 (1966): 299–315.

Sotinel, Claire. "La recrutement des évêques en Italie aux IVe et Ve siècles. Essai d'enquête prosopographique." In *Vescovi e pastori in epoca teodosiana,* volume 1, 193–204. Rome: Institutum Patristicum Augustinianum, 1997.

———. "Le personnel épiscopal. Enquête sur la puissance de l'évêque dans la cité." In *L'évêque dans la cité du IVe au Ve siècle: Actes de la table ronde de Rome (1er et 2 décembre 1995),*

edited by Eric Rebillard, 105–26. Rome: École française de Rome, 1998.

———. "The Christian Gift and Its Economic Impact in Late Antiquity." In *Church and Society in Late Antique Italy and Beyond,* 1–23. London: Aldershot, 2010.

Spalinger, Anthony. "Some Revisions of Temple Endowments in the New Kingdom." *Journal of the American Research Center in Egypt* 28 (1991): 21–39. DOI: 10.2307/40000570.

Stadermann, Christian. *Gothus: Konstruktion und Rezeption von Gotenbildern in narrativen Schriften des merowingischen Gallien.* Stuttgart: Franz Steiner Verlag, 2017.

Stambaugh, John E. "The Functions of Roman Temples." In *Aufstieg und Niedergang der römischen Welt: Geschichte und Kultur Roms im Spiegel der neueren Forschung,* Vol. 2: *Principat,* edited by Hildegard Temporini and Wolfgang Haase, 554–608. Second series. Berlin: de Gruyter, 1978.

Stancliffe, Clare. "From Town to Country: The Christianisation of the Touraine, 370–600." In *The Church in Town and Countryside,* edited by Derek Baker. Studies in Church History 16 (Oxford: Blackwell, 1979), 43–59. DOI: 10.1017/S0424208400009852.

Stebnicka, Krystyna. *Identity of the Diaspora: Jews in Asia Minor in the Imperial Period.* Journal of Juristic Papyrology Supplements 26. Warsaw: Faculty of Law and Administration of the University of Warsaw, the Institute of Archaeology of the University of Warsaw, and Fundacja im. Rafała Taubenschlaga, 2015.

Stocking, Rachel. *Bishops, Councils, and Consensus in the Visigothic Kingdom, 589–633.* Ann Arbor: University of Michigan Press, 2000. DOI: 10.3998/mpub.16864.

Story, Joanna. "Lands and Lights in Early Medieval Rome." In *Italy and Early Medieval Europe: Papers for Chris Wickham,* edited by Ross Balzaretti, Julia Barrow, and Patricia Skinner, 315–38. Oxford: Oxford University Press, 2018. DOI: 10.1093/oso/9780198777601.003.0025.

Subrahmanyam, Sanjay. "Agreeing to Disagree: Burton Stein on Vijayanagara." *South Asian Research* 17, no. 2 (1997): 127–39. DOI: 10.1177/026272809701700204.

Tedesco, Paolo. "Economia monetaria e fiscalità tardoantica: una sintesi." *Annali dell'Istituto Italiano di Numismatica* 62 (2016): 107–49.

Tjäder, Jan-Olof. *Die nichtliterarischen lateinischen Papyri italiens aus der Zeit 445–700*, 2 volumes. Lund: Gleerup, 1955–82.

Thompson, E.A. *The Goths in Spain*. Oxford: Clarendon, 1969.

Tomás-Faci, Guillermo. "The Transmission of Visigothic Documents in the Pyrenean Monastery of San Victorián de Asán (6th-12th centuries): Monastic Memory and Episcopal Disputes." *Antiquité tardive* 25 (2017): 303–14. DOI: 10.1484/J.AT.5.114864.

Tomás-Faci, Guillermo, and José Carlos Martín-Iglesias. "Cuatro documentos inéditos des monasterio visigodo de San Martín de Asán (522–586)." *Mittellateinisches Jahrbuch: Internationale Zeitschrift für Mediävistik* 52, no. 2 (2017): 261–86.

Toneatto, Valentina. *Les banquiers du seigneur: Évêques et moines face à la richesse (IVe–début IXe siècle)*. Rennes: Presses universitaires de Rennes, 2012.

Velázquez, Isabella. "Jural Relations as an Indicator of Syncretism from the Law of Inheritance to the Dum Inlicita of Chindaswinth." In *The Visigoths from the Migration Period to the Seventh Century: An Ethnographic Perspective*, edited by Peter Heather, 225–80. Woodbridge: The Boydell Press, 1999.

Wallace-Hadrill, J.M. *The Long-haired Kings, and Other Studies in Frankish History*. London: Methuen, 1962.

Ward-Perkins, Bryan. *From Classical Antiquity to the Middle Ages: Urban Public Building in Northern and Central Italy AD 300–850*. Oxford: Oxford University Press, 1984.

———. *The Fall of Rome and the End of Civilization*. Oxford: Oxford University Press, 2006.

Wataghin Cantino, Gisella. "Monasteri di età longobarda: spunti per una ricerca." In *XXXVI Corso di cultura sull'arte ravennate e bizantina: seminario internazionale di studi sul tema:*

Ravenna e l'Italia fra Goti e Longobardi, Ravenna, 14–22 aprile 1989, 73–100. Ravenna: Girasole, 1989.

Webster, David. *The Fall of the Ancient Maya: Solving the Mystery of the Maya Collapse.* London: Thames and Hudson, 2002.

Weidemann, Margarete. *Das Testament des Bischofs Berthramn von Le Mans vom 27. März 616.* Mainz: Habelt, 1986.

Weiner, Annette. *Inalienable Possessions: The Paradox of Keeping-While-Giving.* Berkeley: University of California Press, 1992. DOI: 10.1525/california/9780520076037.001.0001.

West, Gerald. "Tracking an Ancient Near Eastern Economic System: The Tributary Mode of Production and the Temple State." *Old Testament Essays (OTE)* 24, no. 2 (2011): 511–32.

Westall, Richard. "Constantius II and the Basilica of St. Peter in the Vatican." *Historia* 64, no. 2 (2015): 205–42.

Wickham, Chris. "Aristocratic Power in Eighth-Century Lombard Italy." In *After Rome's Fall: Narrators and Sources of Early Medieval History,* edited by Alexander C. Murray, 153–70. Toronto: University of Toronto Press, 1998. DOI: 10.3138/9781442670693-013.

———. *Framing the Early Middle Ages: Europe and the Mediterranean 400–800.* Oxford: Oxford University Press, 2005.

———. "The Other Transition: From the Ancient World to Feudalism." In Chris Wickham, *Land and Power: Studies in Italian and European Social History, 400–1200,* 7–42. London: British School at Rome, 1994.

Wipszycka, Ewa. *Les ressources et les activités économiques des églises en Égypte du IVᵉ au VIIIᵉ siècle.* Brussels: Fondation Égyptologique Reine Élisabeth, 1972.

———. *The Second Gift of the Nile: Monks and Monasteries in Late Antique Egypt.* Warsaw: University of Warsaw, 2018.

Wiśniewski, Robert. "Clerical Hagiography in Late Antiquity." In *The Hagiographical Experiment: Developing Discourses of Sainthood,* edited by Christa Gray and James Corke-Webster, 93–118. Boston and Leiden: Brill, 2020. DOI: 10.1163/9789004421332_005.

————. "How Numerous and How Busy Were Late-Antique Presbyters?" *Zeitschrift für Antikes Christentum* 25, no. 1 (2021): 3–37. DOI: 10.1515/zac-2021-0011.

————. "The Last Shall Be Last: The Order of Precedence Among Clergy in Late Antiquity." *Sacris Erudiri* 58 (2019): 321–37. DOI: 10.1484/J.SE.5.119459.

Wood, Ian. "Creating a 'Temple Society' in the Early Medieval West." *Early Medieval Europe* 29, no. 4 (2021): 462–86. DOI: 10.1111/emed.12498.

————. "Entrusting Western Europe to the Church, 400–750." *Transactions of the Royal Historical Society* 23 (2013): 37–73. DOI: 10.1017/S0080440113000030.

————. "Land Tenure and Military Obligations in the Anglo-Saxon and Merovingian Kingdoms: The Evidence of Bede and Boniface in Context." *Bulletin of International Medieval Research* 9–10 (2005): 3–22.

————. "Teutsind, Witlaic and the History of Merovingian *precaria.*" In *Property and Power in the Early Middle Ages,* edited by Wendy Davies and Paul Fouracre, 31–52. Cambridge: Cambridge University Press, 1995. DOI: 10.1017/CBO9780511628665.004.

————. "The Early Medieval West as a Temple Society." *Rivista di Storia Antica* 11 (2019): 107–34.

————. "The Ecclesiastical Politics of Merovingian Clermont." In *Ideal and Reality in Frankish and Anglo-Saxon Society,* edited by Patrick Wormald, 34–57. Oxford: Blackwell, 1983.

————. "The Legislation of *Magistri Militum*: The Laws of Gundobad and Sigismund." *La forge du droit. Naissance des identités juridiques en Europe (IVe–XIIIe siècles), Clio@Themis* 10 (2016): 1–16.

————. *The Priest, the Temple and the Moon in the Eighth Century.* Brixworth Lecture. Brixworth: Friends of All Saints' Church, 2008.

————. *The Transformation of the Roman West.* Leeds: ARC Humanities Press, 2018.

Wood, Jamie. *Politics of Identity in Visigothic Spain: Religion and Power in the Histories of Isidore of Seville.* Brill's Series on the Early Middle Ages. Boston and Leiden: Brill, 2012. DOI: 10.1163/9789004224322.

Wood, Susan. "Bishops and the Proprietary Church: Diversity of Principle and Practice in Early Medieval Frankish Dominions and in Italy." In *Chiese locali e chiese regionali nell'alto medioevo, 895–912. Settimane di Studio del Centro Italiano di studi sull'Alto Medioevo, Spoleto* 61. Spoleto: Fondazione Centro italiano di studi sull'alto medioevo, 2014.

———. *The Proprietary Church in the Medieval West.* Oxford: Oxford University Press, 2006. DOI: 10.1093/acprof:o so/9780198206972.001.0001.

Yarrow, Simon. "Economic Imaginaries of the Global Middle Ages." In *The Global Middle Ages,* edited by Catherine Holmes and Naomi Standen, 214–31. Past and Present 238, Supplement 13. Oxford: Oxford University Press, 2018. DOI: 10.1093/pastj/gty029.

Index